Masculinity in Contemporary New York Fiction

Masculinity in Contemporary New York Fiction is an interdisciplinary study that presents masculinity as a key thematic concern in contemporary New York fiction. This study argues that New York authors do not simply depict masculinity as a social and historical construction but seek to challenge the archetypal ideals of masculinity by writing counter-hegemonic narratives.

Gendering canonical New York writers, namely Paul Auster, Bret Easton Ellis, and Don DeLillo, illustrates how explorations of masculinity are tied into the principal themes that have defined the American novel from its very beginning. The themes that feature in this study include the role of the novel in American society; the individual and (urban) society; the journey from innocence to awareness (of masculinity); the archetypal image of the absent and/or patriarchal father; the impact of homosocial relations on the everyday performance of masculinity; male sexuality; and the male individual and globalization.

What connects these contemporary New York writers is their employment of one of the great figures in the history of literature: the flâneur. These authors take the flâneur from the shadows of the Manhattan streets and elevate this figure to the role of self-reflexive agent of male subjectivity through which they write counter-hegemonic narratives of masculinity. This book is an essential reference for those with an interest in gender studies and contemporary American fiction.

Peter Ferry received his Ph.D. from Queen's University Belfast in 2012. He has published articles on the flâneur, Freud and masculinity, fatherhood, and the sociological value of the study of men and masculinities in a range of literary and sociology journals. He is currently employed at the University of Cordoba, Spain.

Routledge Transnational Perspectives on American Literature

Edited by Susan Castillo, King's College London

1 **New Woman Hybridities**
Femininity, Feminism, and International Consumer Culture, 1880–1930
Edited by Ann Heilmann and Margaret Beetham

2 **Don DeLillo**
The Possibility of Fiction
Peter Boxall

3 **Toni Morrison's *Beloved***
Origins
Justine Tally

4 **Fictions of the Black Atlantic in American Foundational Literature**
Gesa Mackenthun

5 **Mexican American Literature**
The Politics of Identity
Elizabeth Jacobs

6 **Native American Literature**
Towards a Spatialized Reading
Helen May Dennis

7 **Transnationalism and American Literature**
Literary Translation 1773–1892
Colleen Glenney Boggs

8 **The Quest for Epic in Contemporary American Fiction**
John Updike, Philip Roth and Don DeLillo
Catherine Morley

9 **The Literary Quest for an American National Character**
Finn Pollard

10 **Asian American Fiction, History and Life Writing**
International Encounters
Helena Grice

11 **Remapping Citizenship and the Nation in African-American Literature**
Stephen Knadler

12 **The Western Landscape in Cormac McCarthy and Wallace Stegner**
Myths of the Frontier
Megan Riley McGilchrist

13 **The Construction of Irish Identity in American Literature**
Christopher Dowd

14 Cities, Borders and Spaces in Intercultural American Literature and Film
Ana Mª Manzanas and Jesús Benito

15 American Utopia and Social Engineering in Literature, Social Thought, and Political History
Peter Swirski

16 Transnationalism and American Serial Fiction
Edited by Patricia Okker

17 Nature, Class, and New Deal Literature
The Country Poor in the Great Depression
Stephen Fender

18 Travel and Dislocation in Contemporary American Fiction
Aliki Varvogli

19 Nabokov, History and the Texture of Time
Will Norman

20 The Transnationalism of American Culture
Literature, Film, and Music
Edited by Rocío G. Davis

21 Utopia and Terror in Contemporary American Fiction
Judith Newman

22 Occupying Space in American Literature and Culture
Static Heroes, Social Movements and Empowerment
Ana Mª Manzanas and Jesús Benito

23 Identity, Diaspora and Return in American Literature
Edited by Maria Antònia Oliver-Rotger

24 Cold War American Literature and the Rise of Youth Culture
Children of Empire
Denis Jonnes

25 Masculinity in Contemporary New York Fiction
Peter Ferry

Masculinity in Contemporary New York Fiction

Peter Ferry

Routledge
Taylor & Francis Group
NEW YORK AND LONDON

First published 2015
by Routledge
711 Third Avenue, New York, NY 10017

and by Routledge
2 Park Square, Milton Park, Abingdon, Oxon OX14 4RN

Routledge is an imprint of the Taylor & Francis Group, an informa business

Library of Congress Cataloging-in-Publication Data

Ferry, Peter, 1982–
Masculinity in contemporary New York fiction / Peter Ferry.
pages cm. — (Routledge transnational perspectives on American literature ; 25)
Includes bibliographical references and index.
1. American fiction—20th century—History and criticism. 2. American fiction—21st century—History and criticism. 3. Masculinity in literature. 4. Sex role in literature. 5. Men in literature. 6. Flaneurs in literature. 7. New York (N.Y.)—In literature. I. Title.
PS374.M37F47 2014
813'.609353—dc23
2014015081

ISBN: 978-1-138-01604-0 (hbk)
ISBN: 978-1-315-79398-6 (ebk)

Typeset in Sabon
by Apex CoVantage, LLC

MIX
Paper from responsible sources
FSC www.fsc.org FSC® C013056

Printed and bound in Great Britain by
TJ International Ltd, Padstow, Cornwall

For Julia, Peter, Sean, Joseph, Lucia, and Ryan

Contents

Acknowledgements

Special thanks first and foremost must go to Professor Brian Caraher for his belief in both myself as a research scholar and the research project that has culminated in this book. I will always be grateful for his wisdom and guidance and, most importantly of all, for his time on Thursday afternoons. Spending an hour or two in his company was always hugely nerve wrecking but incredibly inspiring. These moments, in many ways, were the highlight of the project.

I'd like to thank the Department for Employment and Learning in Northern Ireland for the three-year funding that made this project possible. I will be forever grateful to the Helen Ramsey Turtle Group, as it was their scholarship, awarded to me in 2011, that made my research trip to New York City, the visit to the Shere Hite Archive in the Schlesinger Library, Radcliffe Institute, Harvard University, and my appearance at the 2012 American Men's Studies Conference in Minneapolis possible. This research trip to the United States was a dream come true and an essential experience that made this book what it is.

I'd also like to pay tribute to the organisers of the conferences that gave me the opportunity to present my research during the project. The planners of the "Performing the Invisible: Masculinities in the English-Speaking World" conference at the Université Sorbonne Nouvelle Paris 3 in September 2010 gave me much needed confidence at an early stage of this journey. Moreover, this baptism of fire led to my first publication. Presenting an overview of my research in masculinity in New York fiction in March 2012 at the 20th American Men's Studies Association (AMSA) Conference at the University of St. Thomas in Minneapolis, Minnesota was a standout moment of this project. The warmth and generosity of this group of researchers on men and masculinities confirmed to me that I was involved in an innovative and vibrant research community. I'd also like to display my gratitude to the organisers of the "Masculinities in Motion—Men and (E)Quality of Life" conference at the University of Oslo, Norway, May 2012. Their generosity in awarding me one of the 2012 "Masculinities in Motion" awards to attend the conference helped me finalise the structure of this project in a welcoming and supportive environment. Presenting papers at the "Working Through Psychoanalysis: Freud's Legacy in Art, Cinema, Literature in Popular Culture" conference at the University of Leeds in April 2011, and at the Spanish Association of Anglo-American Studies (AEDEAN) conference in Barcelona in November 2011, allowed me to refine my research and reflect upon my methodological approach to reading men and masculinities in literature.

I'd like to express my gratitude to the staff in the Stephen A. Schwarzman Building and particularly those involved with the Paul Auster Collection of Papers, which forms part of the Henry W. and Albert A. Berg Collection of English and American Literature at the New York Public Library. I am also extremely thankful for the hospitality of the professionals of the Experimental Archives Project working on the digitisation of the Shere Hite Archive in the Schlesinger Library, Radcliffe Institute, Harvard University. I was the first researcher to access the archive, and the research conducted there was absolutely essential in the writing of Chapter 3 of this book. Special thanks must also be given to the staff at the Health and Social Care Library in the MDEC Building, Altnagelvin Hospital, Derry, for saving me a lot of time and hassle with my many inter-library loans.

I'd also like to thank everyone at Routledge. The comments of the anonymous reviewers of the proposal were incredibly perceptive and insightful and have quite simply made this book better. The series editors, editorial assistants, copy editors, and the other staff involved in the publishing of this book have my eternal gratitude. Their professionalism has made this a fantastically smooth process and I hope to work with them all again.

Finally I owe a huge debt to my family. Writing a book is mostly a solitary exercise and of course you need to be self-motivated and, in many ways, self-reliant; ultimately, however, it is a selfish endeavour and cannot be completed without the sacrifice of others. My parents, John and Isobel, have never questioned any of my hugely questionable ideas or decisions and have always been there when I needed them. The in-laws, Julia and José Luis, have been a huge support with the children and I will always be grateful. And I hope my grandmother Avril knew that she was number one in my eyes too! Finally it goes without saying that this book is for Julia and the kids. I believe that no matter what research interest you have, or what subject you are writing a book about, at the end of the day you are really writing about yourself; therefore I hope we all might agree it has been worth it and that writing this book has made me a better husband and dad. I'll keep trying.

An earlier version of Chapter 2 appeared as "Reading Manhattan, Reading American Masculinity: Reintroducing the Flâneur with E. B. White's *Here Is New York* and Joshua Ferris' *The Unnamed*," in *Culture, Society and Masculinities* 3.1 (2011): 49–61. An earlier version of Chapter 3 appeared as "Paul Auster and Models of American Fatherhood: Reading Counter Hegemonic Father Figures in Auster's Fiction," in *Paul Auster:*

Special Issue of Critical Engagements (UK Network for Modern Fiction Studies), ed. Mark Brown (Lulu, 2013). Some material appeared in "Writing Men: Recognising the Sociological Impact of Counter-Hegemonic Masculinities in American Fiction," *Masculinities and Social Change*, 2.2 (2013): 146–166.

1 Introduction

Finding Yourself in New York

New York City is the greatest city in the world. Thanks to a Research Training Support Grant from the Department for Employment and Learning in Northern Ireland, the generosity of the scholarship awarded to me by the Helen Ramsey Turtle Group at Queen's University Belfast, the much-appreciated contribution from my parents, and, of course, the understanding of my wife and young children, in March 2012, I fulfilled my lifetime ambition of spending one month as a New Yorker. I had always imagined myself arriving onto the shores of the New World like my Irish ancestors on a large steamship to see man's image of himself emerge slowly into view. As I sat in a cramped cabin—alas an air cabin, not a ship cabin—watching the little airplane edge frustratingly slowly across the Atlantic Ocean on the tiny screen in front of me, I experienced that sense of nervous excitement of those arriving into the unknown of New York City for the first time. This, of course, is one of the great paradoxes of the experience of the first-time visitor to New York. Everyone knows New York. Everyone has a connection to New York. Everyone's favourite movie, sitcom, cartoon, band, song, stand-up comedian, chat show, magazine, podcast, and, dare I say, even book is most likely to be inspired by New York, set in New York, produced in New York, or remains interminably connected to New York.

Unbeknownst to that only child growing up in a small town in Northern Ireland in the 1980s, New York would become a reference point in every stage of my formative years. The first cartoon that I became obsessed with was *Teenage Mutant Ninja Turtles,* the story of Leonardo, Donatello, Raphael, and Michelangelo, four teenage crime-fighting, pizza-loving turtles who lived with their father, the rat Splinter, in the New York City sewers. The first movie that my dad took me to see at the local cinema, on the eve of my eighth birthday, was the live-action film version of the cartoon. One of my first toys was the car from one of the great 1980s New York City movies, *Ghostbusters* (1984). The Ectomobile, also known as Ecto-1, was the distinctive white 1959 Cadillac Miller-Meteor that Peter Venkman, Ray Stanza, Igon Spengler, and Winston Zeddemore used to catch the spectres and spirits that terrorised Manhattan. The first grown-up film that my dad let me watch one Christmas in the early 1990s was *Batman* (1989). Tim

Burton's reboot before reboots of Gotham's urban detective delved into the dark side of Bruce Wayne's struggle with the issues surrounding his dual identity. Burton's gothic re-imagining is still my favourite interpretation of the greatest superhero of them all.

Moving into my teenage years in the 1990s, U.S. sitcoms became an unexpected obsession. While *Friends* was a cultural phenomenon in the U.K., due mainly to it being a window into the lives of six good-looking thirty-somethings struggling in the city (but still able to afford pretty luxurious Manhattan apartments!), I also remember watching lesser appreciated shows such as *Mad About You, Caroline in the City, Spin City, Just Shoot Me!,* and *King of Queens.* It wasn't until the arrival of the era of the box set during my undergraduate years in the new millennium that I discovered what is undoubtedly the greatest New York City sitcom of them all: *Seinfeld. Seinfeld* was more than an obsession. After studying during the day and working the local petrol station in the evening, I would spend each night living New York with Jerry Seinfeld, George Costanza, Elaine Benes, and Cosmo Kramer. *Seinfeld* is more than a sitcom; it is an extremely acute critical investigation into New York social behaviour. I identified wholeheartedly with the skits that satirise our obsession with absurd social etiquette. The four main characters are far from sympathetic city dwellers, and that is exactly the point. As Jerry puts it somewhat sarcastically in the fifth season episode "The Dinner Party": "The fabric of society is very complex, George." The overarching influence over the characters for the full nine-season run of *Seinfeld,* as they struggled with the inanity of everyday adult life, was New York City. *Seinfeld* couldn't have been set anywhere else.

New York also had a major influence on me in terms of the music I listened to growing up. Certainly New York doesn't have the same grassroots rock identity as other American cities such as Seattle or Detroit; New York is more of a musical melting pot and more often than not the place that young artists find themselves gravitating towards in search of other, like-minded musicians on the long road to creative and/or commercial success. The New York band that made the biggest impression on me in my guitar playing years was The Strokes. Their debut album, *Is This It?* (2001), is arguably the finest indie-rock album of the opening decade of the twenty-first century. Along with the New Wave revivalists of that time, such as Interpol and The Yeah Yeah Yeahs, The Strokes echoed the urgency and the attitude of the great New York bands such as The Velvet Underground, The Ramones, The Talking Heads, Television, and Blondie. The Strokes were the perfect pin-up garage rock band, a group of five good-looking Manhattan boys whose infectious melodic riffs gave people around the world a taste of New York City cool.

To this day New York remains a cultural referent for me. *The New York Times* Sunday Book Review is the place I go to first to read about the latest works of fiction and nonfiction. *The New Yorker* magazine is my cultural compass for keeping up with the latest critical thinking on the changing

American landscape in areas such as politics, culture, and literature. The *New Yorker* Fiction Podcast keeps me company on my commute. And now, as a father of five, New York continues to find its way into my everyday life through my children. The most scratched DVD in our house is the Sam Raimi–directed *Spiderman* (2002). As a photographer capturing everyday images of the city, as well as a crime fighter intent on keeping the New York City streets safe, Spiderman is possibly the ultimate New York *flâneur*; he is the superhero who uses the very physicality of the city itself to move around as he watches and protects the people of New York. What Raimi's film succeeds in doing so well is exploring the developing masculine identity of the boyish Peter Parker. With Tobey Maguire as this sympathetic young everyman, Peter Parker is forced to deal with his changing body in his teenage years, the move into responsibility and adulthood following the loss of his father figure Uncle Ben, and the (sexual) development of his relationship with the girl-next-door Mary Jane Watson. At this stage, however, my kids just like the fact that he gets to wear a cool costume!

Clearly New York has been a huge influence in my life. Echoing in my head as I arrived into Manhattan was the resonating line from Colson Whitehead's urban sketch of the great city, *The Colossus of New York* (2003): "you start building your private New York the first time you lay eyes on it" (4). I started building my New York as I lugged my suitcase up the steps at 79th Street and Broadway into the bright spring sunlight of the Upper West Side. At that moment I felt what in many ways has become cliché in describing the experience particular to the first-time New Yorker taking his or her first steps in the city: beginning to move within the unique energy of the people, the sensory overload created a weird sensation of both moving within the throng while feeling somewhat detached and distant from those people enveloping me. On my way to the studio apartment I was to rent on 82nd Street and Columbus Avenue, I found refuge in the safety of a Starbucks on Amsterdam Avenue. Looking out through the window at the everyday Manhattanites passing by, I realised that while New York had been my city growing up in cartoons, TV shows, sitcoms, music, and movies, finally arriving here it felt both oddly familiar and yet a surreal fiction.

The primary objective of my time in New York was to consult the Paul Auster collection of papers from the Henry W. and Albert A. Berg Collection of English and American Literature at the New York Public Library. I had the honour and the pleasure of spending hours in the inspirational Room 320 on the third floor of the Stephen A. Schwarzman Building, Fifth Avenue at 42nd Street. Being able to see, touch, and smell Auster's notebooks, correspondence, and private materials was an exhilarating experience. In particular, the postcards and letters sent between Auster and Don DeLillo gave an intimate insight into the developing relationship between two of New York's finest living writers; from Auster's initial reverential tone in the first contact between the two to their later lighthearted quips about the Mets, book tours, and trips with their wives. Getting this close to Auster in terms of understanding the process of his writing was an opportunity that I am incredibly grateful for and one that has left a mark on how I now read and appreciate Auster's narratives.

Despite the self-discipline and diligence I mustered to go through the wealth of materials in the Auster archive, after a stretch of long days I found myself hankering to return to the city streets. I fell very easily into the rhythm of making my daily commute on the South Ferry–bound 1 train down to 42nd Street and Fifth Avenue from what had become my station on West 79th and Broadway. I soon realised that it was these journeys that were beginning to define my New York. I began to step off the subway at random stops and experience that sense of lightheaded wonderment as I climbed out of the subway into the glare of the spring sunshine. Arriving at street level, what strikes you is how blue panels covering construction work blanket the New York City sidewalks. New York is truly E.B. White's city that is both "changeless and changing" (*Here Is New York* 48). If I returned to New York tomorrow, it would not be my New York from 2012. Nor would I expect it to be. New York is a living organism; the people who walk the city streets under the sprawling skeleton of endless scaffolding are the blood in its veins.

On the first day trying to make my way to the Public Library, in my sleepy haze I went left instead of right and found myself standing in the middle of Times Square. The idea that I had to make my way past the blazing spectacle of the Disneyfication of New York in all its glory to get to the distinguished solemnity of the Stephen A. Schwarzman building, established in the nineteenth century and currently the second largest public library in the United States and the third largest in the world, was in many ways telling of the New York experience. The city is so vast that I wasn't able to see half of what I had intended to see and yet in many ways I saw twice as much as any tourist ticking off the famous New York landmarks. This idea of the need to walk a city in order to understand a city underpins William B. Helmreich's recently published sociological study, *The New York Nobody Knows* (2013). Helmreich, to his eternal credit, walks every street of the five boroughs, a gruelling project that he estimates as having led him to walk about 6,000 miles over four years! Helmreich is certain that his decision to walk the city—as crazy, dangerous, and daunting as that might sound—was absolutely fundamental in the success of his project. For him it was this ethnographic method of direct observation of the buildings, the people, and the little everyday happenings that walking allows, as well as having the opportunity to stop and chat with random folk, that enabled him to truly touch upon the uniqueness of New York City:

> Walking is critical to the task because it gets you out there and lets you get to know the city up close. However, you cannot merely walk *through* a city to know it. You have to stop long enough to absorb what's going on around you. And the only way to do that is to immerse yourself in it—spending as much time as possible in the city streets. (Helmreich 3)

Taking a wrong turn, if such a thing even exists in this city, is to stumble upon something that adds to your New York. New York rewards those willing to walk the city streets.

And still on the days I spent in downtown Manhattan, or on Fifth Avenue, or in the Upper East Side on "Museum Mile," or in a deli in front of the Flatiron Building, or on the Brooklyn Bridge looking back at Manhattan, I was always happy to return to what had become my pocket of New York in the Upper West Side. New York demands a lot from its people but it gives back so much more. My New York was the New World coffee shop on Columbus. Crazy customers? Yes. Discombobulated service? Yes. Overpriced breakfasts? Yes. But good coffee, decent pastries, and the perfect window counter to sit and watch people of New York walk their dogs towards Central Park. The P&K Laundromat on Amsterdam Avenue was a godsend with great service, lightning fast turnaround, and out-of-this-world folding of my shirts, trousers, and smalls. The Chirping Chicken satisfied my cravings on Saturday nights in front of the box watching the Knicks. The Dead Poet is highly recommended by many as the cool quirky artsy bar, but I preferred watching soccer with some pub grub a few doors down in the Gin Mill. Popping into The Zingone Brothers grocery store, an old mom-and-pop store that has been selling produce on Columbus Avenue since 1927, became a daily ritual. If it is good enough for Jerry Seinfeld, then it was good enough for me! Reading the article "A Zingone in Every Aisle," published recently in the *New York Times,* had me welling up with pride.[1] This was my New York!

I left the Big Apple on a cold, blowy Sunday evening to make my way to Boston, where I would spend time with the Shere Hite Archive in the Schlesinger Library, Radcliffe Institute for Advanced Study, Harvard University. As I looked wistfully out the window while the train weaved its way past downtown Manhattan, I was happy that walking the city had answered the main premise of my research: that is, to know New York is to walk New York, and to walk New York is to know something greater, something deeper about your inner self. Letting myself fall into the rhythm of the city I began to see the city and see myself in the city. While in principle the flâneur may come to New York as a stranger with the primary objective of documenting the city, eventually it is the city that adopts the flâneur and encourages this social observer to not only muse upon the spectacle of the external that envelops him but also to reflect upon the impact of the city on his own individual identity. It is the city that fosters the creation of these narratives that make us who we are, whether we are first-time visitors, long-time city dwellers, or distant but firmly attached admirers of New York. To paraphrase and add to Meyer Berger's maxim that each man finds his own meaning in New York, in the finely attuned acts of walking and writing the city each man also finds his own meaning in himself.[2]

This might go some part of the way to explain why the contemporary New York writers that are the focus of this book—Paul Auster, Bret Easton

Ellis, and Don DeLillo—engage with the literary figure of the flâneur in their critical investigations into masculinity in the city. The choice of authors for this study is a very deliberate one. Auster, Ellis, and DeLillo are the heavyweights of the contemporary canon. They enjoy a degree of commercial and critical crossover not experienced by what some may call difficult "literary" writers. Despite Auster, Ellis, and DeLillo featuring strongly on modules and courses of American fiction, up to now gender and masculinity have been criminally overlooked in the critical reading of these literary greats. Gendering these writers underlines the fact that Auster, Ellis, and DeLillo are white, heterosexual, middle-class, educated men writing white, heterosexual, middle-class, educated men.[3] And yet this is something that remains criminally overlooked. It appears that the call of Michael Kimmel, one of the leading figures within the field of Masculinity Studies, still rings true:

> to men . . . gender often remains invisible. Strange as it may sound, men are the "invisible" gender. Ubiquitous in positions of power everywhere, men are invisible to themselves. ("Invisible Masculinity" 29)

Using this as a springboard, as much as it is absolutely crucial to study the representations of marginalised and subordinate masculine groups, there is the need to challenge the privilege of invisibility that the hegemonic group of men in society enjoy. The act of gendering these works of fiction not only enables us to understand how masculinity is an overlooked central theme of these writers, but also underlines the sociological value of the novel as a self-reflective device for challenging established patterns of the performance of masculinity.

With such a focused study on only three authors, there may be concerns regarding the narrow range and scope of this study. The range of issues that feature in the subsequent chapters should allay any such qualms. Gendering the works of Auster, Ellis, and DeLillo illustrates how their explorations of New York men and masculinities are tied into the principal themes that have defined the American novel from its very beginning. These include: the role of the novel in American society; the individual and (urban) society; the journey from innocence to awareness (of masculinity); the archetypal image of the absent and/or patriarchal father; the impact of homosocial relations on the everyday performance of masculinity; male sexuality; and the male individual and globalization. And it is here that we reach the crux: reading these novels through a gendered lens alongside the work of sociologists dedicated to the study of men and masculinities—namely Raewyn Connell, Michael Kimmel, and Shere Hite, amongst the many others that also influence the readings in this book—will underscore how Auster, Ellis, and DeLillo occupy a unique and valuable position in the development of our understanding of the social construction of masculinity and the role of fiction in this project. As writers of fiction, they are able to go beyond the limits of cold, hard statistical data of other disciplines to analyse the processes that shape the everyday experience of the New York male. Crucially, as this study will argue, it is their engagement with the literary figure of the flâneur that powers their self-reflective narratives. The flâneur allows these writers to be observers, readers, and writers of the contemporary condition; it is by focalising their meditations on the New York male through this figure that these writers are able to be both part of the crowd and yet manage a degree of critical distance. It is this approach that is fundamental in their ability to produce narratives that ultimately promote the possibilities of counter-hegemonic performances of masculinity.

The third chapter of this book, "'The Son Saves the Father': Counter-hegemonic Father Figures in Paul Auster's Fiction," explores the centrality of the theme of fatherhood in Paul Auster's writing. Finding the meaning of masculinity in part through walking the city is a major trope in Auster's texts.[4] As Auster comments in *Winter Journal* (2012), the act of walking provides the writer an opportunity for reflection. Auster is clear about the importance of flânerie in his journey towards understanding his own masculine identity: "for that is how you see yourself whenever you stop to think about who you are: a man who walks, a man who has spent his life walking through the streets of cities" (59). The male characters in Auster's novels are often taken out of New York to other locations—to Vermont, the Midwest, the capitals of western Europe, or the deserts of New Mexico. It is notable, however, that these journeys fail to offer a sense of self-understanding, and Auster's male figures end up returning to New York.[5] It is in the city that Auster's male figures reject the entrenched hegemonic ideal of the absent father and engage in a counter-hegemonic active father role. Reading the models of fatherhood from selected Auster texts, from *The New York Trilogy* (1987) to more recent works, such as *The Brooklyn Follies* (2005), *Man in the Dark* (2008), and *Sunset Park* (2010), this chapter explores the developing trend of Auster's protagonists as counter-hegemonic in their desire to be a father, their regret of losing the father role, or, recognising the self-realising power of fatherhood, seeking to engage in second-chance fatherhood as a surrogate father figure.

The fourth chapter reevaluates the sociological power of Bret Easton Ellis' *American Psycho* (1991). The first question that arises is whether we might even class Ellis as a "New York writer." The majority of Ellis' novels have been set outside of New York, be it Los Angeles in *Less Than Zero* (1985), *The Informers* (1994), and *Imperial Bedrooms* (2010); New Hampshire in *The Rules of Attraction* (1987); London, Paris, and Milan in *Glamorama* (1998); and the fictional Midland County in *Lunar Park* (2005). Moreover, Ellis is nowadays probably more closely associated with Hollywood, due to his screenwriting career and infamous Twitter persona. And yet it seems that Ellis is fated to be best remembered for his satirical portrayal of 1980s Manhattan in *American Psycho*. The chapter "'Because I Want to Fit In': The Influence of the Male Peer Group in Bret Easton Ellis' *American Psycho*" presents Ellis' seminal text as his (self-)reflexive examination of homosocial relations in the male peer group in relation to the Manhattan male's attempt to adhere to the ideal of masculinity in 1980s yuppiedom. The protagonist of the novel, Patrick Bateman, has become a figure firmly fixed into pop-culture consciousness. Bateman is not only a cursor of the Manhattan male of the period but appears as a precursor of the sense of "aggrieved entitlement"[6] that would come to dominate the performance of the white American male in media, culture, and society in the contemporary era.[7] Reading Patrick Bateman as a flâneurial figure brings to the fore the intricacies of his performance of his masculinity when he leaves the social spaces of the bars, clubs, restaurants, and his Wall Street office—the spaces in which his masculinity is constantly challenged by his peers—and begins to stalk other Manhattan males on the New York City streets. Seeing Patrick take on a flâneurial role underlines the symbolical value of the attacks on other Manhattan males as a reaction against the challenge to his perceived fixed position in New York society as a successful Wall Street male.

There are clear flâneurial sentiments in Don DeLillo's fiction. DeLillo's view of the novel is that of the arena within which the discourses that shape and inform the social realities around us are absorbed, digested, and addressed. As DeLillo remarks, "writing is a concentrated form of thinking. I don't know what I think about certain subjects, even today, until I sit down and try to write about them. Maybe I wanted to find more rigorous ways of thinking" (Begley, n.p.). DeLillo, reflecting upon his role as writer, intimates that engaging in this activity turns the everyday citizen into the flâneur:

> Words on a page, that's all it takes to help him separate himself from the forces around him, streets and people and pressures and feelings. He learns to think about these things, to ride his own sentences into new perceptions. (Begley, n.p.)

The fifth chapter "'A World Citizen with a New York Pair of Balls': The Global Hegemonic Male in Don DeLillo's *Cosmopolis*" presents Eric Packer, the protagonist of *Cosmopolis* (2003), as the flâneur through which DeLillo critiques the impact of the discourses of globalization upon the Manhattan male's sense of his masculinity. It is the tension between the global and the local that comes to characterise Packer, a twenty-eight-year-old multibillionaire asset manager and currency trader, as he moves through the streets of New York. Inside his white stretch limo, Packer's masculinity is defined by his literal and figurative detachment from other individuals in Manhattan. It is in the act of stepping outside of the limo, and adopting the role of flâneur, that Packer not only begins to "see" other people in Manhattan, but also to "see" himself. It is in becoming the flâneur that Packer recognises the impact of his performance as a global hegemonic male in Manhattan through the self-reflective journey into his masculine selfhood.

Before embarking on the critical analysis of the centrality of the theme of masculinity in the works of Auster, Ellis, and DeLillo, the opening second chapter of this book, "Walking Manhattan, Writing Masculinity: (Re-)Introducing the New York Flâneur with E. B. White's *Here Is New York* and Joshua Ferris' *The Unnamed,*" introduces the main strands of this study. The first section charts the development of the flâneur through the course of modernity from the aimless wanderer to the sociologically conscious critical investigator. The second section engages with a classic piece of flâneurial writing on New York City, E. B. White's *Here Is New York* (1949), to illustrate the power of the flâneur to see men and masculinity in the city. The third and final section rebuffs the current critical attitude of the dissolution of the cultural relevance of the contemporary flâneur with a close reading of Joshua Ferris' *The Unnamed* (2010). What may initially appear to be two profoundly divergent texts to (re-)introduce the flâneur, E. B. White's *Here Is New York* and Joshua Ferris' *The Unnamed,* demonstrate that the New York flâneur has existed, and continues to exist, as a counter-hegemonic methodological tool through which the discourses of power that shape American masculinity are dramatized and, crucially, made visible.

NOTES

1. See Bigar.
2. See Berger to get a sense of the Pulitzer Prize–winning journalist's great love affair with the city.
3. Ellis has always been cannily ambiguous regarding his sexuality, something that he continues to play with to this day in his Twitter-charged media persona.
4. New York is a central character in Paul Auster's novels. When this is put to Auster by Bill Corbett, Auster replies, "Yes, this is my town; it's my place. I love it and hate it; I want to leave and I want to stay. . . . The frenzy of the place at times, the poverty of the place, the ambitiousness of the place, the shallowness of the place and yet everything I say about it can be contradicted" (Auster and Corbett, n.p.).
5. The majority of readings that focus on the movement of the Auster protagonists through the urban spaces of New York seem to underline this point. Tim Woods, in his excellent essay "'Looking for Signs in the Air': Urban Space and the Postmodern in *In the Country of Last Things*," discusses the politics of place and urban spatiality in Auster's dystopian visions of the city. While Woods cites the preoccupations of Auster's fiction as "memory, place, walking, the relation of body to mind, [and] texts as spaces" (152), there is a notable lack of reference to the construction of masculinity in these urban spaces.
6. See Kimmel 2013.
7. Ellis continues: "Patrick Bateman seems to embody something about masculinity that was blooming at a certain point in the late '80s to early '90s. This kind of damnification of the male. This obsession with male narcissism and beauty. Men being looked at in a way that women had been looked at for decades" (Coreno).

2 Walking Manhattan, Writing Masculinity

(Re-)Introducing the New York Flâneur with E. B. White's *Here Is New York* and Joshua Ferris' *The Unnamed*

THE FLÂNEUR AS SOCIOLOGIST: MASCULINE DISCOURSES AND THE FLÂNEUR

Richard D. E. Burton sums up critical opinion on the origins of the flâneur by stating that "no figure belongs more thoroughly to Paris, and the nineteenth century, than the flâneur" (1). While flânerie began as the pastime of a seemingly passive languid Parisian ambler, the flâneur has evolved during the course of modernity to enjoy various reinterpretations. Beginning with Flaubert's "disinterested idler," to Balzac's "flâneur-artiste" and Baudelaire's "lyrical poet," "anonymous artist," and "philosopher," the flâneur has evolved into Walter Benjamin's "detached reporter" and Edgar Allan Poe's "urban detective." Contemporary readings of the figure have emphasised the role of the flâneur as "sociologist," in the view of David Frisby, or "analytic form" according to Chris Jenks. As a sociological type engaged in the analysis of urban discourse, the flâneur, as Deborah Parsons elaborates, continues to exist "in theoretical and historiographical means, as a model for [our] own methodology and the cultural climate we are studying" (228). This section of the chapter will address the shifting role of the flâneur before arriving at the crux of the analysis of the sociological value of this figure: the flâneur continues to exist as a vital tool for the writer intent on exploring the grand narrative of the social construction of masculinity in society.

In the years before the French Revolution (1789–1799), Louis Sébastien Mercier wandered the streets of Paris. Mercier's disorganized, fragmented, and mesmerizing flâneurial masterpiece was *Tableaux de Paris,* published in twelve volumes between 1781 and 1789.[1] *Tableaux de Paris* is a celebration of the French capital but by no means does it shy away from the filth and squalor experienced by many in the city streets. It is a work that highlights the need for social regeneration, both of the Parisian urban landscape and the Parisian individual himself. Edmund White, in his tribute to the "paradoxes of Paris" with his book *The Flâneur* (2001), praises Mercier for placing the "practical and noble goals" (34) of urban renewal at the core of his flâneurial conclusions.

Honoré de Balzac is identified as the writer who transformed the flâneur into a truly respected urban personage.[2] As Balzac's flâneur exclaims in *La Comédie humaine,* "To stroll is to vegetate; to flâneur is to live" (930). Balzac's celebration of the flâneur-artiste created the model from which later writers would shape the literary figure of the flâneur. This urban wanderer became established in Parisian urban discourse in the nineteenth century in modest-looking, paperbound, pocket-sized volumes. Walter Benjamin argues that these pieces, written with the intention of detailing social changes brought about by the French Revolution, simply sketched the "types" that could be found walking the streets of Paris: "from the itinerant street vendor of the boulevards to the dandy in the opera-house foyer, there was not a figure of Paris life that was not sketched by a *physiologue*" (*Selected Writings* 18).[3] Benjamin, however, dismisses the flâneurial writings of these times as "a basically petty-bourgeois genre from the ground up . . . nowhere did these physiologies break through the most limited horizons" (18). Benjamin underlines their lack of critical depth in stating that "the long series of eccentric or simple, attractive or severe figures which the physiologies presented to the public in character sketches had one thing in common: they were harmless and of perfect bonhomie" (*Charles Baudelaire* 37).[4] The legacy of these pieces of flâneurial literature, however, was to introduce writing focused on social commentary of the urban individual, writing that was taken to the next level by one of Benjamin's heroes: Charles Baudelaire.

Charles Baudelaire's seminal text in terms of the study of flânerie is the essay "The Painter of Modern Life" (1863). In Baudelaire's view the flâneur has a specific task: "he makes it his business to extract from fashion whatever element it may contain of poetry within history, to distil the eternal from the transitory" (2). For Baudelaire the drive behind this need was the flâneur's desire to illustrate "that quality which you must allow me to call 'modernity.' . . . By 'modernity' I mean the ephemeral, the fugitive, the contingent, the half of art whose other half is the eternal and the immutable" (13). The protagonist of the piece, the anonymous Monsieur C. G., is not simply a "man of the world" (6) but "a man of the whole world, a man who understands the world and the mysterious and lawful reasons for all its uses" (7). He enters the crowd as though it were a "mass of electrical energy," with this flâneur appearing as a "mirror to the crowd itself," a "kaleidoscope gifted with consciousness" (9):

> The crowd is his element, as the air is that of birds and water of fishes. His passion and his profession are to become one flesh with the crowd. For the perfect *flâneur,* for the passionate spectator, it is an immense joy to set up house in the heart of the multitude, amid the ebb and flow of movement, in the midst of the fugitive and the infinite. (9)

Flâneurial activity was not simply the act of seeing the city but (re)producing these visual experiences on paper. As Baudelaire states, "Few men are gifted with the capacity of seeing; there are fewer still who possess the power of expression" (12). The sociologist David Frisby affirms the range of skills and abilities that are developed daily by the active flâneur: "an investigation of *flânerie* as *activity* must therefore explore the activities of observation (including listening), reading (of metropolitan life and of texts), and producing texts" ("The Flâneur in Social Theory" 82). Benjamin regards Baudelaire as the key figure in early flâneurial writing, as it is Baudelaire who gives voice to the shock and intoxication experienced by the individual in the modern city.

Benjamin does not accept Baudelaire's assertion, however, which makes reference to Edgar Allan Poe's renowned flâneurial tale, as the flâneur existing as the "man of the crowd" ("The Painter of Modern Life" 7). According to Benjamin, "the man of the crowd is no flâneur. In him, composure has given way to manic behaviour. Hence he exemplifies, rather, what had to become of the flâneur once he was deprived of the milieu to which he belonged" ("On Some Motifs on Baudelaire" 172). In contrast to Baudelaire's urban writer being "one flesh with the crowd," Benjamin's flâneur exists outside of the masses, a detached reporter casting his gaze upon those affected by the distortion of time and space that is characteristic of modernity. This inside-outside dichotomy is a key insight in understanding Benjamin's stance on the flâneur. Benjamin regards the act of flânerie as a series of paradoxical oppositions, a reading that is evident in *The Arcades Project*. An encyclopaedic project that Benjamin worked on for thirteen years, from 1927 until his death in 1940, *The Arcades Project* argues that the growth of popularity of flânerie can be linked to architectural change in the city of Paris. Benjamin's analysis marks a shift in the thinking of the role of the flâneur. Benjamin argues that this reinvention as urban detective is of great benefit to the flâneur:

> it does him a lot of good socially, for it legitimates his idleness. His indolence is only apparent, for behind this indolence there is the watchfulness of an observer who does not take his eyes off a miscreant. Thus, the detective sees rather wide areas opening up to his self-esteem. He develops reactions that are in keeping with the tempo of a big city. (*Selected Writings* 22)

This new role of watchful observer hints at the role of detective that would come to define the flâneur in a rapidly developing capitalist society driven by the masculine and masculinizing forces of commodification and consumerism.

The success of the flâneur as the urban detective begins with Edgar Allan Poe. Walter Benjamin called Poe's "The Man of the Crowd" (1840) "an X-ray of a detective story" (*Selected Writings* 27). Dana Brand, in his fine work *The Spectator and the City in Nineteenth-Century American Literature* (1991), argues that critics have overlooked the link between the flâneur and the creation of Poe's urban detective, C. Auguste Dupin. Brand cites the earlier attempts to connect Dupin to Voltaire's Zadig, the links to four articles possibly read by Poe that were published in the *Gentlemen's Magazine* in 1838, entitled "Unpublished Passages in the Vidocq, the French Minister of Police," or indeed the possibility of Dupin being a romanticized self-portrait of Poe. In answer to these readings Brand persuasively presents the flâneurial behaviour and habits displayed by Poe's Dupin—the most notable being his distance and invisibility from the crowd, his appetite for urban observation, and his techniques of reading the urban condition (95–99). Rather than existing as a copy of earlier flâneurial figures, Poe's urban detective, Brand suggests, transcends the traditional figure of the flâneur.[5] Highlighting that the only language of the flâneur is that of the city—"every object or person has no life or meaning other than that which the flâneur attributes to him, her, or it" (99)—Poe's detective becomes "a metareader of urban languages" (99). He is able to read reality in greater complexity by analysing varying interpretations of truth; he is able to see what is both not there and what is. Instead of naively believing that he can be all-seeing, the urban detective, a flâneur 2.0, becomes "a panoramic interpreter of interpretations" (102). The flâneur is no longer satisfied with reading the surface but looks to the hidden complexities lying below the superficial. The role of the urban detective is to impose an interpretative order upon the chaotic.

Poe, writing in the mid-1800s, decided to set "The Man of the Crowd" in London—a city, at this time, that symbolized the order and rationality of a modern metropolis for the American people. As William Sharpe argues, Poe plays on the literary device of the immensity of the setting of London for "a New York audience who will read their city's future into London's fictive present" (*New York Nocturne* 70). Poe's anonymous narrator sits in a café observing the swarm of city dwellers surging past his window, taking time to categorise the different people that he sees. He happens to spot an old man moving among the masses and decides to follow him. The significance of "The Man of the Crowd" lies in its positioning within the historical lineage of flâneurial writing as a meta-critical pointer towards the role of the flâneur and his reading of the city. Brand argues that Poe's critique of the flâneur's method of representing modern cities enables him to develop a new method of transcending flâneurial limitations: "Inventing a new genre, and a new urban spectator, in response to changes that may have been taking place in the public understanding of cities, Poe offered new models for reading and consuming the city" (79). The concept of the flâneur thus reacts to the changing characteristics of the modern metropolis. Brand sees the urban detective not as a contradiction or rejection of the flâneur but as a "dialectical adaptation" of him. The detective is a construction that is better adapted to the changing aesthetic and intellectual needs of the reader. The city "is still a spectacle, and the model for consciousness that can consume the spectacle is still a detached reader and connoisseur of a social world with which he has no desire to interact" (105). The arrival of gaslight opened up a new subgenre of the nocturnal urban sketch, with writers revelling in the sensationalism of inner-city "truths" lit up by artificial light.[6] These stories finally gave way to that typified by Poe's "The Man of the Crowd," with the assumption that the activities illuminated in the flâneur's writing are not only to be observed but also morally questioned. The flâneur became a literary device that embodied method, deduction, and reasoning whilst existing as the holder of intellect and a wider understanding of the functioning of society. The flâneur was both one with the crowd and detached from it, reading the past of the city while existing entirely in the present, and in a position to shape the public landscape with his own private psyche during his flâneurial performance.

As Poe, an American, was writing his flâneurial tale set in London, an Englishman, Charles Dickens, was writing his flâneurial experience in New York City. Charles Dickens is traditionally considered a "London" writer, having spent the majority of life in this grand metropolis.[7] Yet Dickens also spent time abroad, most notably in terms of his clear flâneurial impulses, in Paris and New York. Grahame Smith investigates the symbolic significance of London and Paris in Dickens' writing.[8] Smith supports his exploration of the particular resonance of Paris with Peter Ackroyd's fine research on Dickens in the French capital. In Ackroyd's estimation, Paris was "Dickens' own vision of the world"—a city that fulfilled "Dickens' own need for light and brilliancy"; the arena in which "the world is turned into a spectacle" (qtd. in Smith). London, on the other hand, provided a spectacle of a different kind. As Smith argues, "if Ackroyd is right in claiming that Paris fulfilled Dickens' 'own needs for light and brilliancy,' we could argue that London fulfilled his equally strong need for darkness and confusion." Smith's view is clear: in a Dickensian reading of these grand urban labyrinths, Paris symbolises the theatrical richness of the metropolis, the daily display of urban parade. London, on the other hand, appears as a spectacle in which all human life is characterised by the negative aspects of relentless urbanization. Building upon this reading, Dickens' flâneurial reportage of his experience in New York should also be considered alongside London and Paris in any investigation into the symbolic significance of the city for Dickens. Reading *American Notes*, Dickens' writing on New York offers a crucial insight into another aspect of the city experience: the particular type of male subjectivity that populates the urban arena.

Dickens visited America twice in his lifetime. Although it is widely considered—somewhat fairly it might be said—that Dickens' main motivation for visiting the United States was financial, while there Dickens commented on the social conditions of the New World.[9] *American Notes* is the published product of Dickens' flâneurial wanderings from his first visit to America between January and June of 1842. Chapter 6 of this work is dedicated to what Dickens describes as "the beautiful metropolis of America" (80): New York City.

Uncovering the social realities of urban living was a central concern that drove Dickens' flâneurial missions in London and Paris. New York City was no different. Michael Hollington's article "Dickens the Flâneur" argues for a sociological drive in Dickens' writing of his novels.[10] The sociological implications that Hollington refers to are played in the "sets of oppositions" (78) that, in his view, characterise the activity of the flâneur. Hollington reads flânerie as a "paradoxical form of activity" (74), an activity which he sees as having a "negative capability permitting a special heightened form of observation" (74).[11] Hollington highlights Boz, Master Humphrey, and The Uncommerical Traveller as the three principal examples of the literary figure of the flâneur offering a sense of meaning within the chaotic fictional urban landscape. As Hollington states, "we might expect elsewhere, then, some correlation between the *flâneur* as the mediator of the disparate stimuli of the street and the narrator as the uncoverer of the mysteries of the plot and the extremes and contradictions within it" (83). Employing the first-person plural narrative mode "we" to engage the reader in his flâneurial experience, Dickens makes general comments on the layout and condition of the New York City streets. He takes on the role of social investigator, noting the degradation of the living conditions endured in various areas of the city, no more so than in his exploratory visits to the public institutions of New York.

The great focus of Dickens' chapter on New York is his characterisation of the male that inhabits this burgeoning city of the New World. Dickens identifies the various New York men that shape and are shaped by the public sphere. He does not shy away from underlining the hegemony within New York society that is formed around the categories of race, class, and financial power. Dickens mocks those who see themselves as privileged among the ever-increasing mass of people: he sees a southern republican who "swells with Sultan pomp and power" (81); the "Yorkshire groom, who has not been very long in these parts, and looks sorrowfully round for a companion pair of top-boots" (81); and the "Byrons of the desk and counter" (81) standing impotent in their inability to approach the ladies of certain dress and bearing. Dickens also identifies the marginalised male figures in New York society at that time. He mentions the Negro coachmen displayed as trophies by their white masters (81); the prisoners in the Tombs treated inhumanely and driven to suicide (83); and "the corpulent black fiddler" and his friend who "play a lively measure" (91). Dickens also praises the "honest service" of two Irish labourers, constructing their story of loyalty, sacrifice, and determination to create a better life for their families. Dickens displays his strong admiration for these men, for it is these men that achieve self-definition and self-improvement through their commitment to regenerating their urban environment:

> For who else would dig, and delve, and drudge, and do domestic work, and make canals and roads, and execute great lines of Internal Improvement! Irishmen both, and sorely puzzled too, to find out what they seek.

> Let us go down, and help them, for the love of home, and that spirit of liberty which admits of honest service to honest men, and honest work for honest bread, no matter what it be. (81)

The lasting image from Dickens' reportage of New York City is that of the "solitary swine" (86). Dickens was not exaggerating when he wrote of the presence of pigs in the streets of Manhattan. Photographs show pigs wandering through the city streets until 1900.[12] Dickens, our flâneur, sees the particular types of New York male projected in these animals. On Broadway he comes upon this pig wandering the streets alone:

> Here is a solitary swine lounging homeward by himself. He has only one ear; having parted with the other to vagrant-dogs in the course of his city rambles. But he gets on very well without it; and leads a roving, gentlemanly, vagabond kind of life, somewhat answering to that of our club-men at home. (86)

Throughout this section Dickens' writing is both fiercely critical and yet highly comical: "They are the city scavengers, these pigs. Ugly brutes they are; having, for the most part, scanty brown backs, like the lids of old horsehair trunks: spotted with unwholesome black blotches" (87). Although he begins by identifying the pig with the "club-men at home" (86), he also sees these swines as perfect projections of other categories of urban male, particularly as a "republican pig" (86). These "gentlemen hogs" (86) lounging around the streets of Broadway are a satirical swipe at the New York gentry who remain completely oblivious to the reality of the social inequality in Manhattan: "He is in every respect a republican pig, going wherever he pleases, and mingling with the best society, on an equal, if not superior footing, for everyone makes way when he appears, and the haughtiest give him the wall, if he prefer it" (86). Dickens, as we can see, is writing about a particular type of male subjectivity that inhabited the New York City streets.

Dickens' piece of urban observation transposes the literary figure of the flâneur from the streets of Paris to the city of New York. William Sharpe writes:

> In New York, however, Dickens abandoned aesthetic detachment, gave vent to a personal sense of outrage, criticized rather than lauded public institutions, and expressed shock that such a social order be allowed to exist. Although his penchant for comparison occasionally imparts the sense that New York is a second-hand London, Dickens is vivid enough in short stretches to seem to have got the gist of New York's misery a decade before Melville, and a half-century before Jacob Riis. In his best moments, what Dickens adds to the urban sketch is an apprecia-tion for the humanity of his subjects; he provides compassion without

condemnation. But his sympathy for the poor and the imprisoned, and his indignation at the conditions which they are forced to endure, ring discordantly in a tradition where enthusiasm of any sort is usually reserved for wonder at the vastness and variety of the city itself. ("A Pig upon the Town" 14)

Dickens' employment of the flâneur illustrates the power of taking a figure associated with the European literary tradition and placing him within the New World to open up the great American metropolis to sociological investigation. Dickens' flâneur underlines the fact that as an observer, a reader, and a writer of the city, the flâneur is also a constructor of male subjectivity. The entire existence of the writer is based upon this dialectic; in other words, existence no longer lies in living in the city, but writing in the city. These textual representations, as Baudelaire proposed, allow the reader to see the city's complexities in greater clarity and to recognise these external societal issues as reflections upon the inner issues of the writer himself: "the external world is reborn upon his paper, natural and more than natural, beautiful and more than beautiful, strange and endowed with an impulsive life like the soul of its creator" ("The Painter of Modern Life" 12). Flânerie, therefore, can be split into three interrelated activities: first, the flâneur is an observer of the people, a spectator of social activities, an onlooker within the social arena of the metropolis; second, with this information, he is a reader of the city, its architecture, and its spatial configurations; and third, and arguably most significantly, the flâneur is also the writer of the city, the producer of textual representations of the metropolis. The city and the individual live a dual existence—the physical and the textual—and it is the textual representations that offer key insights into the contemporary experience of the male individual in the city.

From this historical mapping of the development of the flâneur, it is clear that a sociological drive has underpinned flâneurial activity since its very beginning. As I mention above, Louis Sébastien Mercier highlighted the social plight of the average Parisian. Balzac has been credited as being a pioneer in the writings of the flâneur. David Harvey, in his study of flânerie, asserts that "Balzac's flâneur is more than an aesthete, a wandering observer, he is also purposive, seeking to unravel the mysteries of social relations and of the city" (*Paris* 56). Walter Benjamin argued that social awareness ran through the writing of Baudelaire, not merely artistic or commercial interests. This sociological strand is continued in the writing of Benjamin himself. David Frisby maintains that not only did Benjamin attempt one of the first histories of the flâneur, but in looking at Benjamin's own reflections upon the methodology for *The Arcades Project,* he also produced an analytic of flânerie that reveals certain links between this activity and the sociologist's investigation into the sociological world (89). Benjamin suggests that this figure is able to grasp concrete historical experience (*Erfahrung*) and not merely subjective lived-out experience (*Erlebnis*) and produce illuminating pieces of literary text (Frisby, *Cityscapes of Modernity* 40). It is the act of writing, therefore, that allows the flâneur a deeper reflection upon what has been seen and experienced, and it is this activity that is the key component of the act of flânerie. As Benjamin puts it, "the flâneur observes and seeks the meaning of his modernity" (16). To this, perhaps we might add that in observing modernity, the flâneur also finds the meaning of his masculinity.

FINDING THE MEANING OF MODERNITY AND MASCULINITY IN MANHATTAN: E.B. WHITE'S *HERE IS NEW YORK*

Curiously New Yorkers did not initially consider their city as flâneurable. The first American incarnation of the flâneur was the ex-pat flâneur; the people of the city in the 1840s devoured American reprints of the city sketches of their European cousins with writers such as Washington Irving and Nathaniel Parker Willis sending back their experiences of the intoxication of London and Paris on the urban individual.[13] However, as New York City became the particularly American elaboration and intensification of the urban developments seen in London and Paris, the New York City flâneur began to recognise his city as the ideal urban arena.[14] The flâneur was also tied into the development of the identity of New York as the emerging urban metropolis. It could be argued that it is for this reason that this literary figure, originating in Paris, enjoyed great success when transposed into the American arena. During this period Cornelius Mathews, one of the leaders of the self-coined "Young America" movement, argued for a literature that truly represented American identity. Mathews called for a new literary style that focused on "the crowded life of cities, the customs, habitudes, and actions of men dwelling in contact" (qtd. in Burrows and Wallace 692). Burrows and Wallace, in their Pulitzer Prize–winning *Gotham* (1999) make the claim that Mathews' *Career of Puffer Hopkins* (1842) "was the first fictional attempt to capture the colour of New York, as its flâneurial hero wandered about from fancy shops to dingy alleys, exploring the city's various worlds" (692). William Sharpe's reading of the flâneur in the United States is worth quoting in full:

> The flâneur thrived in the United States, where his glorification of commerce and benign sense of the crowd brought him closer to the cultural mainstream than his dandified European cousin had been. The urban spectator represented a culmination of the forces transforming the United States into the preeminent industrial civilization, a place where trade could live in apparent harmony with civic ideals. Dwelling on the commercial spectacle, the flâneur propagated the all-important links between looking and consuming, and between consumption and greatness. (*New York Nocturne* 43)

With the emergence of gaslight in the 1840s and new printing presses in the 1850s, it was the journalist writers of this period, the flâneurs, who guided readers into the very heart of the city. As the years passed and New York grew, George Foster, Herman Melville, Edgar Allan Poe, and Walt Whitman wrote telling tales that led New York to become the most visually represented city in the country.[15] As Walt Whitman famously proclaimed, Manhattan was "the great place of the Western Continent, the heart, the brain, the focus, the main spring, the pinnacle, the extremity, the no more beyond of the new world" (Rubin and Brown 19).[16] New York was the centre of diversity and progress, the frontline of American development, pulling the country and its people into the future. The rapid growth of the city led these flâneurs to turn their attention inward to examine the link between the city and the individual. There is one text that remains the classic piece of flâneurial writing on the city in its depiction of the masculine power discourses at play in the urban metropolis: E. B. White's *Here Is New York* (1949). In fifty-four compact and powerful pages, White portrays not only the poetry found in the great city but the reality of everyday survival in a place that is a unique energy. Gendering White's march, it becomes clear that White is not only writing about the urban environment but also about how masculinity both shapes and is shaped by New York.

Here Is New York is widely lauded as White's love poem to the grand metropolis of Manhattan, a man-made construction of social and theatrical wonder. White paints New York as the centre of the modern world, a global city, an exhibit of the changing landscape in the melting pot of modern life. As much as it is a tribute to the city itself, I would like to propose that the condition of male subjectivity emerges as the central theme of White's classic flâneurial text. It is not coincidental that White riffs on the various types of male figures that perform within this urban arena:

> New York is the concentrate of art and commerce and sport and religion and entertainment and finance, bringing to a single compact arena the gladiator, the evangelist, the promoter, the actor, the trader and the merchant. (19)

Sitting in a "stifling hotel room in 90-degree heat" (20), White locates himself in the city in relation to what may seem at first glance as a random list of famous figures from that era:

> I am twenty-two blocks away from where Rudolph Valentino lay in state, eight blocks from where Nathan Hale was executed, five blocks from the publisher's office where Ernest Hemingway hit Max Eastman on the nose, four miles from where Walt Whitman sat sweating out editorials for the Brooklyn Eagle . . . (20)

White goes on to list other New York celebrities, both male and female, but these first examples are telling. Within these few lines White is appropriating his personal experience of Manhattan alongside famous male figures that represent varying categories of masculinity: Rudolph Valentino, the Italian movie star sex symbol; Nathan Hale, a spy for the Continental Army during the American Revolutionary War, who has been long considered an American war hero after being captured and executed by the British Army; Ernest Hemingway, the American writer whose fiction depicts the struggles of men attempting to maintain traditional notions of masculinity; and Walt Whitman, the New York poet whose work is often read as an exploration of male sexualities in the metropolis. White's method of making sense of his being within this city of modernity is telling. He defines his own experience by measuring it alongside other male figures who form their identities in their struggles in New York.

New York is not a capital city. It is neither a national capital nor a state capital, but it is often regarded as the capital of the world in terms of commerce, art, and culture. New York City's social transformation occurred in a spectacularly short space of time, in which it experienced incredible levels of immigration and urban development. As White states, "It is a miracle that New York works at all" (31). White recites the disasters that should have befallen New York during this period of rapid growth: "New York should have destroyed itself long ago, from panic or fire or rioting or failure of some vital supply line in its circulatory system or from some deep labyrinthine short circuit"; "Long ago the city should have experienced an insoluble traffic snarl"; "It should have perished of hunger"; "It should have been wiped out by a plague starting in its slums or carried in by ships' rats"; "It should have been overwhelmed by the sea" (32). This chiming refrain is a ringing declaration of the city's defiance in the face of seemingly inevitable collapse. What drives this defiance is the power of the city to defy the odds, to face up to adversity, and to become even stronger. This unique strength of character is based on the special relationship between New York City and its people.

At various points in *Here Is New York*, White emphasises the protective nature of the city. White sees New York City, and in particular Manhattan, as succeeding in "insulating the individual (if he wants it, and almost everybody wants or needs it) against all enormous and violent and wonderful events that are taking place every minute" (22). To those suffering "a deficiency of spirit" it can offer "sources of excitement for spiritual sustenance and maintenance of morale" (25). Ultimately White believes that the city's inhabitants "find in New York a protection" (25). The issue of the dialectical relationship between Manhattan and the urban individual is a central theme of *Here Is New York*:

> On any person who desires such queer prizes, New York will bestow the gift of loneliness and the gift of privacy. It is this largess that accounts for the presence within the city's walls of a considerable section of the population; for the residents of Manhattan are to a large extent

> strangers who have pulled up stakes somewhere and come to town, seeking sanctuary or fulfilment or some greater or lesser grail. (19)

White's view of New York City as being able to provide "the gift of loneliness and the gift of privacy" is often cited by critics of contemporary New York as proof of a better time when the city was less crowded, less fractious, and less tense. Roger Angell, in the introduction to the 1999 edition of *Here Is New York,* laments the changes that Manhattan has experienced since the original publication date of White's flâneurial text in 1949:

> I'm not sure that New York in 1999 can offer "the gift of loneliness and the gift of privacy," the way it did in the book. It's hard to feel private in the surging daily crowds at the Metropolitan Museum of Art, say, or lonely in a side street packed solid with gridlocked traffic. (White 11)

I would suggest, however, that the opening passage in *Here Is New York* is White's comment on the ability of New York, and in particular Manhattan, to offer the budding flâneur the ideal arena for observing, reading, and writing the grand metropolis. Michael Hollington notes in his application of Benjamin's theory of flânerie to the writing of Charles Dickens that "the flâneur on the street embodies and becomes aware of the paradox that urban man is at his most isolated and private in the midst of a crowd" (79). The traditional image of the flâneur is a man of the crowd who is able to move among the masses unopposed and unnoticed. The urban wanderer that inhabits the city streets is able to observe and critique the urban environment that he sees around him. He is not a detached observer but a member of the public mass of people that is turned on to the power of the individual to offer literary representations of the metropolis. I would argue, therefore, that White is suggesting that New York's greatest gift to the urban individual is to offer the opportunity for each inhabitant to become more than a simple city dweller by realising his or her potential as a flâneur roaming the streets of New York. White affirms this once more in the text when he states, "New York blends the gift of privacy with the excitement of participation" (22). Manhattan is presented as the ideal environment for the urban flâneur.

White reaffirms this point by celebrating the power of the metropolis to provide "not only a continuing excitation but also a spectacle that is continuing" (38). White, our urban onlooker, lists the "good many rather splashy events" (22) that have taken place there since he arrived: a man who shot and killed his wife, an air show, a lion convention, various sporting spectacles, a visit of the governor, and the tragic death of a man killed by a cornice. The point White is making is thus:

> New York is peculiarly constructed to absorb almost anything that comes along . . . without inflicting the event upon its inhabitants; so that every event is, in a sense, optional, and the inhabitant is in the

> happy position of being able to choose his spectacle and conserve his soul. In most metropolises, small and large, the choice is often not with the individual at all. (23–24)

There is a sense that the city is somehow aware of its size and power and the fragility of the people that flow through its city streets, the blood through its veins. White is also clear, however, in his warning of the two sides to this relationship. On the one hand New York City may welcome, protect, and nourish its inhabitants. Yet on the other hand, as White warns in the final sentence of the first paragraph of *Here Is New York*, "[New York] can destroy an individual, or it can fulfil him, depending a good deal on luck. No one should come to New York to live unless he is willing to be lucky" (19).

The effects of this rapidly growing metropolis cannot be exclusively positive. As White notes, "New York has changed in tempo and temper during the years I have known it. There is greater tension, increased irritability. You encounter it in many places, in many faces" (51–52). White's focus on the physiognomies of the people echoes Poe's methodological approach to studying the effect of the sprawling urban environment on the everyday individual. White notes that "the normal frustrations of modern life are here multiplied and amplified. . . . There is greater tension and there is greater speed" (52). White is writing about Manhattan in the late 1940s, but his acute awareness of societal conditions of the time foretells the state of this dense urban arena to come, evoking in many ways David Harvey's influential concept of "time-space compression."[17] The power of the discourses in New York to alter the individual's sense of time and space, particularly in relation to the individual's sense of his masculine identity, is a major theme that I will discuss later in my analysis of globalization and the contemporary New York male in Don DeLillo's *Cosmopolis* (2003).

White does not hide the tensions and strains of the urban concentration. He reads the effects of these accelerating forces in this city of modernity in the everyday demeanour of the New York people. New York, in White's view, "has never been so uncomfortable, so crowded, so tense" (52). Crucially, however, White does not reach the conclusion suggested by Elizabeth Wilson of the metropolis leading to the deconstruction of the subject in the urban environment. White celebrates the special relationship between the individual and Manhattan. As White denotes, "Mass hysteria is a terrible force, yet New Yorkers seem always to escape it by some tiny margin. . . . The city makes up for its hazards and deficiencies by supplying its citizens with massive doses of a supplementary vitamin—the sense of belonging to something unique, cosmopolitan, mighty and unparalleled" (32–33). White argues that the urban male need not automatically suffer dissolution of his masculine subjectivity due to the stresses and strains of everyday life in the city. Conversely, it is the very urban environment itself that can offer a sense of (re)generation of selfhood.

Here Is New York also documents one of the underlying dynamics that has characterised the development of Manhattan: the island's experience of creative destruction. White acknowledges that Manhattan "neither looks nor feels like it did twenty-five years ago" (48), with railways having been pulled down and Broadway's "bony structure" of hotels and shops now "largely disappeared under the neon lights and letters and the frozen custard façade" (48–49). Although White laments the absence of the old haunts he would frequent as a resident in the heart of the city, he does not dwell overly on the past. Rather *Here Is New York* recognises the progress that the city is making, with the "slums gradually giving way to the lofty housing projects—high in stature, high in purpose, low in rent" (50–51) and other housing developments "lifting people far above the street, standardizing their sanitary life, giving them some place to sit other than an orange crate" (51). White is not completely ignorant of the reality of this urban restructuring. He acknowledges that "thousands of new units are still needed and will eventually be built, but New York never quite catches up with itself, is never in equilibrium" (51). Despite these urban traumas, the city maintains its special relationship with its people, a quality not normally associated with an expansive urban metropolis. White, walking its streets, each area "a city within a city within a city" (35), locates this special quality of the city and its people in the communities that make up New York.[18] As we are taken around these insulating pockets of community, we see and hear the expressions of merging cultures from "the open windows of the drum and saxophone parlours" (38). This is the beauty of the borough of Manhattan. It finds expression of its plurality and cultural diversity through seemingly natural and spontaneous artistic means. It is the plurality of the population and the diversity of its competing categories of masculinity that makes New York City the archetypal city of modernity. As White remarks, "the city is like poetry: it compresses all life, all races and breeds, into a small island and adds music and the accompaniment of internal engines" (29).

In White's estimation, the dialectic between the subject and the urban environment gives New York City a distinctive tripartite character that he sets out as follows:

> There are roughly three New Yorks. There is, first, the New York of the man or woman who was born here, who takes the city for granted and accepts its size and its turbulence as natural and inevitable. Second, there is the New York of the commuter—the city that is devoured by locusts each day and spat out each night. Third, there is the New York of the person who was born somewhere else and came to New York in quest of something. (25–26)

Of these three, White chiefly celebrates the third version, as "it is the third city that accounts for New York's high-strung disposition, its poetical deportment, its dedication to the arts, and its incomparable achievements"

(26). I would argue that the other versions of New York are equally as significant in providing an insight into the mentality of the New York City people. The "turbulence" experienced in the "first New York" that White refers to is later expanded in more detail: "The subtlest change in New York is something that people don't speak much about but that is in everyone's mind. The city, for the first time in its long history is destructible" (54). White notices a change in the mentality of the people, a wariness of their vulnerability. Moreover, considered in the context of the terrorist attack on New York City on September 11, 2001, White's insight takes on an eerily prophetic tone: "A single flight of planes no bigger than a wedge of geese can quickly end this island fantasy, burn the towers, crumble the bridges, turn the underground passages into lethal chambers, cremate the millions. The intimation of mortality is part of New York now in the sounds of jets overhead, in the black headlines of the latest edition" (54). Hal Foster, reflecting on Rem Koolhaas' "retrospective manifesto" for Manhattan, *Delirious New York* (1978), suggests "the attack on the World Trade Centre—of the two jets flown into the two towers—was a dystopian perversion of this modernist dream of free movement through cosmopolitan space. Much damage was done to this great vision of skyscraper and city—and to New York as the capital of this dream" (146). The vulnerability of New York and its people is an observation that White reinforces in the text. Under "the cold shadow of planes" (56), this "stubborn fact of annihilation" (54) is illustrated with an unsettling image: "It used to be that the Statue of Liberty was the sign-post that proclaimed New York and translated it for all the world. Today Liberty shares the role with Death" (54). This is the universal dilemma of modernity that hints at the complex existence of the modern metropolis. Whilst appearing on the exterior to have a hard shell shaped by growing capitalist strength, the inner insecurities remain, formed and maintained by the predominantly unmediated, or arguably even unmediatable, array of societal discourses. It may later prove possible to take this analogy further and apply it to the reading of Manhattan and constructions of contemporary American masculinity found in the selected novels of this study.

Despite delving into the darker areas of New York City inhabitants' psyches, at the heart of White's writing on New York City is the belief in the beauty and vitality of this unique metropolis. This is evident when White gives his highly critical view on the people that define the "second New York," that of the commuter. White is highly critical of this version of the Manhattanite. Despite spending a significant period of their day moving through the city streets, White makes clear that "the commuter dies with tremendous mileage to his credit, but he is no rover" (27). In White's estimation, the commuter cannot appreciate the terrain of the city, repeatedly retracing his or her steps in the entrances and exits shared by millions of others. As White scolds, the commuter "discovers nothing much about the city except the time of arrival and departure of trains and buses" (27).

He is unable to claim some undiscovered treasures, as "he has never come suddenly on anything at all in New York as a loiterer, because he has had no time between trains" (27).

This flâneurial rhetoric employed by White should not be dismissed as rose-tinted idealism. *Here Is New York* demonstrates the power of the concept of the flâneur as a methodological approach that marries socio-economical, anthropologic, and psychological insight with the ability to communicate in a simple and direct manner. White's flâneurial instincts, driven by the beating pulse of this "capital of modernity," move him through the labyrinth as he writes the city and the condition of male subjectivity. As White begins *Here Is New York* commenting on the link between the city and its people, he also ends *Here Is New York* with his final proclamation of New York as "the City of Man" (56). Certainly on one level this would seem a pun on *Man*hattan, but it also refers to the changing social and political landscape of New York City at the time. In 1947 it was decided that the permanent headquarters of the United Nations would be situated in the Turtle Bay area of Manhattan. Manhattan, in housing the United Nations headquarters, can be considered both factually and figuratively as the location of what White terms "the Parliament of Man" (55). It is in Manhattan that diplomacy, democracy, and international relations among men would be situated. Manhattan became the arena in which male subjectivity would be debated and defined.

(RE-)INTRODUCING THE CONTEMPORARY NEW YORK FLÂNEUR WITH JOSHUA FERRIS' *THE UNNAMED*

Contemporary research on the flâneur has read this literary figure as a casualty of postmodernity. Zygmunt Bauman ("Desert Spectacular"), Jean Baudrillard, and Graeme Gilloch have led the call for the death of the flâneur, a view crystallized in Gilloch's article "The Return of the 'Flâneur': The Afterlife of an Allegory" (1999). Attaching his reading of the flâneur to the lineage of the great theorists of flânerie, specifically Walter Benjamin, Gilloch states his intention to explore "how and why such an eccentric and arcane allegorical figure has become a key trope in contemporary social and urban analysis" (101). Gilloch argues that Benjamin saw the flâneur as an allegory "[capturing] the world, not in its fullness and perfection, but in its decay and fragmentation" (102). It is at this point the postmodern alarm bells begin to ring. "Decay" and "fragmentation" are arguably two of the buzzwords of cultural theorists seduced by the fatalist strand of postmodern poetics, and this proves an early indicator of the tone of the article to come.

To his credit Gilloch makes a persuasive point in highlighting the influence of Franz Hessel on the thinking of Benjamin and, I would argue, the study of the flâneur as a literary figure. Hessel was a firm believer in the textuality of the city, and Gilloch acknowledges how "the city is transformed into a semiological universe, a mass of hieroglyphs and emblems, which are discerned and deciphered by the flâneur. The city becomes a text to be read in passing" (105). Citing David Frisby, who praises the writing of Benjamin for providing an analytic of flânerie that reinvents the flâneur as sociologist, Gilloch fixes the flâneur as the general model for urban exploration and enquiry. Gilloch even goes as far as to suggest that our contemporary era calls for a resurrection of the flâneur. However, whether this is a heroic reinvention or merely a simulated by-product of the period is less clear. Rejecting any suggestion of the power of the flâneur to offer acute critical insight, Gilloch states:

> The return of the figure is symptomatic of the postmodern. The *flâneur* no longer perambulates as a pedestrian, but circulates as a sign. As the *flâneur* comes to adopt more and more guises, proliferating as a trope, an allegory for more and more tenuous figures and experiences, it becomes a pure sign, a signifier freed from, bereft of, any specific signified. (108)

Reading this mission statement, the influence of the postmodern theorists name-checked above is quite clear. Using the lexis of the post-structural school of thought, the flâneur in this contemporary postmodern era, which Gilloch sees epitomised by Baudrillard's *America* (1988), is not a propagator of progress. The flâneur has regressed once more into the languid strolling sign, walking aimlessly amidst the attractions of flashing neon lights promising instant satisfaction and excitement but ultimately delivering empty experiences.

Those interested in the issue of masculinity and the flâneur also maintain this position. The self-proclaimed propagators of "postmodern feminist discourse" in the 1980s and 1990s, Elizabeth Wilson, Janet Wolff, Griselda Pollock, and Priscilla Parkhurst Ferguson, argued that the flâneur, as the voice of modernity, has always existed as the voice of masculinity, and as such, should be read as the ultimate tool in the preservation of patriarchal dominance in society.[19] Janet Wolff gets directly to the point: "the literature of modernity describes the experience of men" (37). Wolff explicitly genders the writing of the most influential figures that have shaped this literary figure: "the influential writings of Baudelaire, Simmel, Benjamin, and more recently, Richard Sennet and Marshall Berman, by equating the *modern* with the *public,* thus fail to describe women's experiences of modernity" (37). Wolff uses the example of George Sand, who in 1831, with the desire to experience Parisian life and to learn about art, culture, and society, was forced to dress as a boy in order "to give herself the freedom she knew women could not share" (41).[20] As Wolff states, "the disguise made the life of the *flâneur* available to her; as she knew very well, she could not adopt the non-existent role of the *flâneuse.* Women could not stroll alone in the city" (41).

Priscilla Parkhurst Ferguson builds on Wolff's main argument with her research on the power discourses that she sees as defining flâneurial activity: "There is another reason for excluding women from the fraternity of *flâneurs:* women are essential components of the urban drama that the flâneur observes. A woman idling on the street is to be 'consumed' and 'enjoyed' along with the rest of the sights that the city affords" ("The *Flâneur* On and Off the Streets of Paris" 28). As Parkhurst Ferguson comments, "Balzac introduces the topic of flânerie in the *Physiologie du marriage* (1829) with conjectures about a woman glimpsed in the street" (28). It is therefore possible to argue that from its very beginning the flâneur has been engaged, whether consciously or not, in the power discourses that shape masculinity. The "male gaze," in objectifying the female individual, ensures that the male figure sustains his hegemonic status.

Elizabeth Wilson's contribution to the discussion on the issue of gender and the flâneur focuses on the notion that it is the city itself that forms and deconstructs the flâneur's masculinity. Wilson, echoing Georg Simmel's influential essay "The Metropolis and Mental Life" (1903),[21] argues that the urban labyrinth leads to a "disintegrative effect" on masculinity:

> From this perspective, we might say that there could never be a female *flâneur,* for this reason: that the flâneur himself never really existed, being but an embodiment of the special blend of excitement, tedium and horror aroused by many in the new metropolis, and the disintegrative effect of this on the masculine identity. The *flâneur* does indeed turn out to be like Poe's Man of the Crowd—a figure of solitude, he is never alone; and, when singled out, he vanishes. He is a figure to be deconstructed, a shifting projection of angst rather than a solid embodiment of male bourgeois power. . . . He floats with no material base, living on his wits, and, lacking the patriarchal discourse that assured him of meaning, is compelled to invent a new one. ("The Invisible Flâneur" 109)

It is at this point that we have perhaps reached the crux of this postmodern argument. Gilloch argues that the flâneur, so deeply embedded within the world of simulacra, is unable to extract himself from the staged artifice of contemporary society. The flâneur is implicated within the overstimulation of urban discourse. He is a sign devoid of any signified. The flâneur is not an urban hero. Gilloch is clear about the sociological power, or lack thereof, of this social observer, this everyday journalist, this urban detective: "*Flânerie* is not a mode of resistance" (108).

In contrast to contemporary deconstructors of the sociological power of the flâneur, I would argue that what drives the flâneur is not simply the desire to observe his urban surroundings and produce aesthetically pleasing literary reflections of this environment or, indeed, to maintain a hegemonic position in the objectification of others; conversely, this study will argue that the flâneur is the writer of the counter-narrative. Certainly masculinity is an issue fundamentally linked to the figure of the flâneur and his writing on the city, but in contrast to the suggestion that it is masculine power discourses that lead to the deconstruction of the flâneur, the flâneur in the contemporary New York novel illustrates that it is the act of walking and writing the city in which the flâneur finds the meaning in his masculinity. The flâneur is a conscious observer, an avenue into a reading of the everyday, and a propagator of the possibilities for change. Stefan Morawski, in his essay "The Hopeless Game of Flânerie," proclaims the figure of the flâneur as "the last intellectual" (Morawski 187). Morawski's flâneur is the individual who will not surrender to the total lure of modern-day Manhattan. In lieu of the typically postmodern drives of instant gratification and mindless stimulation, Morawski adds definitively: "The *flâneur* as the artist's (the intellectual's) probe and shield is today super-heroic in his challenge to the drills of our civilization, the narcotizing market supply of idiocies, the lifestyle-tied shibboleths" (187). In a historical period when fatalistic prophecies were fashionable, it is reassuring that there was a voice willing to speak in support of the flâneur. Yet I would distance my position from Morawski's view that the flâneur need occupy an elevated position of intellectualism. The flâneur is not the last intellectual but the everyman. Gilloch, in his annihilation of the contemporary flâneur, argues, "the flâneur returns as a definitive postmodern figure" (108). I would reformulate that statement to say that the flâneur returns as the definitive figure of what some might call our postmodern age. The flâneur is not negated by postmodernity but has a particular postmodern sensibility; that is, he is conscious of the various discourses at play within contemporary society. Although not necessarily in control of them, he does not exist outside of them. He is an observer, he is a consumer, but most importantly he is a self-reflexive figure who studies, and who should be studied, as a device that underlines the sociological value of literary representations of masculinity in contemporary New York fiction. This raises a key question: How does the flâneur lead us into new avenues of studying contemporary American masculinity represented in novels based in Manhattan?

The sustained significance of the flâneur as a tool for examining the social construction of masculinity is finely illustrated with a look at Joshua Ferris' *The Unnamed* (2010).[22] Ferris' first novel, set in a recession-hit ad agency in Chicago, *Then We Came to the End* (2007), satirises the absurdities of office culture and the interactions between people forced into the constrictive stressful environment of the office. Yet beyond its appearance as a comedy of manners, the novel also deals with the intricacies of the social relationships between differing groups of men within this microcosm of the office. The sharp cultural insights that define *Then We Came to the End* are further developed in Ferris' "The Dinner Party" (2008), a short story published in *The New Yorker.* Although appearing to share the comedic sensibility of *Then We Came to the End*, there is a sharp shift in the tone of the piece toward a darker rumination on the underlying tensions in social relationships. "The Dinner Party" can therefore be identified as the transitional piece in the published work of Ferris. The satirical social commentary of *Then We Came to the End* is transposed and transformed through "The Dinner Party" into a more sociologically charged questioning of the effects of contemporary existence within an all together different social arena in *The Unnamed:* the streets of Manhattan.

The protagonist of *The Unnamed* is Tim Farnsworth, an extremely successful partner of a law firm in the heart of Manhattan. He has the perfect family, the perfect house, and the perfect job. However, Tim begins to develop a condition that disturbs this ideal existence: without warning, regardless of where he is or what he is doing, and unable to control it, he gets up and walks. At first this may seem no more than a gimmick employed to drive the narrative. However, this trope enables Ferris to study the contemporary cultural climate and its shaping of masculinity in New York.

The Unnamed engages with one particular strand within the field of critical men's studies: masculinity in the workplace.[23] The law firm is a gendered institution. Its structure, practices, values, and language reflect these socially established notions of masculinity. Furthermore, it is a gendering institution in that it creates masculine identities that are shaped by the various discourses at play. Tim is the archetypal hegemonic male. He is white, middle class, and, as a city lawyer, has a job that gives him a high degree of power and influence. It is Tim's job that is central to his masculine identity. His increasingly sporadic impulse to walk, however, raises various problems that force him to re-evaluate his masculinity in twenty-first–century Manhattan.

Tim lives to work. Even in his darkest moments, exhausted and broken after another endless bout of walking, and having been found by his wife curled up by the side of the road, he repeats his mantra, "I have to go in" (14). Tim strives to adhere to the hegemonic ideal of authentic American manhood of the "breadwinner" and "self-made man." Having worked his way up the firm from a junior position to partner, it is clear that he believes that it is work that defines him:

> The trial, that was the point. The clients. The casework. The war room. He took on a few pro bono causes. And he worked in midtown amid the electricity and the movement. And his view of Central Park was breathtaking. And he liked the people. And the money was great. And the success was addictive. And the pursuit was all-consuming. And the rightness of place was never in doubt. (37)

Despite the fact that "there were no official hierarchies among partners at Troyer, Barr" (56), it is evident that performing within the hierarchical system is ingrained into the psychology of the male employees. Tim's self-positioning within this hierarchical masculine framework is played out in his interactions with the law firm's managing partner, Mike Kronish. Kronish occupies the top position, but Tim's masculine ego makes him believe that he is above all others in the firm. This masculine power struggle is evident in their every exchange. When coming face to face with his corporate adversary, it is Kronish's physicality that is prominent, especially when compared with Tim's physical state after spending another night walking the city streets: "[Kronish] seemed to hover. Proximity to him felt like sudden contact with a grizzly bear risen up on its hind legs" (56). It is not only his physical stature but also his ability and willingness to push himself to the limits of physical endurance that Tim begrudgingly admires. Tim is extremely envious of the fact that Kronish once worked a twenty-seven–hour day, which "made Tim want to leap across the desk and eat his lucky, healthy heart" (57).

Tim's egotistical nature is shaped and driven by his obsession with achieving a more dominant hierarchical position. Collinson and Hearn term this "careerism."[24] Its destructive force is best illustrated in the trial of R.H. Hobbs. Hobbs, whose private equity firm provides a lot of business for Troyer, Barr, is accused of stabbing his wife to death. The general consensus within the company is that he is innocent. The evidence against him is entirely circumstantial, and the district attorney only manages to bring charges against him by the skin of his teeth. Tim believes that he is the lawyer to ensure that Hobbs will be acquitted, and yet, as the court date approaches, the worsening of Tim's condition means that Tim pays little attention to the case. Even with Hobbs arriving into the law firm and breaking down in Tim's office, with Tim unable to show any compassion, "He didn't know what to say" (74), Tim remains adamant in his repeated refusals to allow any other lawyer to take on the case. Moreover, later in the novel, a man claiming to know details about the murder approaches Tim. Not only does the man suggest that he is involved, he also has a knife, which he hints at being the murder weapon. Tim, however, is unable to find out for certain if this nameless man in the street is a suspect in the case, as his uncontrollable urge to walk returns. Eventually Kronish has to take overall control of the case, but by that point it is too late. Hobbs is convicted and ultimately takes his own life in prison.

Michael Kimmel argues that men view masculinity as "a defence against the perceived threat of humiliation and emasculation in the eyes of other men" ("Masculinity as Homophobia" 135). It is this fundamental component of the performance of masculinity that makes Tim continue to go to even greater lengths to hide his condition from his colleagues. After finally admitting his condition, and hoping for some sense of compassion, Tim is sacked from the firm. He loses his position as partner and finds he has been replaced by a new up-and-coming lawyer, "that kid," Masserly: "Peter's favourite . . . with that air of entitlement that some junior associates acquire when they sense they are favoured by one or another partner" (123). The irony is, of course, that Tim is describing himself years before when he got his break by "impressing the right people" (37). Yet the work that he took so much pride in, that defined him, has now been rejected and, to his complete disbelief, repeatedly "guffawed" at (177).

Tim's dismissal is due to the development of his condition—the "unnamed" to which the title of the novel refers. Experts within a range of medical disciplines offer Tim a variety of causes: dietary deficiencies (38); psychiatric problems (38); naturopathic issues (38); a possible reaction to his environment (39); and the suggestion of a genetic cause (40). The failure of science to explain what is happening to Tim is summed up with one physician's definitive diagnosis: "There is no laboratory examination to confirm the presence or absence of the condition . . . so there is no reason to believe the disease has a defined physical cause or, I suppose, even exists at all" (41). It is finally given a name: "benign idiopathic perambulation" (41), that is to say, a need to walk that arises spontaneously from an unknown cause.

Future readings of the novel will most probably focus on the physical and psychological deterioration of Tim as the narrative develops. Reading his condition as a strict medical illness is, in my view, somewhat of a reductive approach to this complex flâneurial character and ignores what Tim's narrative gives us in terms of his counter-hegemonic performance. I would argue that the cause of Tim's condition is more in line with the diagnosis of the bodhisattva who offers a sociological insight into Tim's malaise:

> The bodhisattva has encouraged him to look deeply into his reliance upon technology. Email and PDA, cell phone and voice mail were extensions of the ruinous consuming self. They made thoughts of the self instantaneously and irrepressibly accessible. Who's calling me, who's texting me, who wants me, me, me. The ego went along on every walk and ride, replacing the vistas and skylines, scrambling the delicate meditative code. The self was cut off from the hope that the world might reassert itself over the digitized clamour and the ego turn again into the sky, the bird, the tree. (49)

The origin of Tim's condition may be uncertain, but it does affect every area of his life. He loses his position in his law firm, his marriage breaks down, and his daughter sees him, at least initially, as a freak. A possible answer to the riddle may be that it is a manifestation of the subconscious desire that Leslie Fiedler underlines as the key theme of American fiction: the male's escape from the responsibilities of society. Following the example of the hegemonic male literary figure Huck Finn, Tim also makes his way through the wilderness. Yet, in contrast to the natural wilds of the forest, Tim's wilderness is the streets of Manhattan: "for everywhere was a wilderness to him who had known only the interiors of homes and offices and school buildings and restaurants and court houses and hotels" (247). The metropolis is Tim's wilderness but one that he calls home.

With the various tenets of what shaped Tim's understanding of his masculinity disintegrating around him, it is his reinvention as the urban spectator that provides Tim with a renewed sense of self. The city becomes his sanctuary but also his subject of study. Outside the closed capsule of the office environment, Tim begins to recognise the patterns of hegemony that shape the performance of the urban male. Tim's observation is so acute that he identifies the dual categories of hegemonic masculinity: "external hegemony," i.e., the dominance of the hegemonic male group over women, and "internal hegemony," i.e., the dominance of the hegemonic male group over other males.[25] This dual hegemony is played out in key scenes: first, Tim listens to the conversations between two Latina girls. He recognises that these girls are part of "the subculture of women who did not get the respect they deserved from men" (151); second, later that day, he also overhears two men talking. Although they are speaking English, he struggles to hear exactly what they are saying: "He got only the tone of complaint. He understood that the speaker had been wronged in some way, and that the injustice was more than just a minor slight" (153). This is a striking metaphor for the awakening of Tim. A lawyer, gifted in the use of language, able to listen to clients, and to understand, interpret, and shape their cases into convincing narratives, is unable to make out what the average man in the street is saying:

> He strained to recall a single exchange—on the street, from the next table in a restaurant—overheard in all the years he had lived in the city, within the inescapable nexus of babble he had sat in most of his life, and not one came to mind. Not one. Had he never unplugged his ears of the self-involvement that consumed him about work, when he wasn't sick, or about sickness, when he couldn't work? Had he never listened? (151)

Tim, evolving into the New York flâneur, begins to recognise the power of observation, the self-educating power of watching, and perhaps more importantly, the self-nourishing potential of urban narratives for him and his ill wife:

> For the first time he began to pay attention to the things he saw on the walks so that when he returned to her, he had observations of the outside world to share. They were fleeting, they were middles without beginnings or ends, but they were diverting—for him to witness, for her to hear. (287–288)

The urban wilderness becomes Tim's place of refuge. He returns to the city with Jane after she recovers from cancer. Leaving their eight-bedroom mansion, they move into a one-bedroom apartment in the heart of the city, "a tenth of the size of their house in the suburbs" (184). Leaving behind all "their stuff," letting go of his masculine pride in wanting to assert himself as the dominant member of the law firm, and realising that he doesn't need to feel any greater sense of social status, Tim begins to delight in the small details of urban living. He repairs his relationship with his wife and becomes a father to his daughter. The smells and sights of the inner-city streets, in particular, their "physical touch," gives Tim, the contemporary flâneur, "a greater containment of the world" (188).

When initially roaming the streets of Manhattan, Tim had been an aimless wanderer, dominated by his own self-interest and paying little attention to those around him. Echoing the ideas of Morawski, Tim doesn't become a complicit wanderer of the streets. Empty urban delights don't interest him. When opening his eyes to the city the change is telling:

> He realized he might have been doing it wrong for years. He might have seen interesting things had he been able to let go of his frustration and despair. He wondered what kind of life we might have had if he had paid attention from the beginning. (288)

From these two passages there is the clear indication that becoming an incarnation of the flâneur gives Tim a greater sense of selfhood, a belief in the significance of his own existence within the increasingly chaotic and disorientating urban environment. Throughout the narrative, he embodies various flâneurial personas: in the complex internal monologues he is Baudelaire's philosopher; in search of the murder suspect he is Poe's urban detective; trying desperately to get a look at the face of a man walking through the crowded metropolis he echoes Poe's "The Man of the Crowd." Ultimately, Tim is employed by Ferris as a counter-hegemonic figure, a commentator on the dynamics of hegemonic masculinity in New York as we move into the second decade of the twenty-first century.

CONCLUSION: FLÂNERIE IN MANHATTAN, MAKING MODERN MASCULINITIES DISCURSIVE

One of the recurring charges put to this literary figure in the contemporary era is the invisibility of the flâneur. In this introductory chapter, I have aimed to demonstrate that the flâneur symbolizes a creative attitude of urban investigation and inquiry, "a procession from scepticism to sight," in the words of Chris Jenks (*Visual Culture* 149), a shaking off of a typically postmodern blasé attitude and a movement towards a critical appreciation of literary representations of American masculinity shaped in New York City. As Jenks states:

> The flâneur, though grounded in everyday life, is an analytic form, a narrative device, an attitude towards knowledge and its social context. It is an image of movement through the social space of modernity. . . . The flâneur is a multilayered palimpsest that enables us to move from real products of modernity, like commodification and leisured patriarchy, through the practical organisation of space and its negotiation

> by the inhabitants of a city, to a critical appreciation of the state of modernity and its erosion into the post-, and onwards to a reflexive understanding of the function. (148)

The dialectic of flâneurial fiction is grounded in the fact that by writing and reading these texts we become better noticers of life; by immersing ourselves into the detail of flâneurial narratives either as writers or readers we in turn apply this critical consciousness to our experiences in our daily lives. In other words, as better writers or readers of fiction we might become better writers or readers of our own everyday narratives. As Keith Tester suggests, "the activity of the flâneur is essentially about freedom, the meaning of existence (or the lack of a meaning of existence) and being-with-others in the modern urban spaces of the city" (*The Flâneur* 8). These contemporary flâneurs, in writing about the city, are not only writing about themselves, but also writing about the social conditions of their fellow urban dwellers. Put simply, "the flâneur observes and seeks the meaning of his modernity" (16).

While the flâneur satisfies the reporting instincts of the fiction writer, the flâneur is more than a mere reporting device; the flâneur is an interpreter of social discourse, the link between the factual and the fictional. From the overview of the development of the flâneur throughout the course of modernity, the flâneur should be seen as a reflexive literary device operating on two distinct yet interrelated levels: the flâneur is a documenter of his environment, a producer of literary reflections on the modern city. Yet the flâneur is also self-reflexive; he is an analytical agent of subjectivity and masculinity shaped within the urban arena by the various discourses at play. As the following case studies illustrate, Paul Auster, Bret Easton Ellis, and Don DeLillo are not only investigating and interpreting masculinities in their illustrations of the everyday experiences of their protagonists, but in their sociologically charged narratives, they are writing counter-hegemonic alternatives for the New York City male.

NOTES

1. Perhaps the most accessible version of this epic work is the 1999 translated and abridged edition, *Panorama of Paris: Selections from "Le Tableau de Paris."*
2. See Parkhurst Ferguson, "Paris as Revolution" 80–115 and chapter 1 of Edmund White for insightful readings of Balzac.
3. Walter Benjamin has been given many titles: a literary critic, a philosopher of history, an unorthodox Marxist. He has also been labelled a sociologist who has produced influential work on the concept of the flâneur. See Frisby, "The Flâneur in Social Theory."
4. Benjamin continues, "If that sort of thing could be done, then, to be sure, life in the big city was not nearly as disquieting as it probably seemed to people" (*Selected Writings* 21).
5. Also see Werner for in-depth discussion of Poe's engagement with the flâneur.

6. For a study of the arrival of gaslight on literary production in New York City, see Sharpe, *New York Nocturne.*
7. Hollington makes reference to three examples of writers who employed the figure of the flâneur and influenced Dickens: William Blake, de Quincey, and Charles Lamb. See Hollington 75–77.
8. See Smith.
9. The prime objective of Dickens' first voyage, in 1842, was to propose the idea of international copyright of published literature, as his novels were being widely pirated in the United States. He took a second trip to America in 1868 with the view of extending his hugely successful book tour to the New World. Dickens was generally impressed by this burgeoning country but was heavily critical about sanitary conditions, social degradation, and the continued existence of slavery.
10. Hollington writes: "In this essay I shall be concerned less with the psychological aspect of Dickens' street-walking habits than with their broader, more sociological implications, which have significance, I think, for the art of novels" (72).
11. This critical reading is heavily influenced by the writing of Walter Benjamin, in particular Benjamin's work on Charles Baudelaire. Hollington identifies four oppositions that are of particular relevance to Dickens: (a) his consciousness of flânerie as an ambiguous middle term between "purposive" and "non-purposive" activity on the street; (b) his awareness of "solitude" and "multitude" on the street; (c) his experience of interior and exterior space on the street; and (d) his perception of the familiar and the fantastic on the street (78).
12. See Sharpe, "A Pig upon the Town."
13. See Burrows and Wallace 691–711.
14. See Brand 64–78 for a compact overview of the arrival of the flâneur in America.
15. See Sharpe, *New York Nocturne* and Burrows and Wallace 690.
16. Whitman made this statement in the *Aurora*, March 14, 1842.
17. Harvey argues that space and time are basic categories of human existence, and we must realise the human role in their construction from a materialist perspective, i.e., time and space are not detached objective paradigms but social constructs created through material practices. Harvey, a Marxist social geographer, sees social development shaped and reflecting in the flow of capital accumulation. As society continues to develop due to rapid technological and industrial innovation, the paralleled acceleration in commodity consumption and circulation of capital results in a new type of social existence for the individual. Harvey makes the case that this acceleration of capital accumulation and eventual capital overaccumulation changed the way the individual experienced society, creating "processes that so revolutionize the objective qualities of space and time that we are forced to alter, sometimes in quite radical ways, how we represent the world to ourselves" (*The Condition of Postmodernity* 240).
18. A composite of many tiny neighbourhoods, New York enjoyed huge expansion in the late nineteenth century, with population density in urban areas reaching peak levels. In parts of New York City's Lower East Side, the number approached 900 persons per acre, approximately 500,000 per square mile, a number suggested by Kenneth Fox at that time to be the highest residential concentration ever achieved in modern history (38).
19. See Wolff; Wilson, *Sphinx in the City* and "The Invisible Flâneur"; and Pollock 1988. Also see Buck-Morss 1986.

20. George Sand is the pseudonym of Amantine Aurore Lucile Dupin, later Baroness Dudevant, a French writer who is regarded as being the first French woman writer to gain a major reputation. See Tindall.
21. Simmel's essay delineates the psychological conditions created by overwhelming social forces: "The psychological basis of the metropolitan type of individuality consists in the intensification of nervous stimulation which results from the swift and uninterrupted change of outer and inner stimuli" (409–410).
22. Other novels that tell flâneurial tales about life in contemporary Manhattan have appeared in recent years. These include Joseph O'Neill's *Netherland* (2008) and Teju Cole's *Open City* (2011).
23. For comprehensive overviews of studies of masculinity in the workplace, see Cheng and Collinson and Hearn, "Naming Men as Men" and "Men and Masculinities."
24. See Collinson and Hearn, "Naming Men as Men" for their analysis of the concept of "careerism." Notable insights include, "Competition for career progress comes to be synonymous with conventional masculinity. Upward mobility can therefore become a key objective in the search to secure a stable masculine identity" (161).
25. Key research on the development of Raewyn Connell's concept of "hegemonic masculinity" includes Carrigan, Connell, and Lee 1985; Connell 1977, 1979, 1987, 1995, and 2010; Connell and Messerschmidt 2005; Demetriou 2001; Hearn 2004; Howson 2006; Messerschmidt 2012; Moller 2007; Wedgwood 2012; Whitehead 1999.

3 "The Son Saves the Father"

Counter-hegemonic Father Figures in Paul Auster's Fiction

READING AUSTER SOCIOLOGICALLY

As one of the most studied American authors of the past thirty years, Paul Auster is firmly established in the canon of contemporary American fiction. Numerous bibliographies, critical books, special editions of academic journals, academic articles, book chapters, reviews, and newspaper articles have probed Paul Auster's postmodernity.[1] These critiques present the postmodern preoccupations that underpin Auster's novels: identity crises, agency, chance and contingency, memory, trauma, and solitude. The majority of research presents Auster as a writer who indulges in abstract postmodern matters while simultaneously revelling in self-referential postmodern games of authorship, narrativity, language, self-reflexivity, and intertextuality. The common conclusion reached by critics is that Auster's works are self-negating novels of postmodern nihilism, case studies on the fragmentary nature of selfhood.[2] As one critic has remarked on the Auster experience: "One leaves the text and feels that one has been left with nothing" (Martin, "Love Crimes").[3] Moreover, Dennis Barone, in the introduction to what is regarded as the seminal collection of critical essays on Auster, *Beyond the Red Notebook* (1995), argues that Auster's texts "foreground story and narrativity, not 'the sociological moment'" (11).[4]

The suggestion of Auster's novels as sociologically charged texts is a complex issue, made even more complicated by various statements from the author himself. As Auster elaborates in an interview with Christopher Bigsby:

> I feel that in many ways I am absolutely immersed in the American tradition and that I am writing about the same things that my American ancestors wrote about . . . the novels of Melville and Hawthorne, the stories of Poe and the writings of Thoreau, for example, all of whom I am passionately interested in, were not about sociology, which is what the novel has come to concern itself with in the United States. Those writings had a metaphysical dimension, a philosophical dimension to them, which I think has been forgotten and ignored. (Bigsby 31)[5]

Aliki Varvogli supports Auster's point above by highlighting how "Auster shares many preoccupations with his American forefathers, ranging from the investigation into language and its relation to reality to questions of identity, solitude and artistic creativity, and the contrasting views of America that emerge from its cityscapes and the large expanses of nature" (*The World That Is the Book* 22). Varvogli, notably, doesn't make reference to male sexuality or masculinity.

Auster, in an interview with his fellow New York writer Jonathan Lethem, speaks about his approach to writing fiction and once more makes his position clear:

> You see, I'm not a sociologist, and the [American] novel has often concerned itself with sociology. It's one of the generating forces that's made fiction interesting to people. But that's not my concern. I'm interested in psychology. And also certain philosophical questions about the world. (Lethem)

In an unpublished interview with Bill Corbett, Auster reinforces his position:

> There's a certain kind of realism that is dominant in fiction that doesn't interest me at all, the realism of sociology. I think so many novels are written in that spirit and they seem to do best in America. Novels that document an era, that tell us what we wear, what we eat. I find this . . . well, there's a sense of complicity between the reader and the writer that I don't like. People read those books in order to recognise themselves. That's not why I am writing. I try to write stories that ask the questions I am most interested in which are, I suppose, big questions, questions that don't have answers. I'm not sure of anything, and I suppose my books reflect my own doubt about the state of the world. They are poems, fair[y] tales, meditations. ("Interview with Paul Auster")[6]

Varvogli makes the point that Auster's fiction, with *The New York Trilogy* as the prime example, reconciles "realism" with "experiment," and "sociology" with writing that emanates a "metaphysical dimension" (*The World That Is the Book* 4). What I aim to argue, however, is that although Auster may maintain that his fiction concerns itself with metaphysical matters of the human condition, his narratives are firmly anchored in the dynamics of the everyday. This difficulty in determining the sociological drive of Auster's works is further complicated by Auster seemingly contradicting himself by stating that "in the strictest sense of the word" he sees himself as a "realist" (Barone, *Beyond the Red Notebook* 116).[7] Speaking with Christopher Bigsby, he states, "I know people often say of my work that it is improbable and crazy and unrealistic but I consider myself a realist, an absolutely rock bottom, nuts-and-bolts man of the earth. I am not making it up" (18).[8]

Varvogli, in her focus on the textuality of Auster's fiction, refutes this "realist" element in Auster's narratives:

> It is true that many of the characters he creates, and some incidents in his books, come from "real life," and the effect in later novels especially is one of deceptive realism. At the same time, however, Auster's fictions are, if anything, over—determined, full of allusions and references to other books and writers. Even if that were not the case, it would still be problematic to say that his books come out of the real world. (*The World That Is the Book* 6)

But that is exactly the point—underlying any "experimental," "magical," or "deceptive" fabulations in Auster's novels is the "realism" of the social experience of the American male. Auster underlines this point in discussion with Jonathan Lethem about the "higher forms of fiction." Despite his obsession with the "big questions" that he speaks of above, Auster ultimately concedes: "I like the low. I'm very interested in the low, the close to the ground, something that's almost indistinguishable from life" (Lethem). Moreover, Auster reveals, "I think that every one of my books is actually about America. That's the subject that interests me most" ("Interview with Paul Auster"). Moving beyond this, it is not simply America that is the subject of Auster's fiction but more specifically it is New York. When it is put to Paul Auster by Bill Corbett that New York is one of the main characters in his fiction, Auster states, "Yes, this is my town, it's my place. I love it and hate it; I want to leave and I want to stay. . . . The frenzy of the place at times, the poverty of the place, the ambitiousness of the place, the shallowness of the place and yet everything I say about it can be contradicted" ("Interview with Paul Auster").

The closeness of Auster's fictional worlds to our social reality is evident in his more recent work. Speaking about *Sunset Park* (2010), Auster reveals it was his growing interest in the social issues of homelessness and social exclusion that inspired the narrative.[9] The fact remains that Auster's novels are not, nor have they ever been, composed in a vacuum. As Auster acknowledges, "History is present in all my novels. . . . And whether I am directly talking about the sociological moment or just immersing my character in the environment, I am very aware of it" (Neary). In contrast, therefore, to the customary argument that Auster's texts are spinning, self-referential narratives disconnected from their social and historical context, with this chapter I propose that Auster's fiction, from its very beginning with *The New York Trilogy*, is sociologically charged in its examination of the condition of American masculinity.

This shift in Auster scholarship towards recognising the sociological value of Auster's fiction is being realised in new criticism on his work. James Peacock's article "The Father in the Ice: Paul Auster, Character, and Literary Ancestry" (2011) reconsiders the standard approach to reading Auster's novels. To illustrate this development, Peacock offers a telling example from one of his early articles on Auster in which he proclaims, "there can be no reality beyond the self-ratifying circuitry of [Auster's] texts" (363). Peacock champions the move from these "nihilistically postmodern" readings of Auster towards criticism that takes "more ethically orientated views on Auster's writing" (363). Peacock ultimately calls for critics to recognise the potential of Auster's novels as "models for our interpersonal orientation in the real world" (363).

This turn towards the sociological in Auster scholarship is further demonstrated with *The Invention of Illusions: International Perspectives on Paul Auster* (2011). This collection of essays calls for the need to "highlight the political drive of Auster's most recent production" (Ciocia and Gonzalez 4). Paolo Simonetti, in his discussion of Auster's post-9/11 novels, hints at the complex nature of the relation between the philosophical and the sociological in Auster's work:

> It seems that Auster's fiction—not to speak of his poetry—inhabits a Hawthornean "neutral territory," a purely subjective (quite autobiographical) dimension always conscious of the difficult negotiation with a historical reality that, though progressively bracketed by metafictional strategies, violently reclaims its actuality through recent traumatic events. (Simonetti 15)

What we can draw from this reading is that although Auster's novels may be formed within certain postmodern metafictional frameworks, ultimately his fiction is anchored in what Simonetti calls "historical reality," or, as I would put it, everyday social reality. Simonetti concludes that the trajectory of Auster's published work sees the author trying to "reconcile postmodernism and realism and escape the narcissistic inward spiral of self-referring fiction" (32). Although Simonetti is analysing Auster within the context of the last decade of his writing, I would argue that this negotiation has featured in Auster's prose from its very beginning. Certainly Auster's fiction has moved towards politically charged narratives, but the sociological has always been there. The main point to draw from this is that while Auster's fiction may ask many metaphysical questions about the human condition and the nature of existence, it is the sociological investigation in his narratives that supplies the answers. Auster's novels are texts that dramatize the discourses that shape American society, with the dynamics of the social construction of masculinity being one of the major themes.

Mark Brown, in his 2007 study on Auster, writes that "gender does not figure significantly in Auster's work as a theme" (*Paul Auster* 159). Regrettably this statement is representative of the critical attitude towards the leading figures in the contemporary American literary canon.[10] What emerges when we gender the works of Paul Auster is that masculinity must be considered as one of the major themes in Auster's fiction. There is one major thread that ties together Auster's (self-)reflective narratives on the American male experience: the impact and influence of fatherhood on the male individual's understanding of the self. Engaging with Auster in this manner continues the move towards the sociological in the analysis of his texts as dramatizations of the discourses that define the male individual's experience of fatherhood and, crucially, the effect of this on the shaping of his masculinity. Obviously the distinction between the philosophical and the sociological is not clear-cut, and it would be foolish to attempt, particularly within the restrictions of a single chapter, to refute a large proportion of Auster scholarship. What I hope this study will achieve, however, is to stimulate a critical conversation on Auster's depictions of the father role in the shaping of American masculinity. Reading the models of fatherhood from selected key texts alongside the theoretical writings that explore the impact of the historical development of fatherhood on American masculinity will demonstrate that the dynamics of the relationship between father and son play a central role in the male protagonist's understanding of their masculinity in Auster's fictionalised New York. There is one text that is both the literal and symbolic starting point of Auster's fictional reflections upon what it means to be an American father: *The Invention of Solitude.*

THE INVENTION OF SOLITUDE

The Invention of Solitude was Auster's first published prose text, in 1982, and is regarded by many as the cornerstone of Auster's body of work.[11] One concern to address immediately is the fact that *The Invention of Solitude* is generally considered a work of "non-fiction."[12] It has been called a memoir,[13] "a memoir-as-meditation,"[14] "a kind of biography,"[15] and an autobiography.[16] As Auster himself has reflected in an interview with Michael Contat, the classification of the text is not a straightforward issue:

> I never thought of this book as an autobiography—not even as a biography. But I was very conscious of what I was trying to do, which was to write a kind of meditation on how you *might* write a biography. Or, more importantly, how and if anyone can talk about someone else: what you know about other people. This is really what it's about. (Auster and Contat 180)

In many ways, therefore, *The Invention of Solitude* is a meditation on the act of writing. Auster reflects further on the text's existence within the realms of fact and fiction in an unpublished interview with Bill Corbett:

> I've never been able to define it [*The Invention of Solitude*]. If I use any word at all it is meditation. Yes, it's non-fiction but at the same time it's written in the same spirit one would write a novel. I tackled it the way

> a novelist tackles a story, you have to objectify it. You're writing about yourself and what happened to you but at the same time you have to stand outside yourself. ("Interview with Paul Auster")

Taking these points into consideration it is clear that Auster considers *The Invention of Solitude* as his first step towards setting the parameters of the literary representations of fatherhood and masculinity in his fiction.

The critical appreciation of *The Invention of Solitude* supports this view. Pascal Bruckner calls it "both the *ars poetica* and the seminal work of Paul Auster" (Bruckner 27). As James Peacock writes, "Each subsequent novel reprise[s] and extend[s] themes and ideas first addressed explicitly in *The Invention of Solitude*" (*Understanding* 15). Stephen Fredman sets the text as the one in which "Auster confronts all of his central obsessions, obsessions that return in various forms to animate his subsequent novels" (Fredman 7). Aliki Varvogli argues that in *The Invention of Solitude*, "we recognise the questions that Auster will go on asking throughout his work" (*The World That Is the Book* 10). As Bruckner concludes, "To understand him we must start here; all his books lead us back to this one" (27). Auster agrees with these critical readings: "In retrospect I can see that everything I have done has come out of that book. The problems and questions and experiences that are examined in there have been the meat of what I have done since" (Bigsby 22).[17]

It would be foolish, therefore, to overlook *The Invention of Solitude*. Auster is a writer of narratives, and for Auster it is these narratives that allow a unique insight into the subtleties of our everyday existence. This approach to reading Auster ties into the now infamous Auster line: "The anecdote as a form of knowledge" (*Invention of Solitude* 65).[18] It is also important to remember that *The Invention of Solitude* is a work of two parts.[19] Critiques of the text have emphasised the juxtaposition of these sections, both thematically and stylistically.[20] However, it is also necessary to recognise that they are intrinsically linked. The first part, "Portrait of an Invisible Man," is not a simple retelling of his father's life from birth to sudden death. It is a study of the historical conditions that dictated the experience of this man as a father in mid-twentieth-century America. The second part, "The Book of Memory," is Auster's reflection upon his emerging role of father to his son Daniel. There is a noticeable shift from the first half of the text as Auster adopts a third-person perspective by fictionalising himself as the character A. This self-critical distance allows Auster to reflect upon the breakdown of his marriage and the effect of this on his relationship with his son as he moves A., a flâneur reflecting upon his identity, through the streets of New York. It is also the first indication of Auster's belief in the power of fiction to offer sociological critique. Ultimately *The Invention of Solitude* is the inception of Auster's fixation with the impact of the role of father on the shaping of the masculinity of his protagonists in his fiction.

THE AMERICAN FATHER: "PORTRAIT OF AN INVISIBLE MAN"

Paul Auster's father, Sam Auster, died suddenly from a heart attack on January 15, 1979, and Auster writes of feeling an instant "obligation" to maintain his father's memory: "I thought: my father is gone. If I do not act quickly, his entire life will vanish along with him" (*Invention of Solitude* 6). Critics have commended the direct and immediate tone of the "plain prose" of "Portrait of an Invisible Man," viewing it as a frank and forthright memoir of the life of Auster's father.[21] I would suggest, however, that it is not as straightforward as it may first appear. Within this study of literary representations of masculinity, "Portrait of an Invisible Man" is an extremely loaded title. The first element of the title, "Portrait," alludes to issues regarding the authorial intentions of this piece of writing. A portrait is something that represents or resembles a certain subject, the subject of this piece being, of course, Auster's father. Yet "portrait" also suggests an artistic endeavour rather than a simple retelling of events. A portrait is an act of illustrating and interpreting a chosen subject, exposing the complexities and contradictions that lie beneath the surface of the façade. Auster's text, therefore, is not merely a meticulous recording of a man's life. This seemingly objective exercise is infused with subjective reflections that not only frame the father's life but also reveal certain details about the son writing the piece. There is undoubtedly a degree of fact *and* fiction in biographical writing, and Auster is the flâneurial detective trying to piece together the narrative of his father's life.[22] Instead of one fixed idea of his father's masculinity, Auster explores the several unsettled identities that co-existed side-by-side. There is the striking image that Auster uses in the text to emphasise this point. Sorting through his father's belongings, Auster finds a bag of loose photographs. There is one photograph of several men sitting around a table, each of them staring at each other and at nothing, as if they are engaged in a séance:

> And then, as you study the picture, you begin to realise that all these men are the same man. The séance becomes a real séance, and it is as if he has come there only to invoke himself, to bring himself back from the dead, as if, by multiplying himself, he has inadvertently made himself disappear. There are five of him there, and yet the nature of the trick photography denies the possibility of eye contact among the various selves. Each one is condemned to go on staring into space, as if under the gaze of the others, but seeing nothing, never able to see anything. It is a picture of death, a portrait of an invisible man. (33)

The second part of the title, "an invisible man," points to the underlying thematic intentions of this text. The invisibility of Sam Auster resonates on many levels, most notably in terms of his role of "absent father." It also points to the performance, or lack thereof, in relation to his masculinity. As Auster states, his father was "invisible to others, and most likely invisible to himself as well" (7). Auster's view of his father is crystallised in an early passage:

> Devoid of passion, either for a thing, a person, or an idea, incapable or unwilling to reveal himself under any circumstances, he had managed to keep himself at a distance from life, to avoid immersion in the quick of things. He ate, he went to work, he had friends, he played tennis, and yet for all that he was not there. In the deepest, most unalterable sense, he was an invisible man. (6–7)

In social situations his father "remained invisible, a puppeteer working the strings of his alter-ego from a dark, solitary place behind the curtain" (16). Ultimately his father existed within his self-imposed solitude. In Auster's view, his father was "solitary in the sense of retreat. In the sense of not having to see himself, of not having to see himself being seen by anyone else" (17). The "invisible man," therefore, is not solely a pointer to the "absence" of Auster's father. It is also reference to his father's (non-)performance of his masculinity. With *The Invention of Solitude,* Auster sees it as his task to make the social and historical discourses that shape his father's masculinity visible. And, crucially, it is this sociologically charged task that would come to influence Auster's critique of American masculinity and the American father in his fiction.

THE HEGEMONIC IDEAL: SELF-MADE MASCULINITY

The evaluative credentials of "Portrait of an Invisible Man" as a document that critiques traditional American models of hegemonic masculinity is further evident when read alongside one of the key pieces of scholarship on the historical development of American masculinity: Michael Kimmel's *Manhood in America* (1996). In this study Kimmel identifies the cultural shifts that shaped the American male's understanding of what it means to be masculine. Kimmel's underlying message is that the ideological images that defined the American male's early conception of American manhood remain the definition of the hegemonic ideal in contemporary understandings of American fatherhood and masculinity.[23] Kimmel highlights the model of American masculinity that emerged at the time of the American Revolution, which continues to dominate the American male's idea of true American manhood: the self-made man (Kimmel, *Manhood* 13–14).[24]

Kimmel suggests that the term "self-made man" was an American neologism, first coined by Henry Clay in a speech in the U.S. Senate in 1832. In defence of a protective tariff that he believed would enable further enterprise of humble men, Clay praised the humble "self-made men" who achieved whatever they had through diligent labour (*Manhood* 19). As the economic system of the late eighteenth and early nineteenth centuries was first replaced by a proto-industrial economy and then by a factory-dominated culture, more and more men found their identities formed in the world of competitive capitalism. True American masculinity was not something that the everyday male was born with—it was something to be earned and performed repeatedly in the workplace. In other words, masculinity existed only when confirmed in the eyes of other men.[25]

The pressures that underpinned the performance of the male individual from early age are evident in Auster's reflections upon the life of his father. Sam Auster had his first job at age nine and at age eighteen he had a radio repair business with one of his brothers: "Up early every morning, home late at night, and in between, work, nothing but work. Work was the name of the country he lived in, and he was one of its greatest patriots" (*Invention of Solitude* 56). Auster's father believed that it was the straightforward exercise of earning more and more money that defined him as a man. As Auster reflects, "That is not to say, however, that work was pleasure for him. He worked hard because he wanted to earn as much money as possible. Work was a means to an end—a means to money" (56). His father strove towards this hegemonic ideal of the self-made man, measuring his success by the amount of money not only that he had, but more importantly that he earned. Auster recognises astutely the cultural credence of this performance of his father's masculinity:

> He dreamed all his life of becoming a millionaire, of being the richest man in the world. It was not so much the money itself he wanted, but what it represented: not merely success in the eyes of the world, but a way of making himself untouchable. Having money means more than being able to buy things: it means that the world need never affect you. Money in the sense of protection, then, not pleasure. (56)

This passage is loaded with the discourses that impacted upon his father's everyday performance of his masculinity. Money, more accurately, earned money, provided him with protection. But protection from what? Reading the figure of Sam Auster alongside the concept of hegemonic masculinity, more specifically the fundamental idea that men compete within a historically contingent hierarchical framework, Auster indicates that his father's wealth not only allowed his father to validate his masculinity within open society, but it also offered him protection from challenges to his hegemonic status from other males. Money was power, but not in terms of consumer culture—money held a certain currency in the masculine system. Auster paints his father as a man who enjoyed being the better man: "He loved clever little tricks, prided himself on his ability to out-smart the world at its own game" (58). His father, following the creed of the capitalist system that projected the ideological image of the self-made man as the quintessential American male, felt that earning money was the ultimate performance on the path towards reaching the hegemonic ideal.

The establishment of the self-made man ideal in the early decades of the nineteenth century heralded the beginning of a fundamental separation of the public and private spheres in American society.[26] It was at this time in American history that the workplace and the home became intrinsically gendered, with the workplace pronounced male and the home decreed female. Although this ideology and reality of the separation of the spheres was largely white and middle-class, it was imposed society-wide as the American family norm.[27] American manhood performed outside of the home heralded the birth of a new American male: the breadwinner.[28]

In 1820, the term "breadwinner" was coined to denote the responsible American male who strived towards the hegemonic ideal of self-made manhood with the ultimate purpose of supporting his family. The ironic effect of this change on American fatherhood was felt throughout the country. Robert L. Griswold, in the introduction of his study *Fatherhood in America* (1992), states:

> Despite men's differences, breadwinning has remained the great unifying element in fathers' lives. Its obligations bind men across the boundaries of colour and class, and shape their sense of self, manhood, and gender. Supported by law, affirmed by history, sanctioned by every element in society, male breadwinning has been synonymous with maturity, respectability, and masculinity. (2)

The effect of the cultural ideology of the breadwinner role on the father's relationship with his family, more specifically his son, emerges as the key focus of Auster's fictional representations of fatherhood and masculinity. In "Portrait," Auster recognises the consequences of this social pressure on his father's performance as husband and father: "Although he did not shirk his outward duties as a husband (he was faithful, he provided for his wife and children, he shouldered all his responsibilities), it was clear he was not cut out to play this role. He simply had no talent for it" (*Invention of Solitude* 18). The effect of this on his father was evident. Auster speaks of a constant anger inside his father, an anger produced and maintained by the frustrations of the internal conflicts versus the unattainable external ideals of the breadwinner role. His father learned to live behind his masculine façade, appearing calm in public while being "prey to a roiling, unstoppable force of fury within" (32). Auster's father was a man trapped in the greater ideological expectations of hegemonic American manhood. Robert Blauner's study on the working American male, *Alienation and Freedom* (1964), underlines the stresses and strains that Kimmel highlights as the experience of the breadwinner: powerlessness, meaninglessness, isolation, and self-estrangement (*Manhood in America* 175).[29]

The expectations of the breadwinner role had an inevitable effect on father-son relationships: the segregation of the father from the family environment. Griswold points out that "urban and even town residents found that the bond once uniting men with their children had been broken. Increasing numbers of men now spent their days away from home, engaged in what became the defining characteristic of manhood for over a century—breadwinning" (Griswold 13–14).[30] Pleck writes that "the post-war father was seen as a towering figure in the life of his child not so much by presence as by his absence" (91). As Griswold adds, these men were "outsiders" (42), defined by their distance from their children.[31] In the status of outsider, various subjects in Griswold's study point to the lack of displayed emotion of the American father. One particular American son states:

> He was a dutiful father, but he never kissed me, never talked to me and had conversations with me. He never hugged me—he never hugged anybody. He could play solitaire for five, six hours. He had affection but he never showed it. (Griswold 43)

Auster's father enacts this model. At various points Auster laments how his father appears to be unable, if not unwilling, to reveal his inner emotions. In early passages of the text Auster speaks about his father only showing the surface, crippled by the paranoia of revealing feelings or emotions that he felt could be used against him (*Invention* 16).[32] Auster's memories of his father are of a man defined by his working life. The effect of this disconnection on Paul Auster the son is apparent: "The world was a distant place for him, I think, a place he was never truly able to enter, and out there in the distance, among all the shadows that flitted past him, I was born, became his son, and grew up, as if I were just one more shadow, appearing and disappearing in a half-lit realm of his consciousness" (25). Rather than facing up to these issues, Auster's father, "the perpetual outsider" (9), fell into archetypal masculine habits. Many American fathers who felt disconnected from their families at home preferred to spend time after work in masculine social environments such as pubs, billiard halls, bowling alleys, and union halls or lodges of fraternal organizations. Auster reveals that his father had a "reliance on fixed routines" (32), finding comfort in the established masculine rhythms of his daily life: "Reliance on fixed routines freed him from the necessity of looking into himself when decisions had to be made; the cliché was always quick to come to his lips ('A beautiful baby. Good luck with it') instead of words he had gone out and looked for. All this tended to flatten him out as a personality" (32–33). This form of denial became the coping strategy for many American men who found themselves unable to function under the strain of the inherent contradictions of the American father they wanted to be and the American father society dictated they should be.

American fathers often attempted to justify their absence with stories of great adventures and feats of bravery and heroism. Kimmel speaks of the "masculine mystique," an ideal image of true American manhood that each American father aspired to: "that improbable synthesis of sober, responsible breadwinner, imperviously stoic master of his fate, and swashbuckling hero" (*Manhood* 173). In one particular instance Auster's father invents an outlandish account about days that he spent in South America during his youth: "a tale of high adventure, fraught with mortal dangers, hair-raising escapes, and improbable twists of fortune" (*Invention* 23). This element of the performance of the distant father reappears throughout Auster's fiction. Notable examples include the unnamed narrator creating the magical story of travelling to the moon to explain his sudden disappearance to his adopted son Paul. In Auster's *Moon Palace*, Thomas Effing also concocts an epic narrative of his dangerous days as a loner in the desert out west (137–158). Moreover, in *The Music of Chance* (Auster), when Jack Pozzi's father makes a fleeting appearance in his son's life, he brags about his adventures, wealth, and business success (37–44).

A major feature of the relationship between Auster and his father that becomes a key theme in Auster's fiction is the discord between father and son in the performance of their masculinities. Auster's father represents a traditional masculinity in which the values of reason, rationality, industry, diligence, and productiveness are set as true masculine qualities. Conversely, the son represents an emerging American manhood formed by new ideas of masculinity, containing what American fathers from the previous generation might consider traditionally feminine characteristics.[33] Auster turns towards the more "feminine" activity of writing for a living and reveals that his father would simply say that he had "[his] head in the clouds" or "did not have [his] feet on the ground" (*Invention* 64). Firmly shaped by the breadwinning ideology, in his father's view if an activity didn't result in monetary gain it couldn't be considered work. As Auster states, "writing, therefore, was not work, especially the writing of poetry. At best it was a hobby, a pleasant way to pass the time in between the things that really mattered. My father thought that I was squandering my gifts, refusing to grow up" (65). Tellingly, Auster reveals that the only time his father truly appreciated his son's craft was at a meeting with a producer that was sending Auster to Mexico. The producer pays Auster in cash, and Auster reflects, "This was the transaction my father witnessed. For once, I could see that he was impressed" (69). As Auster goes on to state, "I felt it as a triumph, as if I had somehow been vindicated. For the first time he had been forced to realise that I could take care of myself on my own terms" (69). As Auster's father departs once again, they play out the archetypal father-son scene. After witnessing his son acting like a true American male, Auster's father gives his son a big manly handshake and says, "Good luck, son. Knock 'em dead" (69). Auster's reply is poignant: "You bet" (69).

There is one reflection from "Portrait of an Invisible Man" that remains the cornerstone of Auster's reading of his father:

> The rampant, totally mystifying force of contradiction. I understand now that each fact is nullified by the next fact, that each thought

> engenders an equal and opposite thought. Impossible to say anything without reservation: he was good, or he was bad; he was this, or he was that. All of them are true. At times I have the feeling that I am writing about three or four different men, each one distinct, each one a contradiction of all the others. Fragments. Or the anecdote as a form of knowledge. (65)

It is in this short passage that all the themes that dominate Auster's analysis of his father's life and indeed Auster's fictional explorations of fatherhood and masculinity are crystallised. Auster's "portrait" is the impact of the role of father upon the everyday male's performance of his masculinity in mid-twentieth-century America. It is also crucial to realise the self-reflexive nature of "Portrait of an Invisible Man." Although Auster is writing about his father, Auster is also writing about himself and writing about the experience of every American father and American son. Writing a memoir is not simply engaging in an act of revisiting the past. It is an act firmly anchored in the desire of the author to make sense of his observations and explore the conflicts and tensions that define the experience of the subject, in this case, Auster's father, a man trying to negotiate his identity within the web of discourses that promote the hegemonic ideal of self-made manhood. "Portrait of an Invisible Man" is the case-study analysis that is the starting point of Auster's critique of the diverse models of fatherhood as Auster moves on to write counter-hegemonic performances of masculinity in New York.

"THE SON SAVES THE FATHER": "THE BOOK OF MEMORY"

The suggestion of alternative models of fatherhood in Auster's fiction begins in the second part of *The Invention of Solitude:* "The Book of Memory." Despite Auster writing "The Book of Memory" merely six months after "Portrait of an Invisible Man," stylistically these two pieces of writing could not be farther apart. In contrast to the direct prose of Auster's first-person narration in "Portrait of an Invisible Man," there is a shift to a third-person narrator in "The Book of Memory."[34] Auster's decision to fictionalise his experiences as a father with the character "A." has important implications in Auster's exploration of the role of the father in subsequent fictions. It is at this point, following the case-study critical consciousness of "Portrait of an Invisible Man," that Auster realises the power of fiction in exploring *his* emerging role as father:

> It is interesting to find that I didn't begin to write novels until after becoming a father. Despite my efforts, I didn't manage to do this before the birth of Daniel. I think that there's a link between these two facts. (De Cortanze 21)

Auster has explored this further in an interview with Larry McCaffery and Sinda Gregory when talking about his move into writing fiction:

> I'm certain that having children has had a lot to do with it. Becoming a parent connects you to a world beyond yourself, to the continuum of generations, to the inevitability of your own death. You understand that you exist in time, and after that you can no longer look at yourself in the same way. It's impossible to take yourself as seriously as you once did. You begin to let go, and in that letting go—at least in my case—you find yourself wanting to tell stories. (McCaffery and Gregory 13)

It is within his fictional landscapes that Auster illustrates and evaluates the conflicts that characterise the contemporary male's experience as a father in a society in which certain models of fatherhood collide. As James Peacock writes, "To read both parts [of *The Invention of Solitude*] is to watch a fiction-making consciousness evolve" (*Understanding* 17). The desire to understand the role of father appears as one of the major drives that underpins Auster's need to write fiction.

"The Book of Memory" introduced two interrelated themes that come together in Auster's meditations on his masculine identity and role as father: the act of walking and the act of writing:

> He has spent the greater part of his adult life walking through cities, many of them foreign. He has spent the greater part of his adult life hunched over a small rectangle of wood, concentrating on an even smaller rectangle of white paper. (103–104)

Auster first uses the term "flâneur" in *Leviathan* (1992) to describe the wanderings of Bernard Sachs through the streets of Manhattan: "He worked when the spirit moved him (most often late at night), and the rest of the time he roamed free, prowling the streets of the city like some nineteenth-century *flâneur,* following his nose wherever it happened to take him" (40).[35] In *Invisible* (2009), the aptly named Adam Walker wanders not only the streets of Manhattan but also Paris, the birthplace of the urban flâneur.[36] Paris and flânerie become a central focus of the novel with both Walker and Jim, his classmate from Columbia, moving through the Parisian labyrinth (169, 264). Moreover, Cecile Juin, a literary scholar, focuses her research on one of the first flâneurs, Honoré de Balzac (263). Walker goes in search of his identity in Paris before returning to New York. In light of this trope, Pascal Bruckner makes the point that in Auster's novels "wandering is intimacy's helpmate" (29), and in "The Book of Memory" Auster introduces a theme that will become an obsession in his works: nomadism as a means of cloistering oneself; introspection as a means of escape (*Invention* 30).[37] Bruckner fails to develop this point further but appears to suggest that Auster's protagonists, in roaming the New York streets, become flâneurs that seek freedom of the self in the act of self-analysis.

A. adopts the role of flâneur walking through the streets of Amsterdam, London, Paris, and, of course, New York. Beginning with Amsterdam, A., in an unfamiliar environment, first feels that "he was wandering the circles of hell" (*Invention* 91). And yet, as he begins to focus on each step that he takes, he realises that he is "wandering inside himself" (91). Each step takes him further into the very idea of his being, and "far from troubling him, this state of being lost became a source of happiness, of exhilaration. He breathed it into his very bones. As if on the brink of previously hidden knowledge, he breathed it into his very bones and said to himself, almost triumphantly: I am lost" (91). Evolving into a flâneur in the great cities in the world leads A. to see the act of walking as the act of deep meditation on his male subjectivity. In one remarkable passage, A. reflects that although it may seem that at times we are "wandering through a city without purpose" (129–130), as we watch the faces of other people and imagine their lives, and as one step inevitably leads to another step, then one thought leads to another thought until we realise:

> what we are really doing when we walk through the city is thinking, and thinking in such a way that our thoughts compose a journey, and this journey is no more or less than the steps we have taken, so that, in the end, we might safely say that we have been on a journey, and even if we do not leave our room, it has been a journey, and we might safely say that we have been somewhere, even if we don't know where it is. (130)

After these bouts of walking, A. sits at his desk in a room in 6 Varick Street, Manhattan, processing his thoughts with the written word on the page, the act of writing firmly anchored as a method of self-reflection. In the opening passages of "The Book of Memory" we find Auster's fictionalised persona A. struggling to write anything of substance. There is one passage, however, that stands out and becomes the driving force of the text—a passage that teases out the complexities that underpin the connection between writing and fatherhood:

> When the father dies, he writes, the son becomes his own father and his own son. He looks at his son and sees himself in the face of the boy. He imagines what the boy sees when he looks at him and finds himself becoming his own father. Inexplicably, he is moved by this. (85)

It is here that Auster introduces his awareness of the complexities of the negotiation from the role of son to the role of father and the impact of the shifting role on the American male's sense of self.

The narrative that underpins "The Book of Memory" is A.'s separation from his wife and son. Two months after the death of his father, A. suffers the breakdown of his marriage. Auster continues to focalise the trauma of his recent real-life experiences through A.:

> If it was one thing for him to accept this break-up, to be miserable about it and yet to understand that it was inevitable, it was quite another thing for him to swallow the consequences it entailed: to be separated from his son. (107)

One of the classic themes of the American literary tradition is the absent father. Michael Kimmel attributes this trope of the American male's desire to flee fatherly duty to the cultural history of the nation. Kimmel highlights the impact of the American Revolution on the masculine mind-set with the symbolic patricide of patriarchal Father England by the "Sons of Liberty."[38] Auster strives to subvert this archetypal representation of fatherhood in American fiction with new models of the father role that challenge the normalised performance of the American father. One recurring theme in Auster's oeuvre is the effect of this separation on the *father's* sense of his manhood, and it is this that emerges as the main theme in "The Book of Memory."

"The Book of Memory" revolves around various images of the separation between father and son. Auster catalogues various instances of artists who have experienced the tragic death of their sons.[39] There is the resonating image of flyers alerting the public to a missing child in New York, a child who looks remarkably like A.'s son Daniel. There is also the fictional father-son relationship in the story of *Pinocchio*.[40] Whilst narrating this story at his son's bedside, A. notices that it is the image of Pinocchio, the son, saving Gepetto, the father, which captures his son's imagination. It is the passage of reunion, when Pinocchio finally finds Gepetto in the belly of the whale, that resonates, in light of the state of separation that A. and Daniel are suffering. It is Pinocchio, the son, who carries the father on his back. Auster points out that it is embracing fatherhood by having faith in the son that saves Gepetto from certain death. The line that Pinocchio says to his father, which Auster cites, is extremely powerful: "Follow me and have no fear" (*Invention* 142). As A. exclaims: "The son saves the father" (143).

The ultimate message from "The Book of Memory," which Auster will continue to explore in greater depth in later fiction, is that the role of father can save the everyday man from the conflicts and tensions that appear to shape and control the male individual. Becoming a father has lifted A. from the anguish that breaks many men: "A. looks at his son and realises that he must not allow himself to despair. There is the responsibility for a young life, and in that he has brought his life into being" (168):

> In that the world can lead a man to nothing but despair, and a despair so complete, so resolute, that nothing can open the door of this prison, which is hopelessness, A. peers through the bars of his cell and finds one thought that brings him any consolation: the image of his son. And

> not just his son, but any son, any daughter, any child of any man or woman. (168)

Auster sets the tone for his subversion of the archetypal theme of the absent father in his fiction by proposing that being a visible and active presence in the life of the son (or daughter) can save the American father from the internal and external conflicts that historically have characterised the experience of the American male. It is this rejection of the ideological image of the absent father that is the crux of Auster's literary representations of fatherhood in his fiction.

AUSTER'S COUNTER-HEGEMONIC FATHER FIGURES

Fatherhood is a major theme in Auster's most widely read and critiqued work, *The New York Trilogy* (1987). Auster has remarked that "the *Trilogy* grows directly out of" (*The Red Notebook* 107) and *The New York Trilogy* further develops the themes of walking and writing that shape the subtleties of the performance of the father in Auster's worlds. Made up of three texts, *The City of Glass* (1985), *Ghosts* (1986), and *The Locked Room* (1986), *The New York Trilogy* presents male protagonists who are not simply employed in the novel to drive the narrative, as would be expected in Auster's playfully postmodern, yet ultimately indulgent, subversion of the detective fiction genre. Rather these men are flâneurs moving through the streets of New York engaging in self-reflexive analyses of their masculinities.

Quinn, the protagonist of *The City of Glass,* was once married and a father, but now both his wife and son are dead. There are two activities that make up Quinn's everyday routine: he writes and he walks. While writing mystery novels, which feature the "private-eye narrator" (6) Max Work, was "the only thing he felt he could do" (4), we are told that "more than anything else, however, what he liked to do was walk. Nearly every day, rain or shine, hot or cold, he would leave his apartment to walk through the city" (3). Again Auster returns to the sense of the protagonist feeling lost as he walks the streets—but not physically lost—lost in escaping the social pressures that were defining his sense of his masculinity in Manhattan:

> Each time he took a walk, he felt as though he were leaving himself behind, and by giving himself up to the movement of the streets, by reducing himself to a seeing eye, he was able to escape the obligation to think, and this, more than anything else, brought him a measure of peace, a salutary emptiness within. (4)

The loss of the father role still haunts Quinn. Even though he tries to not think about his son, "every once in a while, he would suddenly feel what it had been like to hold the three-year old boy in his arms" (5).

Quinn's narrative in *The City of Glass* begins with a random phone call. On the other end is a voice asking for "Paul Auster. Of the Auster Detective Agency" (7). When Quinn follows up the call, he meets with Peter Stillman Jr. and his wife, Virginia Stillman. They want "Paul Auster" to protect Stillman Jr. from his father, who is about to be discharged from a psychiatric institution. Virginia is fearful that the father will come and seek revenge. Quinn takes on the role with great gusto, as this is his chance to be a father once again. As he reflects:

> If Stillman was the man with the dagger, come back to avenge himself on the boy whose life he had destroyed, Quinn wanted to be there to stop him. He knew he could not bring his own son back to life, but at least he could prevent another from dying. (35)

Quinn, therefore, has the opportunity for second-chance fatherhood by becoming the flâneurial detective, carefully watching and observing the father Stillman Sr. Engaging in this role is a natural fit for Quinn: "He did not stop to think about what he was doing, nor did he analyse the possible implications of this uncustomary act. He felt an urge to record certain facts, and he wanted to put them down on paper before he forgot them" (106). Ultimately, having the protagonist Quinn accept the identity of "Paul Auster," and accept the job of watching Stillman Sr., is a clever metafictional twist. To become a father figure once more, Quinn must become "Paul Auster" and engage in observing, analysing, and reporting back on the behaviour of this hegemonic male father, Stillman Sr. moving through the streets of New York. It is clear that adopting this role of flâneur gives Quinn a sense of being and purpose, as "imagining himself as Auster had become synonymous in his mind with doing good in the world" (51).[41] Taking a step back, this could be read as Auster playfully yet purposefully hinting at the self-actualising power of not only watching but also writing the father. Be it literally with Quinn in the New York City streets a few paces behind Stillman Sr. or figuratively as a writer of fiction, Auster underlines the importance of adopting the role of flâneur to thoroughly investigate the performance of the father.

It is in *The Locked Room* that Auster sets out the confrontation between conflicting models of American masculinity. The first, Fanshawe, is a hegemonic male figure. Similarly to "Portrait of an Invisible Man," there are passages that emphasise the social experiences of Fanshawe, both in his childhood and in later life, that formed his hegemonic status. The key moment in the representation of Fanshawe's masculinity is his reaction to the news that he is to become a father. When his girlfriend Sophie falls pregnant, Fanshawe leaves her: "husbands, after all, deserted their wives every day, and most of them did not want to be found" (202). Adhering to the traditional idea of what it means to be an American male, Fanshawe rejects the responsibilities of fatherhood and escapes from domesticity to his self-imposed solitude. Fanshawe becomes an invisible man.

The second male figure in *The Locked Room* is the unnamed narrator. This figure embodies a distinct model of masculinity. Fanshawe's closest friend during childhood, the narrator was in awe of Fanshawe's hegemonic status. After losing contact with Fanshawe, the narrator is contacted years later by Fanshawe's wife, Sophie. At Fanshawe's request, Sophie asks the narrator to begin work on publishing the absent Fanshawe's manuscripts. As the narrative unfolds, the narrator marries Sophie and takes over the father role to Fanshawe's child. Throughout the text the unnamed narrator praises Fanshawe's literary talents while he scrapes by as a literary critic. Following the success of Fanshawe's novels, the next step is to write Fanshawe's biography. The narrator is, at first, eager to carry out this exercise in literary self-actualisation, a prominent theme in Auster's fiction. At another point in the text he even toys with the idea of taking on Fanshawe's identity. However, in light of his wife's fear of losing him, the unnamed narrator, despite fleeing to France in search of Fanshawe and toiling with the expectations of what it means to be masculine, finally rejects this archetypal masculine role in favour of remaining a visible figure in the life of his wife and son.

What Auster is doing, therefore, at this climactic point of *The New York Trilogy*, is demonstrating the possibilities for the male to achieve a sense of self-worth and happiness in a role that turns away from what has been historically set as the ideal image of American manhood. A scene between the narrator and his adopted son Ben is extremely poignant. About to leave for his final confrontation with Fanshawe, the narrator makes breakfast for Ben and himself. As they discuss the trip, Ben's final message is that the narrator is "just like an emperor. . . . The emperor of little boys" (303). This is a subtle reference to the Holy Roman Emperor Frederick II in *The City of Glass,* the first story in the Trilogy. Quinn learns that Stillman Sr. conducted an experiment on his son in which he restricted the social development of his language. Quinn makes the link with the Emperor Frederick II, who had hoped to discover man's "natural language" by using similar dominating and abusive methods of restricting language from children. These children, as Quinn reports, died before they had spoken a single word. The message that Auster is sending with this link between these narratives is clear. Coming full circle from the representations of the distorted nature of hegemonic dominance of the father, it is simply being there for the son that means that these American men are "emperors" in the eyes of their children.

There is a certain degree of ambiguity surrounding the connection between Fanshawe and the unnamed narrator. Are they two parts of the same person? Is Fanshawe merely an alter ego of the narrator? Or are these two figures fictional components of Auster's own self? While these are understandable approaches to reading the male figures in the text, the sociological value of these figures is unlocked if we consider these two characters as conflicting models of fatherhood in American society with the final triumph achieved by the counter-hegemonic model. Monika Müller, in her reading of *The Locked Room*, states, "the story seems to proceed to a rather benign ending" (160). Müller, I would argue, completely underestimates the significance of the climactic confrontation between these two representations of fatherhood. It is in their final exchange that these conflicting models of masculinity clash. Fanshawe asks the narrator to save the red notebook that he has left for his son Ben. When the narrator rejects Fanshawe's request, Fanshawe exclaims, "He's my son" (311), to which the narrator replies, "No, he's not. He's mine" (311). In this final encounter, the unnamed narrator condemns Fanshawe for deserting his son. This is a significant shift from the narrator's position at the start of the text. *The Locked Room* opens with the narrator reflecting upon the meaning that Fanshawe brings to his own existence, the crucial role of this hegemonic male figure in the understanding of his individual masculinity. And yet, by the end of the text, the narrator rejects Fanshawe, and in doing so, rejects the "ideal" of the American father: "You're a fool, and you deserve to die" (312).

It has been suggested that Auster's fictional representations of American manhood affirm hegemonic ideals of American masculinity. Müller contends that Auster's underlying objective is to juxtapose conflicting models of masculinity: the feminine activity of writing with this masculine role of the breadwinner. The conclusion that Müller arrives at, however, is curious. Müller declares that although Auster may set out to subvert the notions of "macho-masculinity" presented in hard-boiled detective fiction, Auster ultimately "supports masculine hegemony" (161). Turning to Alan Petersen's reading of contemporary masculinity in which the American male is still expected to fulfil the established masculine role of the breadwinner,[42] Müller argues that despite Auster's subversion of "the usual machoism of detective fiction through his ironic presentation of the conventions of the hard-boiled detective novel" (144), the male figures in Auster's fiction ultimately legitimise the hegemonic model of masculinity:

> Yet by insisting that males fulfil their roles as "breadwinner"—or "head of the household"—in spite of all the difficulties they might encounter, he ultimately furthers hegemonical views of masculinity. (144)

Whereas Müller's critique focuses solely on one work of fiction, *The New York Trilogy,* I would argue that analysing the development of this theme throughout Auster's fictions presents a different picture. Looking at Auster's oeuvre illustrates the fact that Auster persists in his critique of the conflicts and complexities that define the American male's experience and, in complete contrast to Müller's assertion, Auster rejects the legitimisation of patterns of hegemony in his proposal of new models of fatherhood and masculinity. With selected texts below, I will evaluate Auster's methodological approach to critiquing the contemporary condition of American fatherhood through the juxtaposition of conflicting models of the father role.

Following *The New York Trilogy, Moon Palace* (1989) dramatizes further the social dynamics that define the performance of the American father.[43] *Moon Palace* offers a clear concentrated critique of the various father "types" that impact upon the protagonist Marco Stanley Fogg. First, there is the figure of Uncle Victor. Uncle Victor, the older brother of Marco's mother, embodies the traditional literary depictions of American males in being "the sort of person who always dreams of doing something else while occupied" (5). Consequently Uncle Victor displays no desire to be a father, feeling that he simply could not fulfil the role: "He knew that fatherhood was beyond him" (5). Despite becoming a surrogate father figure to Marco in the early stages of the narrative, he treats Marco as a buddy rather than a son.

The second father figure in the novel is Thomas Effing. Effing, an old man close to death, appears in the narrative when he employs Marco to read him selected texts from his expansive library. Marco sees Effing as a very complicated man, spending days spouting nothing but bitterness and sarcasm. Marco judges him to be "a tortured soul, as a man haunted by his past, struggling to hide some secret anguish that was devouring him from within" (114). As we find out, the anguish is the fact that Effing's real name is Julian Barber and, following the traditional path of the American male, Barber had abandoned his wife for a journey of self-discovery in the American Midwest. Effing, after returning to New York with a new name and new identity, finds out many years later that his solitary night of passion with his wife before he left on his trip resulted in the birth of his son, Solomon Barber. Effing's anguish, therefore, is due to his regret of being another absent father.

The next father figure in the novel is Effing's son, Solomon Barber. As a characteristic Austerian narrative twist would have it, Effing, Solomon, and Marco discover that they are all connected as Effing's son, Solomon Barber turns out to be Marco's father. Barber, following Effing, is also an absent father. A history professor, his relationship with a student, Emily Fogg, resulted in Marco's birth. Like his father, Solomon also suffers a great degree of pain and suffering due to the lack of a relationship he has with his son. The suffering that he experiences in being an invisible man is represented ironically in the text in his grotesque physical size: "The larger his body grew, the more deeply he buried himself inside it. Barber's goal was to shut himself off from the world, to make himself invisible in the massiveness of his own flesh" (235).

The final father figure in the novel is the protagonist Marco Fogg himself. And it is with Marco Fogg that we reach the crux of Auster's critique of the effect of the father role in this novel. In light of the connections between these characters, and the dominant theme of the absent father in American fiction, a possible reading of the novel would be to focus on the effects of the absent father on the American son. Conversely, Auster's critique is centred on the damaging effects of the father rejecting the father role. *Moon*

Palace posits these conflicting ideas of fatherhood and illustrates the effect of these on the male individual, both psychologically in terms of Thomas Effing, and physically with regard to Solomon Barber's physical condition. It is through Marco Fogg's narrative that Auster focuses his fictionalisation of the significance of the role of father on the contemporary condition of masculinity.

The one guiding light in Marco's life is his girlfriend Kitty. When Kitty falls pregnant, Marco's life changes forever: "the pregnancy dropped like a cannonball into our little pond, and before we could brace ourselves for the shock, our boat had been swamped and we were swimming for dear life" (271). And yet it is in this passage of the novel that Auster fully realises the counter-hegemonic narrative in the novel. In a subversion of the traditional set-up of an impending arrival of a baby resulting in the male character's rejection of the responsibilities of fatherhood, and the mother left to bring up the baby alone, it is Marco who fights to become a father in the face of Kitty's rejection of the baby. In a further inversion of the traditional gender roles, Kitty rejects the baby not only due to her feeling that a baby would come between their love for each other, but because she wants to focus on her career. Whereas the baby appears to be an abstraction to Kitty, for Marco the baby was a life the second that he knew Kitty was carrying it inside her: "Even if it was no larger than a thumb, it was a person, an inescapable reality. If we went ahead and arranged for an abortion, I felt it would be the same thing as committing murder" (271). Marco reaffirms his acceptance of the responsibility of this impending role of father: "But the moment has come, I would say. Like it or not, we've already made a baby, and now we have to deal with things as they are" (272). Auster's representation of this alternative contemporary father role is fully realised in Marco's reaction during their heated exchange:

> I wanted to be a father, and now that the prospect was before me, I couldn't stand the thought of losing it. The baby was my chance to undo the loneliness of my childhood, to be part of a family, to belong to something that was more than just myself, and because I had not been aware of this desire until then, it came rushing out of me in huge, inarticulate bursts of desperation. (272)

At this point, with the possibility of being a father becoming ever more real in Marco's understanding of his masculinity and male identity, he is certain of the effect of Kitty's request to terminate the child will have on his sense of self: "If you kill our baby, you'll be killing me along with it" (272).

With this set-piece scene Auster is not solely proposing that embracing fatherhood can offer a new mode of living, but, even more importantly, that the desire can exist within the American male to engage in new appropriations of the role. Having a child and being an active participant in its upbringing can offer the possibility of looking beyond the closed self and recognise the pivotal role of the present and active father in the socialization of his children. Crucially, the suggestion is that rejecting the standard masculine type of the invisible, detached, forgotten father not only benefits the child, but as Auster goes on to explore in his fiction, it is also fundamental to the counter-hegemonic condition of contemporary masculinity. This is intimated in how flânerie is presented as a self-reflexive self-actualising activity in *Moon Palace* between father and son.

Initially Marco Fogg spends a significant segment of the narrative seemingly involuntarily walking in the streets of New York: "I turned south, paused for a moment, and then took a step. Then I took another step, and in that way I began to move down the street. I did not look back once" (46). Initially Fogg feels that the "grinding demands" (55) of the streets shame him into an awareness of himself as "a vagabond, a pox of failure on the skin of mankind" (56). Central Park becomes the symbolic place of refuge for Fogg, the place of solitude: "If the streets forced me to see myself as others saw me, the park gave me a chance to return to my inner life, to hold on to myself purely in terms of what was happening inside me" (56). Although Fogg tries to justify this life as a glorified "challenge to the American way" (60), this lifestyle leads to his self-destruction. Struck down with a high fever, his life is saved when Zimmer and Kitty finally find him in Central Park.

The power of flânerie is fully realised when it is a shared activity between (surrogate) father and son. One of Marco's main jobs is to push Effing around the streets of Manhattan. As we are told, Effing "looked forward to an excursion through the streets of the neighbourhood with all the enthusiasm of an explorer about to begin a journey to the Arctic" (115). Once outside, Effing, due to his poor eyesight, demands Marco to describe what he could see. While Marco initially sees this as an inane exercise, what Marco comes to realise is that Effing is teaching him how to see. The father figure is not simply training the son to keep his eyes open when moving through the urban jungle, but to see life in the metropolis in particular detail. At first Fogg laments that he "had never acquired the habit of looking closely at things, and now that I was being asked to do it, the results were dreadfully inadequate" (117). Marco even makes reference to Flaubert, one of the great flâneurs who roamed the streets of Paris. Marco begins to embrace the act of not only observing the great metropolis but also describing it in accurate detail:

> the effort to describe things accurately was precisely the kind of discipline that could teach me what I most wanted to learn: humility, patience, rigor. Instead of doing it merely to discharge an obligation, I began to consider it as a spiritual exercise, a process of training myself how to look at the world as if I were discovering it for the first time. What do you see? And if you see, how do you put it into words? (118)

This is a notable transformation in the performance of Fogg in the streets of Manhattan. Moving on from being a young man who sees the city streets as a place of self-loathing and self-negation, Fogg now embraces the city as a place of self-actualisation through the act of observing, interpreting, and describing the minutiae of the urban arena. The crucial point to make, however, is that this transformation occurs in a shared activity with the father figure in his life. Essentially it is Effing, the surrogate father, who is teaching Marco *Fogg,* perhaps another example of Auster playfully naming his characters, how to see.

Auster's focus on the father role pulsates beneath the surface in subsequent fiction. In *The Music of Chance* (1990) Auster, following the subversive narrative of *Moon Palace,* returns to familiar American literary territory with what is essentially a "buddy" narrative.[44] Following the breakdown of his marriage, Jim Nashe initially uses the excuse of his job to leave his daughter with his sister's family. He quits his job and embarks on an Austerian quest of self-discovery before becoming a father figure to his buddy Jack Pozzi. Equally in *Leviathan* (1992), the narrator, Peter Aaron, displays his shame in his inability to live up to the responsibilities of fatherhood: "I took the responsibilities of fatherhood seriously, and the thought of not being able to provide for my wife and son filled me with shame" (53–54). Later, Aaron, when speaking about the breakdown of his marriage, considers staying with his wife for the sake of his son: "Once you became a parent, there were duties that couldn't be shirked, obligations that had to be fulfilled, no matter what the cost" (78–79).

Following *Mr. Vertigo* (1994), Auster's tribute to the fairy tale,[45] and *Timbuktu* (1999), it is in *The Book of Illusions* (2002) that the loss of the father role re-emerges as a major theme.[46] The protagonist of *The Book of Illusions* is David Zimmer, a character who appeared previously in *Moon Palace* to come to Marco Fogg's aid on his journey towards realising his masculine identity. It is not merely friendship that connects these two characters, however, as in *The Book of Illusions* the devastating effects of losing the father role is revisited once again.

David Zimmer is a professor of comparative literature. Balancing work and home life with his wife and two sons, he is succeeding in being an active figure in the household. Zimmer, however, suffers the tragedy of losing his wife and two sons in a plane crash one week short of his tenth wedding anniversary. Following the death of his family, Zimmer concedes, "most of him had died along with them" (6). The opening sequences of the novel detail Zimmer's reaction to this horrific tragedy. He visits his sons' rooms, putting together their puzzles and playing with their toys: "carrying on their little phantom lives for them by repeating the gestures they had made when they still had bodies" (8). Moreover, he spends each night lying awake in the bed of his son Todd. It is clear that the role of father gave Zimmer place and meaning in the world. Having this taken away from him so cruelly, Zimmer disconnects from society, self-destructing in his anguish and sorrow.

What saves Zimmer from his despair is his chance discovery of the silent films of Hector Mann. Mann's roles as the "everyman" in his films, "at the bottom of the social ladder . . . toiling for others in humble low-salaried jobs" (34), reflect the difficulties he experienced surviving in the real world. Following the dominant trope of ekphrasis in Auster's fiction, Zimmer's coping strategy with his loss of the father role is to study, in obsessive detail, Hector's performance in his films. In Auster's multilevel metafictional text, Zimmer's critique of Mann's films appears to provide him a means to a greater understanding of his masculine role in American society. To fully concentrate on writing his book on Mann, Zimmer retreats to the only place in which he feels he can write a text on the social condition of American masculinity: New York City.[47]

The theme of loss that defines Zimmer's experience of fatherhood in the novel is continued with Mann. Not only does Mann explore the tragedy of losing his family in his films, but in his real life Mann has also suffered the loss of a child. In a characteristic Austerian doubling, while Zimmer loses a son called Todd, Mann's son is named Thaddeus Spelling II, or Tad for short. Just as Zimmer's son Todd dies needlessly in a tragic accident, Tad also dies tragically at three years old after an allergic reaction to a bee sting. Mann had been happy, too happy in his view, up to this point. It is after his son's death that Mann eventually goes back to making films in an attempt to grasp some sense of meaning in the events that have defined his time as a father, and more specifically, the loss that has defined his experience as a father.[48] What ultimately connects these two men is their shared experience of the loss of fatherhood. In this multilevel metafictional text, while Mann makes movies to deal with the loss of his role of father, Zimmer studies Mann to also deal with his loss.

SECOND-CHANCE FATHERHOOD

If it is the loss of the father role that underpins the narratives *Moon Palace, The Book of Illusions,* and *Oracle Night* (2003), in which John Trause suffers the breakdown of the relationship with his son Jacob and feels that he had "more or less abdicated his responsibilities as a father" (162), then it is in *The Brooklyn Follies* (2005) that Auster turns towards exploring the idea of second-chance fatherhood.[49] Set in a late 1990s New York that has yet to suffer the tragedy of the terrorist attacks of September 11, 2001, critics have argued that *The Brooklyn Follies* is a highly charged political text.[50] As much as *The Brooklyn Follies* represents Auster's turn towards the political in his post-2000 novels, I would argue that *The Brooklyn Follies* is one of Auster's most *gendered* political texts, with Auster playing out the conflicts between various categories of American masculinity in the narrative. Nathan Glass' re-engagement in the father role sets him as another Austerian counter-hegemonic figure who, in subverting the archetypal masculine rejection of fatherhood, finds a reason to live in the city that he initially returns to in his search for a place to die.

At first it appears that Nat, at sixty years old, is a stock male figure from the American literary tradition. Having majored in English at college, Nat had the "secret ambition" of going on to study literature or journalism. However, he reveals that he "hadn't had the courage to pursue either one" and spent his life chasing the American Dream of the self-made man and breadwinner roles:

> Life got in the way—two years in the army, work, marriage, family responsibilities, the need to earn more and more money, all the muck that bogs us down when we don't have the balls to stand up for ourselves. (13)

From the outset it is evident that Nat's masculinity has been shaped by oppressive hegemonic discourses of self-made masculinity. Nat's attempt to achieve the unattainable ideal of true American manhood, however, has resulted in the dissolution of his marriage, the breakdown in his relationship with his daughter, and his diagnosis with lung cancer. Having given himself up for dead, Nat decides to return to New York to engage in the trademark Austerian activity of male introspection by writing about his life and the historical development of man, a text which he plans to call *The Book of Human Folly:*

> and in it I was planning to set down in the simplest, clearest language possible an account of every blunder, every pratfall, every embarrassment, every idiocy, every foible, and every inane act that I had committed during my long and checkered career as a man. When I couldn't think of stories to tell about myself, I would write down things that had happened to people I knew, and when that source ran dry as well, I would take on historical events, recording the follies of the fellow human beings down through the ages. (5)

At this early stage in the novel, Nat sees the lives of American men as overarchingly negative narratives. As Harry Brightman, another man in the city who has suffered the breakdown of his marriage and is forced to renounce his role of father by his wealthy father-in-law, laments in a conversation with Nat:

> "By the time a man gets to be our age, Nathan, he's little more than a series of exes. *N'est-ce pas?* In my own case, I could probably reel off a dozen or more. Ex-husband. Ex-art dealer. Ex-navy man. Ex-window dresser. Ex-perfume salesman. Ex-millionaire. Ex-Buffalonian. Ex-Chicagoan. Ex-convict." (58)

What saves Nat from this seemingly self-negating 'ex'-istence is his re-engagement in the father role. Nat becomes a father figure to a number of characters in the text. The first relationship, with Tom Wood, is possibly the most significant in terms of what it represents symbolically in a study of the literary representation of masculinity. Tom represents the archetypal young male protagonist of American literature, the naming of the character evoking images of Tom Sawyer or the emblematic resonance of the woods in the theme of masculine retreat from the responsibilities of society that underpins the classic works of American literature. Furthermore Tom's initial views on American manhood reflect the behaviour of the male protagonists of the American canon. Tom's dissertation on "Imaginary Edens," which focuses on the work of Poe and Thoreau within the backdrop of the emerging Civil War, is one of the main tropes of the novel: "It's about non-existent worlds. . . . A study of the inner refuge, a map of the place a man goes to when life in the real world is no longer possible" (14–15). In Tom's critical reading of Poe and Thoreau, "Both men believed in America, and both men believed that America had gone to hell, that it was being crushed to death by an ever-growing mountain of machines and money. How was man to think in the clamour? They both wanted out" (16). In the face of the distorted ideals of capitalism shaping the lives of American men, Tom celebrates Thoreau's desire to "exile himself in the woods—for no other reason than to prove that it could be done. As long as a man had the courage to reject what society told him to do, he could live life on his own terms" (16). At the other end of the spectrum was Poe, who withdrew into "the imaginary room": "a place to read, write, and think. It's a vault of contemplation, a noiseless sanctuary where the soul can at last find a measure of peace" (16). Tom's representation of the standard themes of American masculinity is further characterised in his lack of interest in becoming a father. When Lucy, Tom's niece, arrives on Tom's doorstep in New York alone and refusing to speak, Tom has no interest in becoming a surrogate father to her: "He knew nothing about children, and even if he'd been living in a twelve-room mansion with a full staff of servants, he still wouldn't have had the faintest interest in becoming his niece's substitute parent" (134). Even Nat, at one point, recognises that Tom is "the worst man for the job" (135).

Auster employs Nat to demonstrate an alternative for the American male. In light of the missed opportunities of being a father to his daughter Rachel, it is Nat who takes on the father role. At first there is the idea of sending Lucy to Vermont to her Aunt Pamela, but Nat decides to assume the responsibility of being a father to her in the city: "I cross Pamela's name off the list and appoint myself as Lucy's temporal guardian. Am I better qualified to take care of Lucy than Pamela is? No, in most ways probably not, but my gut tells me that I'm responsible for her—whether I like it or not" (169). They grow closer and Nat begins to appreciate their relationship: "I never once regretted taking her in" (227). As the narrative unfolds, it is revealed that Lucy's initial unwillingness to speak is due to the dominating presence of her surrogate father, David, in the household over both Lucy and her mother, Aurora. The abuse of a child's development of language as a key trope is a further link to *The Locked Room* and Peter Stillman Sr., and yet, in direct contrast to these dominating father figures, Nat realises that his first job in the father role is to encourage Lucy to speak.

Finally, when Lucy's mother Aurora comes to New York to be with her daughter, Nat reflects upon the girls' return to be with her mother in a conversation with Tom to remind him that "a part of Lucy still belongs to us, to each one of us. She's our girl, too, and nothing will ever change that'" (279). It is clear that it is not simply a submission to some sense of social responsibility that leads Nat to act as a father figure to Lucy. Rather it's Nat's realisation that by doing so, by becoming a father to Lucy, and indeed by becoming a father figure to the other characters in the novel, he is no longer defined by the 'ex'-istence of what he was. Nat realises that at this stage in his life, although he may enjoy talking about creating a new life "in the middle of a quiet New England nowhere" (181), in contrast to Tom's view of true male "courage" (16) being demonstrated in fleeing the city to live in the "make-believe sanctuary" (189) of the Hotel Existence in Vermont, their lives are in New York. And it is in the city, under the guidance of Nat, that Tom begins to open himself up to other modes of masculinity. Tom meets Honey Chowder, and this new stage in his life opens Tom to a new model of masculinity under the energetic influence of his wife in New York: "in spite of his predictions to the contrary, Honey didn't wear him out or beat him down or crush his spirit. Day by day, she slowly turned him into the man he was always destined to become" (240).

Auster further explores the importance of being a father with Nat's attempts to repair the broken relationship with his daughter Rachel in Manhattan. In a letter, he asks Rachel to "forgive your stupid father" (61), stating, "of all the people in the world, you're the one who means the most to me. You're the heart of my heart, the blood of my blood, and it torments me to think that my idiotic remarks could have caused any bad blood between us" (61–62). Again the theme of a self-negating sense of existence without being a father to his daughter is realised: "Without you, I am nothing. Without you, I am no one" (62). When they finally reconnect, they do so in midtown Manhattan. Auster highlights the importance of a visible, dependable father for the son or daughter, with Rachel confessing, "if I can count on you now, I think I'll be able to get through anything" (230). This is replicated in Nat's relationship with his niece Aurora. Following her ordeal of being locked in the basement of her own home by her husband, David, Nat offers to pay for therapy sessions to help her cope with this trauma. Aurora's response is poignant:

> she said no, she'd rather just talk to me. Me. The bitter, solitary man who had crept home to Brooklyn less than a year earlier, the burnout who had convinced himself there was nothing left to live for—knuckle-headed

> me, Nathan the Unwise, who could think of nothing better to do than quietly wait to drop dead, now transformed into a confidant and counselor, a lover of randy widows, and a knight-errant who rescued damsels in distress. (284)

Inasmuch as *The Brooklyn Follies* may be read as a political novel, it also explores the gender politics that shaped the American male experience in the period leading up to what many may consider the defining moment of recent American history—the terrorist attacks of September 11, 2001—an event that Auster himself marks out as "a certain moment in our history" (Dupont). Within this historical context, Auster's narrative demonstrates the destructive nature of past social pressures that characterised the social performance of American masculinity and, through the act of re-engaging in the role of father in American society, suggests the possibilities for new models of fatherhood.

Man in the Dark (2008) is another overtly political Auster novel, but the essence of the book is in its exploration of the power of fatherhood. Although there are certain Austerian tropes that underpin the structure of the narrative, there are also notable subversions that point to Auster's re-engagement with the subject of the father role. The dual narratives of this work contest the two major concerns of the novel. First, the protagonist of the novel, August Brill, is largely confined to his bed after a car accident. Unable to sleep, he lies awake at night inventing the second narrative, the story of a man named Owen Brick surviving in a contemporary America engulfed in a brutal civil war following the 2000 elections. Brick's story is clearly a representation of Brill's inner state, the civil war a symbolic reference to the self-conflict that he is experiencing. As much as the novel may seem, therefore, a novel about contemporary American politics, it is another novel concerned with contemporary gender politics.

Brill, following the sixty-year-old Nat in *The Brooklyn Follies,* subverts the model of the standard Auster protagonist at seventy-two years old. The main narrative of the novel concerns his role as father to his daughter Miriam and as a father figure to his granddaughter Katya. Brill should be working on the memoir of his life that he had promised to write after the death of his wife, Sonia. However, in his grief, he rejects any attempts of self-analysis:

> the end of married life, the loneliness of it all, the fucking loneliness after I lost her, and then I cracked up that rented car, destroying my leg, nearly killing myself in the process, maybe that added to it as well: the indifference, the feeling that after seventy-two years on this earth, who gives a damn if I write about myself or not? (13)

With his set-up early in the novel, Auster sets out to challenge the trademark trope of the male figure allergic to domestic responsibilities. This is the first indication of the importance of family life to Brill. Rather than embarking on the typical Austerian literary exercise of masculine self-generation, Brill turns his attention to his family around him.

The fact that this is a novel about gender politics is evident at subsequent key points in the narrative. Following the recurring Austerian trope of ekphrasis, it is in the films that Brill watches with his granddaughter that he channels his reading of the gender roles in American society. Engaging in the father figure role to support his granddaughter Katya after her former boyfriend Titus has been killed in Iraq, Brill reveals his counter-hegemonic views of the roles of men and women in American society through his thoughts on the performances of the male and female characters in the film they are watching:

> They're all about women. How women are the ones who carry the world. They take care of the real business while their hapless men stumble around making a hash of things. Or else just lie around doing nothing. (21–22)

There are various elements in the narrative that subvert traditional gender roles. Before his retirement Brill was a literary critic and it was his wife, Sonia, who was the main breadwinner. A singer, Sonia, spent long periods away from home building her reputation as a live performer. Speaking with his granddaughter Katya, Brill admits that the situation left him "torn down the middle. On the one hand, I was happy for her whenever she got a booking to perform in a new city. On the other hand—just like your mother—I hated to see her go" (151–152). When Sonia gave birth to their daughter Miriam, she went back to work as soon as she could, three months later. Brill acknowledges that she was a good mother, but "she also had her work" (147). As a result of this subversion of the traditional roles within American society, Brill, in an attempt to regain some sense of control over what he considered to be the traditional performance of American masculinity, engaged in "dumb-ass flings and dalliances" (154) in New York. Consequently Brill and Sonia separated. What brought them back together after nine years apart was the second chance to play the role of guardian with the birth of Katya: "You were the one who got us together again" (163). For Brill in particular it was another opportunity to be a father figure that gave him a renewed sense of self-worth and pride in a performance of his counter-hegemonic roles of masculinity. These moments that Brill shares with Katya become the times in which he not only succeeds in telling the story of his life, but he also gains an understanding of the discourses that shaped his masculine behaviour. The conversations that he has with Katya are a form of negotiation, an opportunity to evaluate the realities that have defined his experiences as an American male. Adopting the father figure role saves Brill from the dark moments that pervade his consciousness as he spends night after restless night inventing the narrative of Owen Brick that plays out his regrets and disappointments.

As the novel progresses, the parallel narratives begin to merge and Brill begins to acknowledge that the invented narrative is his fictionalisation of his inner struggles: "the longer I went on, the more I understood how badly I was fooling myself. The story is about a man who must kill the person who created him, and why pretend I am not that person? By putting myself into the story, the story becomes real" (102). At his darkest moment, reflecting upon his self-destruction after the death of his wife, Brill realises that it is his role of father that saves him:

> She left me our child, too, that mustn't be overlooked, the child who is no longer a child, and how strange to think that I'd be lost without her now, no doubt drunk every night, if not dead or on life support in some hospital. (103)

It is the possibility of acting as a pillar of support for both his daughter and granddaughter that takes Brill from the dark solitude of his late-night imaginary worlds into the reality of what American masculinity means for him now. The three generations of this family in the novel are all shaped by their struggle with incomplete narratives: Brill's stuttering memoir; Miriam's doubts surrounding her biography of Rose Hawthorne; and Katya's stalled studies. And it is Brill, by embracing the father figure role in this potentially tense and claustrophobic nuclear environment, who clears Miriam of her doubts regarding her writing and persuades Katya that it is time for her to go back to school.

Man in the Dark contains trademark elements of every Auster novel. What *Man in the Dark* contributes to our appreciation of Auster's fiction is further illustration that the theme of the counter-hegemonic father is now growing ever more prominent in his critique of American masculinity. Probably the Austerian prototypical protagonist will always remain the thirty-something writer who embarks on a quest of masculine self-discovery. Indeed some critics of Auster's fiction have perhaps somewhat unfairly flagged up Auster's preference for a certain mode of narrative.[51] And yet, what is becoming ever more apparent is that it is the fathers of Auster's fiction who are now appearing as the characters of greater depth and complexity. This theme is developed further in *Sunset Park* (2010).

It might be expected for the key narrative of *Sunset Park* to be that of the archetypal Austerian protagonist Miles Heller. Ravaged by guilt following his involvement in a tragic accident in which his stepbrother Bobby was hit by a car and killed, Miles abandons his family. He travels around the United States before eventually ending up in a small abandoned house with a group of other lost souls in Sunset Park, Brooklyn. It is not Miles' narrative, however, that is of key focus. Following the theme of fatherhood in Auster's writing, it is the narrative of Miles' father, Morris, that emerges as the backbone of the novel in its status as case-study analysis of the conflicts and complexities of the role of father in contemporary New York.

The New York of *Sunset Park* is a place of anguished fatherhood. This is evident when Morris makes a return to the city, having spent some time with his recently estranged second wife, Willa Parks, in England. "A lifelong New Yorker" (58), Heller is in Manhattan to attend the funeral of the daughter of one of the only two American authors from Morris' publishing house Heller Books, Marty Rothstein. It is their shared experience as fathers who have lost children that connects these men: "how not to put himself inside her father's skin and suffer the ravages of this pointless death?" (140). Later, when Morris gives his condolences to his friend, in a moment of true emotion, "Marty throws his arms around him and presses his head against his shoulder, saying Morris, Morris, Morris as his body convulses against him in a spasm of breathless sobs" (142). There is a deep emotional connection between the fathers here in Auster's New York.

At the service there is another Auster doubling with Morris meeting Renzo Michaelson, an old friend and godfather to his son Miles. After the service, whilst having lunch with Renzo in a Jewish delicatessen on Broadway, "a throwback to their New York childhoods" (144), it is the pain and suffering associated with the father role that pervades Morris' thoughts. What Auster does with these two characters is to use their meeting to contrast these models of American masculinity. Renzo is in many ways the typical Austerian hegemonic male. A highly respected writer who has enjoyed both critical and commercial success, his attempt to attain this hegemonic ideal has been an empty and lonely experience. While he appreciates that he no longer has to endure the hardships experienced in his early years, even after all his success, "none of it matters to him" (146). In what he feels is an empty and meaningless public persona, he has lost all sense of who he is: "I just want to disappear, he once told Morris, muttering in the lowest of low voices, staring off with a pained look in his eyes, as if he were talking to himself. I just want to disappear" (146). Morris, at this point in the novel, is also suffering a difficult moment in his life with his family seemingly disintegrating around him. Sitting in what Morris calls "the gloomy realm of dead children" (147), the narrator reflects:

> Renzo has no children, two ex-wives but no children, and given what Marty and Nina are going through now, given what he and Willa have already gone through, first with Bobby and then with Miles, Morris feels something close to envy, thinking that Renzo made the right decision all those years ago to steer clear of the kid business, to avoid the unavoidable mess and potential devastation of fatherhood. (146)

The crucial word in this piece, however, is *potential*. As Auster's exploration into these models of fatherhood and masculinity progresses in the novel, what emerges as the main message of the novel is that despite the tensions and conflicts that may characterise the father-son relationship, it is the father role that saves these men from the desire to disappear and, even more importantly, once again gives meaning to the everyday male experience.

Following Marco Fogg in *Moon Palace,* Sidney Orr in *Oracle Night,* and even Ben Sachs in *Leviathan*, Morris wanted to become a father. It was Morris and not Mary-Lee, Morris' first wife, who wanted to have the baby: "She wasn't prepared to be a mother. She was too young. I shouldn't have pushed her into it" (59). Morris follows Nat in *The Brooklyn Follies*, who tells his daughter Rachel that despite the hardships that he experienced in the breakdown of his relationship with his wife, it was all worth it, as "you're the happy ending to the whole tragic story, and because you are who you are, I don't have a single regret about anything. Do you understand me, Rachel?" (233). Morris also demonstrates that it is fatherhood that has proven to be absolutely "necessary" in the development of his masculinity:

> Time had proved that the real purpose of the two years he spent with her was not about building a sustainable marriage, it was about creating a son, and because that son was the single most important creature in the world for him, all the disappointments he'd endured with her had been worth it—no, more than worth it, absolutely necessary. (61)

In the absence of Mary-Lee, it was Morris who brought up his son in the early years. As Willa, Morris' second wife, reflects, "You used to be so close. That's one of the reasons why I fell in love with you—because of how well you loved that little boy" (27). At various points Morris reminisces of their times playing baseball and spending their Saturday mornings in Joe Junior's café. There is one memory, however, that holds particular significance in terms of their father-son relationship: Morris and Miles walking together through Manhattan.

The significance of walking and watching in the relationship between father and son re-emerges in *Sunset Park*. When Miles runs away from home, his father Morris becomes a distant watcher of his son: "always watching from a place where he couldn't be seen . . . keeping himself hidden, watching Miles grow older, watching his son turn into a man" (178). Morris' strategy to cope with Miles' rejection of his father is to create fantasy characters that allow him to ignore the pain and suffering associated with his son leaving the family. There is one character in particular that stands out, the Can Man, whom Morris calls "one of those old, broken-down men who forage among dumpsters and recycling bins for bottles and cans" (179). In this New York of anguished fatherhood, the absurd character of the Can Man can be read as a metaphor for the effect of the loss of the father role on the American male. Morris now sees himself as "a descendent of those fearless people who built the towers of Manhattan, a crazy customer, alas, not quite right in the head, the daft old loon who spends his days pushing his shopping cart through the neighbourhood" (180), a lost soul in a life without purpose.

Sunset Park also points towards the power of walking in the formation and understanding of fatherhood. The pivotal scene sees fourteen-year-old Miles and his father Morris "walking side by side" (56) in Manhattan. The description of their Sunday afternoon saunter is telling in how the father and the son view this intimate moment. To the son Miles, their journey through the West Village has no particular purpose, "just walking for the sake of walking" (56). It is in this moment, however, that the father Morris reveals just how important the father role is in his life. Miles, no doubt affected by his parent's separation at this formative time in his life, begins to question his father about his parent's relationship. While Miles' mother had been reticent about the situation, the narration of the scene often slips into Morris' voice as he decides to be completely honest with his son: "no doubt thinking that his son was old enough to know the facts, and now that the boy had asked the question, he deserved a straight and honest answer" (57). It is here that the major tropes of Auster's treatment of the theme of fatherhood are crystallised. Walking with his son, Morris reveals his desire to be a father, and, despite the tragedy of the breakdown of the relationship between mother and father, Morris is unequivocal that his son is the most important thing in the world to him.

In the final climactic scene in the novel, this message of the significance of the father role is illustrated. After assaulting a police officer and breaking the officer's jaw, Miles flees once again but quickly realises that his only hope now is to call his father. By reaching out to his father, the text ends with their relationship reaching full circle. Morris is once again the supportive, protecting father, giving his son advice on how to deal with this serious situation. Morris tells his son that running is no longer an option: "You don't want to spend the rest of your life running from the police, do you? You've already done enough running. Time to stand up and face the music, Miles. And I'll stand up there with you" (305–306). Miles' reply reflects his male pride: "You have a good heart, Dad, but I'm in this thing alone" (306). Morris, however, breaking the traditional model of American fatherhood, tells Miles that he is there for his son. Auster ends *Sunset Park,* therefore, by indicating that there is an alternative for the American father. Morris may be suffering with problems in his marriage and the difficulties with his business due to the difficult economic climate, but he is once more an active and positive force in his son's life, with Miles making the symbolic journey from his derelict house in which he lived in Sunset Park, Brooklyn, to his father's home in Downing Street, Manhattan.

CONCLUSION

Gendering Auster's fiction underlines fatherhood as a central theme. The methodical and meticulous case-study analysis of his father, Sam Auster, in *The Invention of Solitude* introduces Auster's interest in the discourses that shape the performance of the American father. As I have discussed, "Portrait of an Invisible Man" proves to be a loaded title in terms of Auster's critical investigation of the social construction of masculinity. As Auster's portrayal of his father illustrates, the great irony that characterised the American male of this era was that in their eagerness to become the hegemonic ideal of the "self-made man" they actually became invisible—to others as well as to themselves. What Auster achieves, therefore, with this "portrait" is to make the discourses that shaped his father's masculinity visible. Building upon this, it is the "The Book of Memory" that marks Auster's foray into fictionalising the impact of fatherhood on the contemporary American male's negotiation of his masculinity. Auster's decision to fictionalise his experience as a father underlines the self-reflective nature of his writing; in other words, Auster's objective is more than simple storytelling—it is a form of meditation on the conflicts that shape the American father's sense of his masculinity. It is at this point that Auster introduces the fundamental elements of his depiction of fatherhood that define the representation of these American fathers throughout his body of work. First, these narratives take place in the urban arena of New York. The choice of New York as the setting for these reflections upon the impact of fatherhood leads me to the second key element that features in Auster's depiction of these fathers: Auster employs the activity of walking the streets of Manhattan as a form of self-reflection. These Manhattan males, from the fictionalised Auster in "The Book of Memory" to Morris Heller in *Sunset Park,* embark on these journeys into the city but also into themselves. Becoming flâneurs, they engage in the act of watching, reflecting, and evaluating the discourses that shape their masculinity. The third element that characterises the depiction of fatherhood in Auster's fiction is perhaps the most crucial of all: Auster highlights the possibility of counter-hegemonic models of fatherhood in his fiction. Auster's counter-hegemonic male figures question the archetypal role expected of them as American males and demonstrate the benefits of active and engaged fatherhood. Auster not only suggests the complexity of the father figure in contemporary American fiction but also underscores the benefits of adopting counter-hegemonic practices of active and engaged fatherhood. Auster's narratives uphold Robert L. Griswold's proclamation that "fathering properly pursued is good for you" (6).

NOTES

1. Bibliographies on Auster include Drenttel's and Springer, *A Paul Auster Sourcebook*. For an excellent selected bibliography, see Peacock, *Understanding Paul Auster*. The most notable essay collections include Barone, *Beyond the Red Notebook*; Bloom, *Paul Auster*; and Ciocia and Gonzalez. Special editions of academic journals dedicated to Auster include *Review of Contemporary American Fiction* 14.1 (Spring 1994), *Critique: Studies in Contemporary American Fiction* 39.3 (Spring 1998), and *Critique: Studies in Contemporary*

American Fiction 49.2 (Winter 2008). Well-received focused studies on Auster include Varvogli, *The World That Is the Book*; Brown, *Paul Auster*; and Martin, *Paul Auster's Postmodernity*. For a particularly useful discussion on the "postmodern nature" of Auster's writing, see Merivale.

2. See Alford; Nealon; Auster and Contat; Dow, "Invention of Solitude"; Lethem; Merlob; Martin, *Paul Auster's Postmodernity*.
3. Clancy Martin continues, "The irony vacuums out the content and, with it, our interest. Like the ouroboros, the ancient symbol of a dragon swallowing its own tail, the book consumes itself, and disappears."
4. Also see Irwin 1994.
5. Auster's connection to the American literary tradition is another major focus of research on his work. See Marling for an analysis into Auster's links to Hawthorne's *Fanshawe* under the subheadings of author/narrator, intertext, erasure, and inheritance. For further investigation into the link between Auster and Hawthorne, see Swope. For a discussion on Auster's and Thoreau's interest in solitude, see Ford. For a juxtaposition of Auster's *Moon Palace* with Whitman and Emerson, see Weisenburger. Also see Varvogli, *The World That Is the Book* and "Exploring Fictions" on Auster's *Leviathan* and the Age of Emerson. For a study on Auster and Melville, see Ramalho de Sousa Santos.
6. Unpublished interview with Bill Corbett accessed from the Auster Archive at the Henry W. and Albert A. Berg Collection of English and American Literature, Stephen A. Schwarzman Building, New York Public Library. I refer to this material throughout the chapter as "Interview with Paul Auster."
7. There are debates concerning Auster's "realism." Malcolm Bradbury calls Auster's fiction "experimental realism." Varvogli calls Auster's work "deceptive realism." See Bradbury; Varvogli, *The World That Is the Book*.
8. See Bigsby. See Brooker, who has also argued that Auster's fiction is cemented in its concern for lived social relations.
9. Homelessness is not just a theme in *Sunset Park* but also features in earlier texts, such as *Timbuktu* (1999) and *Moon Palace* (1989). In *Moon Palace* Marco Fogg runs out of money and sleeps rough in Central Park. Fogg views it as a place of regeneration, an oasis of solitude away from the responsibilities of city life. The reality, however, is that he almost dies. Apart from the symbolic nature of homelessness, Auster is also aware of the greater social issue of homelessness. As Auster states in an npr.org interview, "The more I thought about it, the more I meditated, the more I saw that this problem was growing into an enormous social problem in the United States" (Neary).
10. See Ferry 2011b.
11. See Barone, "Auster's Memory"; Baxter; Dow Adams; Dow.
12. Auster himself refers to *The Invention of Solitude* as a work of non-fiction in his 2005 interview with Jonathan Lethem.
13. The American editor of *Granta*, John Freeman, in an interview with Auster, calls *The Invention of Solitude* "one of the classic literary memoirs of all time."
14. See Fredman 7.
15. See Peacock, "Understanding" 15.
16. See Dow.
17. Dennis Barone, in his introduction to *Beyond the Red Notebook*, makes the fair point that although *The Invention of Solitude* is a hugely significant text, it would be easy to be blinded by the permanence of the themes that underpin the novel in detriment to recognising the developments and shifts in Auster's fiction. Barone writes, "*The Invention of Solitude* may be read as Auster's chosen and invented mythology, as the first cause of all his subsequent works.

But to do so leads to a certain danger in the consideration of his writing. To understand his first prose work in this way may cause one to misread his other prose works, to see too much continuity and not enough change" (14). In answer to his concerns, as I comment in this chapter, there has been a notable shift in the focus of Auster's fiction in the last ten years toward more explicit socio-political concerns at the centre of his narratives. The fact remains, however, that the major themes that pervade his fiction, notably the effect of fatherhood on the shaping of masculinity, begin with *The Invention of Solitude*.

18. James Peacock, in his analysis of *The Book of Illusions*, comments: "It is a conventional notion, but for Auster a vital one: art does not simply imitate life, but can influence it. . . . One might accuse Auster of being simplistic, but he has a sincere belief that the roles adopted in the creation and consumption of art have a direct bearing on the roles we play in life, to the extent that there is very little in the end to distinguish between them" (*Understanding* 159).
19. Auster explains the circumstance of how they were written separately but published together. See Auster and Contat; Barone, *Beyond the Red Notebook* 106.
20. See Peacock, *Understanding* 15–17.
21. See Peacock, *Understanding* 17.
22. See Porter. Also, in an article that engages with *The Invention of Solitude* to frame a study of "the psychological consequences of writing a 'father's biography,'" Carolus van Nijnatten touches on the question of fact and fiction in biography writing (van Nijnatten, 244–250).
23. See also Demos; Rotundo; Pleck.
24. It may be tempting to use "masculinity" and "manhood" interchangeably, but I believe that there is a subtle distinction between the terms. Kimmel acknowledges this distinction: "*Manhood* had been understood to define an inner quality, the capacity for autonomy and responsibility, that had historically been seen as the opposite of *childhood*. Becoming a man was not taken for granted; at some point the grown-up boy would demonstrate that he had become a man and had put away childish things. At the turn of the century, *manhood* was replaced gradually by the term masculinity, which referred to a set of behavioural traits and attitudes that were contrasted now with a new opposite, *femininity*. Masculinity was something that had to be constantly demonstrated, the attainment of which was forever in question—lest the man be undone by a perception of being too feminine. Masculinity required proof, and proof required serious effort, whether at the baseball park, the gymnasium, or sitting down to read *Tarzan* or a good western novel" (*Manhood in America*, 81–82). Put simply, I will use "manhood" to refer to the idea of an ahistorical essence of what it means to be a man, whereas "masculinity" will refer to the historically constructed identity performed in everyday society.
25. Kimmel also points out that at this time in American history a new cultural trend appeared that sold this ideology to the American male: "By the 1840s and 1850s a veritable cult of the Self-Made Man had appeared, as young men devoured popular biographies and inspirational homilies to help future Self-Made Men create themselves. John Frost's *Self Made Men in America* (1848), Charles Seymore's *Self-Made Men* (1858), and Freeman Hunt's *Worth and Wealth* (1856) and *Lives of American Merchants* (1858) provided self-making homilies, packaged between brief biographies of poor boys who made it rich" (Kimmel, *Manhood in America* 19).
26. Kimmel writes on the implications of the "separation of the spheres" for the American family. See Kimmel, *Gendered Society* 113–121.

27. See Kimmel, *Gendered Society* 121.
28. See Kimmel, *Gendered Society* 119–127 and *Manhood in America* 11–29. Kimmel dates the arrival of the masculine figure of the breadwinner between 1810 and 1820 (*Manhood* 15).
29. Kimmel also cites the pressures of being a successful breadwinner as a source of tension and conflict (*Manhood* 174–176).
30. Such broad generalizations can mask certain critical variations. Griswold discusses the racial and class differences in his study *Fatherhood in America* (1992). Ultimately, the breadwinner role permeates all facets of American society.
31. Critics of the historical development of fatherhood cite Alexis de Tocqueville's written reports on the condition of the relationship between father and son in his visit to the United States in the 1830s. See Pleck 88–89.
32. Another interesting element of the depiction of fatherhood in "Portrait of an Invisible Man" is Sam Auster's relationship with his daughter. In contrast to the distance between Auster and his father, a distance created by his father, the relationship between father and daughter has a distinctive dynamic that Auster revisits in his later fictional work. Auster's sister was a lost soul, a drifter, "a miniature Ophelia, already doomed, it would seem, to a life of constant inner struggle" (*Invention* 25). She was more sensitive to the breakdown of the relationship between their father and mother, and Auster reports that she would repeatedly ask their mother if "she loved daddy." From her birth Auster reports that his father "pampered" his sister (27). She was his "little angel" (27). When she suffered a series of terrible breakdowns, Auster's father's reply was typical. Again he believed that work would benefit her and get her back on the straight and narrow: "What she needs, he would say, is to get a job, to clean herself up, to start living in the real world" (27). It appears evident that he is unable to make a true emotional connection with his daughter. He is unable to realise that she needed a different support system. He remained adamant that "there was nothing wrong with her" (27). He refused to pay for her to go see a psychiatrist, preferring to buy expensive vitamins and offering her to come and live with him in his house. Relenting after another stay in hospital, she found that her father had not changed. He stuck to his routine, staying out of the enormous family house all day. Underlying his typical masculine behaviour, Auster felt that his father did suffer. As Auster states, "Unlike everything else he ever came up against, my sister's illness finally *moved* him—but only to leave him with a feeling of utter helplessness" (29).
33. Pleck comments on the social unease at the rise of maternal influence during World War II. See Pleck 90–93.
34. In the interview with Jonathan Lethem, Auster states, "The first part of that book is written in the first person, and then I started the second part in the first person as well. But there was something that I didn't like about it. I couldn't understand why I was dissatisfied. I wrote, I wrote, I wrote and then I had to stop. I put it away, meditated for several weeks, and understood that the problem was the first person. I had to switch to the third. Because in the first part I was writing about somebody else—my father. I was seeing him from my point of view. But, in the second part, I was mostly writing about myself. By using the first person, I couldn't see myself anymore. By shifting to the third person, I managed to get a certain distance from myself, and that made it possible for me to see myself, which in turn made it possible for me to write the book. It was very strange" (Lethem).
35. *Leviathan,* as a highly politically charged text, uses the figure of the flâneur and the trope of watching and being watched in its meditation on the power discourses at play in the act of watching.

36. It is R.D.E. Burton who states, "No figure belongs more thoroughly to Paris, and the nineteenth century, than the flâneur" (1).
37. The effect of place on the individual is a major area of interest in Auster scholarship. See Wesseling; Kirkegaard; Alford; Woods; Varvogli, *The World that Is the Book*; Seidl; Gilloch and Kilby; Brown, *Paul Auster*. Also see chapter 5 of Martin, *Paul Auster's Postmodernity*, "Postmodern Modes of Social Identity: Paul Auster's Evocation of Urban Dislocation, Estranged Solitude, Collective Diversity."
38. The patriarchal father, rejected during the American Revolution, reemerged through George Washington, who was immediately elected as what Kimmel has named the "Symbolic Father" of the new country (*Sexual Self* 143). Since then, Americans have needed father figures, in this case political fathers to keep the fantasy of social and national stability, even if such presidential father figures have often proved to be distant, aggressive, and/or punitive. Paradoxically, then, fatherhood in American culture and politics has often been seen as a punitive, albeit socially necessary, authority. Little wonder that fathers in American fiction, when/if present, tend to be represented as a distant or punitive authority as well. As the editors of *Naming the Father* have noted, "At century's end, one thing seems clear about fatherhood: although we miss it, we can recreate its authority only either as an absence or as a failed relation" (Bueno, Caesar, and Hummel 2). Also see Armengol, "Where Are the Fathers in American Literature."
39. These include the death of Rembrandt's son Titus due to disease, Sir Walter Raleigh's son Wat killed in battle, and Mallarme's Anatole.
40. The fairy tale is a recurring motif in Auster's fiction. Indeed Auster goes as far as to state: "I would say that the greatest influence on my work has been fairy tales, the oral tradition of storytelling" (*The Red Notebook* 140).
41. Stillman's father, also named Peter Stillman, is about to be released from a psychiatric hospital where he was incarcerated after being judged insane following a fire at the Stillmans' apartment. It was at this moment that the authorities discovered that Stillman had been conducting a cruel experiment on his son. Stillman had been denying his access to language in a bizarre experiment to find "God's language." Virginia, however, believes that the fire was deliberate and that Stillman may return to kill his son.
42. See Petersen.
43. In the unpublished interview with Bill Corbett, Auster reveals that the writing of *Moon Palace* began in college: "But when I was in college I started writing a novel which was the seed of *Moon Palace*. I worked on it very hard off and on for years. It never worked but the main characters were there, Effing and Fogg, the main characters were there even if they had other names, and the structure of the story was the same."
44. As Leslie A. Fiedler has highlighted, canonical works of American literature have maintained the theme of men's rejection of women and sexuality in favour of male comradeship outside of society: "Where woman is felt to be a feared and forbidden other, the only legitimate beloved is the self. Pure narcissism cannot, however, provide the dream and tension proper to a novel; the mirror-image of the self is translated in the American novel . . . into the comrade of one's own sex, the buddy as *anima*" (Fiedler 348).
45. Auster states in an interview with Ashton Applewhite, "If there is any book that *Mr. Vertigo* is connected to, it's Pinocchio. In some odd way you could say that Walt is Pinocchio, Master Yehudi is Gepetto, and Mrs Witherspoon is the Blue Fairy" (Applewhite).
46. Helena Wahlström highlights the pivotal concept of the loss of the child as Auster's investigation into fatherhood. Speaking in the context of Auster's film *Smoke* (1995): "For his protagonists the loss of a child results in a

rupture in paternal identity, and the crisis of the protagonist is profound . . . they suffer in solitude" (89).

47. As Zimmer states, New York City is the place "least likely to wear on my nerves" (27).
48. As Mark Brown comments, "In *The Book of Illusions,* both Zimmer and Hector use film to suspend the reality of loss" ("Portrait of a Soul in Ruins" 233).
49. Helena Wahlström supports the view of the crucial thematic concern of the father in Auster's fiction: "Throughout his authorship, Paul Auster has been engaging with the meanings of fatherhood" (89). It is Auster's film *Smoke* that is the focus of her analysis of the representations of alternative models of the father in Auster's fiction. In her view, "*Smoke* also positions Auster firmly in the 'social' of the US in the 1990s, and the film appeared in the middle of ongoing debate over fatherhood and fatherless in that decade" (94). Wahlström also argues that "the potential for reconciliation between men—also between fathers and children—is emphasised in the text, which seems to point in the direction of a progressive idea of masculinity, away from its conventional encoding in dominant US discourses as based upon solitude, individualism, and competitiveness" (93). Ultimately, *Smoke* turns away from the traditional model of the absent or authoritarian model of the father to focus on "men's need for companionship, comfort, and domestic contexts" (94).
50. See Varvogli, "Worst Possibilities"; and Simonetti. Simonetti cites David Hellman's suggestion that *The Brooklyn Follies* is "probably the first authentic attempt to deal with the post-Sept. 11 world."
51. See James Wood's review of Auster's *Invisible,* "Shallow Graves: The Novels of Paul Auster," which quickly turns into an overall critique of Auster's fiction.

4 "Because I Want to Fit In"
The Influence of the Male Peer Group in Bret Easton Ellis' *American Psycho*

Since its publication in 1991, *American Psycho* has become one of the most studied works of contemporary American fiction.[1] As an often automatic inclusion on university syllabi, it could be argued that *American Psycho* is an overappreciated text. To put it bluntly, why revisit this novel once again? What relevance does it have twenty-plus years later? As the fictionalised "Bret Easton Ellis" asks in *Lunar Park* (2005), "What's left to say about *American Psycho* that hasn't already been said?" (Ellis 12).

The furore that surrounded the release of *American Psycho* is well documented, and so there is no need to cover old ground here.[2] The perception of *American Psycho* as a "controversial" novel, however, has endured. The prominence of this attitude is reflected in the tone of recent studies on Ellis and his fiction, particularly Naomi Mandel and Alain-Philippe Durand's *Novels of the Contemporary Extreme* (2006), Sonia Baelo-Allué's *Bret Easton Ellis's Controversial Fiction* (2011), and Naomi Mandel's *Bret Easton Ellis: American Psycho, Glamorama, Lunar Park* (2011). Mandel introduces her reading of *American Psycho* by stating: "*American Psycho* is easily one of the most controversial novels of the twentieth century" (1). This idea of the novel as controversial has shaped the lens through which critics continue to read Patrick Bateman, the protagonist of *American Psycho* and pop-culture phenomenon. Critiques of Patrick's masculinity have been carried out through the prisms of the gothic, grotesque, or serial killer traditions in American literature.[3] Attempts to ground the novel within its wider social and cultural context have been markedly few. The possible exception to this trend is the work of Georgina Colby. In *Bret Easton Ellis: Underwriting the Contemporary* (2011), Colby highlights Ellis' process of "underwriting" as his method of "critiquing the socio-political structures of late capitalism" (1). As Colby points out, Ellis is not simply a writer of surfaces or "blank" narratives[4]; rather Ellis' first-person narratives are vehicles for reflection upon the social processes of the contemporary era as they "function to disclose the ways in which the contemporary political and cultural apparatus affects the individual" (1). There has been a gradual infiltration of the view of Ellis as a *literary* figure, with his fiction now featuring in various interdisciplinary fields of research. As Mandel notes, "[Ellis'] name appears with increasing frequency in recent scholarship on violence and representation, literature and ethics, writing and responsibility, globalization and terror" (1). It must be stated, however, that Mandel makes no mention of the study of men and masculinities.

The limited number of studies that grapple with the representation of masculinity in *American Psycho* read the protagonist through a postmodern lens as a figure representing what has become somewhat of a cliché: the contemporary "crisis of masculinity." As Mark Storey argues:

> The narrative is deeply mired in the "crisis of masculinity," exploring the creation of an identity in a postmodern world in which the concept of identity has changed. In the impossibility of that postmodern creation, Ellis shows us the monstrous heart of masculinity at the outer limits, a frenzied pomophobia[5] that, instead of re-establishing Bateman's identity and sense of order, serves to draw him further into the realm of chaotic unreality. (58)

Storey sees Patrick Bateman as a construct, an exemplar of unstable and incoherent masculinity in a world in which the traditional patriarchal language systems are unable to function as they attempt to adapt to postmodernity (59).[6] While I would agree with Storey's view that Ellis "critiques traditional masculinity in the most intense way possible" (71) with a character who experiences a "chaotic, hysterical perception of the world" (71), Storey echoes the fashionable readings that render Patrick Bateman as a non-entity, particularly the now ubiquitous critique of Patrick by Elizabeth Young:

> Patrick *is* a cipher; a sign in language and it is in language that he disintegrates. . . . He is a textual impossibility, written out, elided until there is no "Patrick" other than the sign or signifier that sets in motion the process that must destroy him. (119)

Certainly Patrick Bateman is a character that Ellis uses in his satirical critique of a particular strand of New York masculinity of the era, but it is too simple to shatter Patrick Bateman and read him as a fragmented subject. Rather, placing the character in context, in terms of the era and its place in the historical development of American masculinity, sets Patrick as the exemplar of the young Manhattan male experiencing the severe social realities of the pressure to achieve the hegemonic ideal of New York Wall Street manhood.

A notable contribution to the study of the sociohistorical value of *American Psycho* is Thomas Heise's "*American Psycho:* Neoliberal Fantasies and the Death of Downtown" (2011). Heise sees the novel as a portrait of the neoliberal free market economics that were shaping the American landscape of that era. Turning away from the typical readings of Patrick Bateman, Heise argues, "Bateman is best understood not as a misogynist or a racist or even a serial killer but as Ellis' fantasy of the quintessential neoliberal subject" (144). Despite Heise's useful reading of this Manhattan male, he too slips into the standard critical jargon of *American Psycho,* arguing that Patrick is "less flesh and blood than he is a discursively produced matrix of verbal utterances which have coagulated into the shape of a person, more a corpus of words than corporeal" (151). Ultimately, in Heise's view, "there is no there *there,* only an empty vessel into which prefabricated ideas, rhetorics, and styles have been poured" (151–152).

Another "gender-specific analysis" (378) of *American Psycho* is Berthold Schoene-Harwood's "Serial Masculinity: Psychopathology and Oedipal Violence in Bret Easton Ellis' *American Psycho*" (2005). Schoene-Harwood sets out his article as an attempt to "pathologize modern masculinity" (378) by identifying masculinity as

> an ideologically motivated gender construct that, by endorsing and legitimizing the realization of certain, possibly genetic, male dispositions as a fixed set of behavioural norms and imperatives, promotes a type of male subjectivity that displays conspicuous similarities to Asperger's Syndrome and high-functioning autism. (379)[7]

Schoene-Harwood's approach appears to provide a welcome shift away from post-structuralist deconstructions of the character. As Schoene-Harwood states refreshingly: "it is important to see it not as the portrayal of an individual person *in extremis,* but as a case study of the predicament of a particular type of man within a specific socio-historical context" (381). Similarly to Byers' concept of pomophobia, Schoene-Harwood also underlines Patrick's "male hysteria" (394) as a sociological condition of 1980s Manhattan, in which the standard hegemonic order was experiencing a "paradigm shift" (380).

Alex E. Blazer makes the first move towards underlining the significance of homosocial relations in the novel. In "*American Psycho, Hamlet,* and Existential Psychosis" (2011), Blazer attempts to account for the "psycho" in *American Psycho* by exploring the notable absence of parental figures in the novel. Blazer sees the absent father as the "psychotic trigger" (40) that leads Patrick to the violent assertions of his masculinity in the novel. Without the civilising effect of his father socializing the son into the symbolic social order, Patrick's seeming "psychosis" is centred in his "basic self-destructive instincts" (47), the acts of graphic violence "a delusion in which he remains trapped" (47). Blazer argues that the lack of a stable familial structure leads Patrick to "self-destruct."

Assessing these readings of masculinity in *American Psycho,* there has been some movement towards analysing Patrick's performance in the novel sociologically. *American Psycho* should not be deemed controversial in itself but appreciated as a sociologically charged satirical examination of the social discourses that defined the performance of hegemonic masculinity in 1980s New York City. Approaching *American Psycho* as a social document underscores Ellis' intention of critiquing the everyday performance of the Manhattan male with the creation of the protagonist of the novel, Patrick Bateman.

"BECAUSE . . . I . . . WANT . . . TO . . . FIT . . . IN"

What drives Patrick Bateman's performance in *American Psycho* is his attempt to attain the unattainable: the contemporary ideal of hegemonic masculinity. The crux of this problematic obsession, however, lies in the fact that Patrick believes that his masculine status can be affirmed only in the eyes of his peers.

As a novel about status, and the affirmation of masculinity in homosocial relations, "Because . . . I . . . want . . . to . . . fit . . . in" (Ellis 228) stands as the resonating line from *American Psycho*. This underlying concern of the Manhattan male is revealed when Patrick goes for lunch with his ex-girlfriend Bethany. Outside the closed environment of everyday life on Wall Street with his male colleagues, Patrick opens up to Bethany. As the conversation swings around to work, Bethany is quizzical about Patrick continuing to work at Pierce & Pierce:

> "And you're at . . . P & P?" she asks.
> "Yes," I say.
> She nods, pauses, wants to say something, debates whether she should, then asks, all in a matter of seconds: "But doesn't your family own—"
> "I don't want to talk about this," I say, cutting her off. "But yes, Bethany. Yes."
> "And you still work at P & P?" she asks. Each syllable is spaced so that it bursts, booming sonically, into my head.
> "Yes," I say, looking furtively around the room.
> "But—" She's confused. "Didn't your father—"
> "Yes, of course," I say, interrupting. "Have you had the focaccia at Pooncakes?"
> "*Patrick.*"
> "Yes?"
> "What's wrong?"
> "I just don't want to talk about . . ." I stop. "About work."
> "Why not?"
> "Because I hate it," I say. "Now listen, have you tried Pooncakes yet? I think Miller underrated it."
> "Patrick," she says slowly. "If you're so uptight about work, why don't you just quit? You don't have to work."
> "Because," I say, staring directly at her, "I . . . want . . . to . . . fit . . . in." (228)

It is Patrick's need to be accepted within the masculinity-affirming environment of Manhattan that is the main narrative drive of the novel. Patrick's performance within the internal hegemonic framework, that is to say the hierarchical framework within which male groups compete with other male groups, underlines the conflicts and tensions that shape the male individual's understanding of his masculinity in this era.[8] As Ellis states in an interview in which he discusses his experience of New York City during this period:

> Consumerist success was really the embodiment of what it meant to be a cool guy—money, trophy girlfriends, nice clothes, and cool cars. It all seemed extremely shallow to me. Yet at the same time you have an urge to conform. You want to be part of the group. You don't want to be shunned. So when I was writing that book as a young man, I was having this battle with conforming to what was then yuppiedom—the yuppie lifestyle—going to restaurants and trying to fit in. I think *American Psycho* was ultimately my argument about this. (Coreno)

A central dynamic of "yuppiedom" was the desire to fit in. Ellis reaffirms this view on two occasions in a recent interview in *The Paris Review* by stating that the novel is "pretty much 385 pages of a young man in a society he doesn't believe in and yet wants to be a part of" (Goulian 183). Moreover, speaking of Patrick's obsession with the 1980s pop artists that appear in the text, Ellis states, "the reason that Patrick loves this music, and wants to tell us about it in excruciating detail, is because he wants to fit in" (176). What emerges as the central concern of the novel, then, is the paradox that shapes American masculinity: man's desire to write his individual narrative while simultaneously seeing masculine status as something that can be affirmed only through the recognition of his male peers.[9]

To fully develop this key aspect of the performance of Patrick Bateman's masculinity in *American Psycho,* I will contextualise Ellis' depiction of the Manhattan male by engaging with the findings of the research on 1980s American male sexuality by the sexologist, sociologist, and cultural historian Shere Hite. Hite's study of American masculinity and male sexuality in the 1980s and early 1990s in *The Hite Report on Male Sexuality* (1981), as well as Hite's overlooked follow-up research ten years later with the "21st Century Man Questionnaire" (1992) and the findings in the subsequent report "Today's Men" (1993), underline the issues that impact upon the American male's understanding of his masculinity. Using Hite's work as a framework for a reading of the dynamics of hegemonic masculinity in *American Psycho,* this will allow a two-part study of what I see as the key interconnected passages in the novel: Patrick's interactions with his peers in the scenes in the restaurants, clubs, and offices in Wall Street, and his subsequent movements through the New York City streets in his role of self-reflective flâneur. This approach to reading Patrick's performance illuminates how it is the shaping of Patrick's masculinity within his peer group that drives his more complicated performance as a flâneur on the streets of Manhattan later in the novel. This approach moves away from the standard readings of *American Psycho* as a "controversial" novel to posit the text as a social document that critiques the realities experienced by the Manhattan male of this era. Patrick Bateman's first-person narration sets him as the urban flâneur reporting the experience of the hegemonic group of Wall Street males at a time when traditional models of manhood were being challenged by the emergence of other masculinities in New York.

SHERE HITE AND THE STUDY OF AMERICAN MALE SEXUALITY

Since the late nineteenth century, sexology, "the science of desire," has sought to determine the underlying drives that shape sexual behaviour. A broad and often contradictory tradition, the study of sexuality, led by sexologists such as Richard von Krafft-Ebing,[10] Havelock Ellis,[11] Sigmund Freud,[12] Alfred C. Kinsey,[13] and Masters and Johnson,[14] propagated the "essentialist" view of sexuality as an entirely biological drive in all human beings. This view of sexuality has been challenged in the last forty years as being "reductionist" and "deterministic": "reductionist" in the sense that it simplifies the complexities and intricacies of the everyday into a set of universal experiences; and "deterministic" by insisting on the fixed nature of sexuality, with the individual rendered a product of inner impulses.[15] The emergence of new social movements in the 1970s, namely second-wave feminism and the women's liberation movement, set out to challenge what they viewed as the repressive controlling nature of the sexual tradition. It was their efforts that paved the way for an alternative view of sexuality as a historical construct shaped by social discourses. The types of questions that emerged, such as "How is sexuality socially constructed?," "What is the symbolic power of sex in society?," and "What is the relationship between sex and power?," remain fundamental in contemporary studies of masculinity and male sexuality.[16]

The period of great change in the study of sexuality in the United States occurred between the decades of the 1930s and the 1960s. With the publication of *Sexual Behaviour in the Human Male* (1948) and *Sexual Behaviour in the Human Female* (1953), Alfred C. Kinsey captured the public's imagination with his study of human sexual behaviour.[17] Despite Kinsey's biologically deterministic philosophy, and the methodological issues surrounding his studies, the great contribution that Kinsey made was to be the first to publish a study on American sexual behaviour that offered an insight into the variation of sexual behaviour in the everyday lives of the American people. Kinsey's work was later consolidated by Masters and Johnson, but their naturalisation of marital sex led to various questions regarding the wider ideological impact of their work. While Kinsey appeared to suggest that any sexual behaviour should be considered normal, Masters and Johnson's naturalisation of certain sexual behaviours would be challenged later for its bias and exclusivity.[18]

The biological, essentialist methods of studying sexuality were disputed in the 1970s as new voices began to emphasise the impact of social and cultural ideologies on the understanding of sexuality. Sociologists began to argue for the need to see sexuality as a process of negotiation shaped in the complexities of social practices. John Gagnon and William Simon,[19] one-time students of the Kinsey Institute, turned the biologically deterministic model on its head by arguing that sexuality was like any other social process shaped by societal discourse.[20] Although almost all of Kinsey's data was organized by cultural and social factors, it was fundamentally biologically driven in its behaviourist paradigms. Gagnon and Simon's development of "sexual scripts,"[21] that is, the organised sets of discourses that control, regulate, and give meaning to sexual behaviours, would remain the dominant paradigm in the study of the social construction of sexuality.[22] In "The Sexual Self in Late Modernity," Stevi Jackson champions Gagnon and Simon's *Sexual Conduct* (1973) as the first social constructionist approach to sexuality, predating other variants deriving from post-structuralism and postmodernism.[23] Jackson makes the notable comment that Gagnon and Simon's approach argued for the positive impact of the social in the shaping of sexuality, presaging the Foucauldian hypothesis of the social solely repressing sexual drives. Furthermore, Gagnon and Simon's approach to understanding sexuality undermined psychoanalysis by demonstrating how sexuality is interwoven in the fabric of everyday life rather than originating in an unknowable unconscious. Rather than the past determining the present, Gagnon and Simon underlined the self as being constantly "in process," repeatedly constructed and reconstructed in the negotiation and interaction with others. This shift provided a new theoretical framework for studying sexuality and gender that enabled sociologists to document systematically the historical legitimisation of patriarchy[24] and analyse the distribution and manipulation of power in the social shaping of gender and masculinity.[25] It is this framework that paved the way for Shere Hite.

Shere Hite has an important place in the historical lineage of the study of sexuality in the United States, and yet she is largely absent from historical mappings of scholarship on masculinity and male sexuality.[26] Hite's interest in the social shaping of sexuality began with her research into the sexual lives of American women. From the years 1972 to 1976 Hite distributed a questionnaire that sought to challenge the patriarchal image of female sexuality by underlining the individual experiences of the American female. For the first time women were given the platform to speak about their personal experiences of sex and sexuality without being filtered through a male lens. Hite enabled the American female population to speak directly on how they defined their own sexuality and what female sexuality actually meant to them. The main finding that emerged from Hite's research was that 70% of women do not experience orgasm from intercourse alone. This was a groundbreaking insight at the time that challenged the patriarchal ideologies that had shaped the studies of sexuality led by Alfred Kinsey and Masters and Johnson, specifically the notion that women who were unable to achieve orgasm directly from intercourse were suffering from a "sexual dysfunction."[27] Conversely, Hite demonstrated how sexual intercourse had become imbedded within a political formation that privileged male pleasure and, in doing so, underlined the grander cultural significance of the position of women in the act of intercourse. To put it succinctly, the woman's role in the bedroom reflected her role in wider society. Before Foucault it was Hite who was linking sex to the cultural and historical discourses and traditions in our social system.[28]

Following the critical and commercial success of *The Hite Report on Female Sexuality* (1976), Hite set out to demystify the American male's understanding of his masculinity with *The Hite Report on Male Sexuality* (1981). Hite emphasised the cultural construction of masculinity, dispelling the stereotype of an overpowering, biological male sex drive to underscore the myriad factors in male sexual socialization that pressure men to live up to a mythic hegemonic ideal. In the preface to *The Hite Report on Male Sexuality,* Hite underscores the importance of studying male sexuality to gain a greater understanding of the impact of masculinity in the shaping of society:

> "Male" sexuality is central to the definition of masculinity—and masculinity is central to the world-view of the entire culture—in a sense, *is* the culture. Therefore, what we are looking at in this book is far more than male sexuality; it is a way of life, the world itself, a culture in microcosm. To discuss sex is to discuss our most basic views of who we are, what we want life to be, and what kind of a society we believe in. (xvii)

The relevance of *The Hite Report on Male Sexuality* in a reading of hegemonic masculinity in *American Psycho* is further evidenced in a look at the breakdown of men that make up Hite's study. The majority of the participants in Hite's research are from what might be considered the hegemonic group of the New York male population. The statistical breakdown of the participants in Hite's study in terms of age, race, and geographical location is particularly interesting: 35% of the men involved were between the ages of 22 and 34, the vast majority of participants were white (83.6%), and New York appears as the most represented city in the study (xxvii–xxix).

The main strength of Hite's methodological approach to studying masculinity was once considered its fundamental weakness: the informal questionnaire format. And yet it is the anonymous nature of these informal questionnaires, as well as the open-ended nature of her questions, that underpins Hite's success. With these questionnaires Hite encouraged American men to reflect upon their everyday experiences attempting to live up to the hegemonic ideals of American manhood. The extensive answers emphasised the complex nature of the American male experience and went beyond the reductive nature of earlier studies of masculinity and male behaviour.[29] Hite moved away from cold statistical data to provide a platform for men to write a collective, cultural narrative of the male experience. As Hite comments, her objective was "to find more subtle meanings underneath the easily quantifiable parts of the replies, and to keep intact each individual's voice so that men would retain direct access to communicating their feelings with the reader, thus reinforcing the integrity of the study" (xix). Gladys Engel Lang supports Hite's intentions by arguing that Hite allowed "thousands of people to speak freely instead of forcing them to choose from pre-selected categories—in essence, predefining them, as with so many studies" (485). Here was a sociologist, or cultural historian, as she prefers to be known, who was not speaking with a single authorial voice but was acting as a channel for the American male individual to write his narrative on the conflicts and tensions that defined the experience of the male subject in American society.[30]

Following *The Hite Report on Male Sexuality,* Hite returned to the analysis of the social construction of American masculinity in a study conducted at the beginning of the 1990s. In "Post-modern Masculinity," published in *Penthouse*, Hite set out her aim to challenge the "century of stereotypes" that had defined the United States in the twentieth century, no more so than in the typecasting of the American male. Hite prefaces the publication of the "21st Century Man Questionnaire" by underlining the impact of the discrepancy between the images of the ideal American male projected in American propaganda and the experience of men in the real world: "what better time to take a new look at men than during the last years of *the* century obsessed with questions of gender role change and definition?" (102). The key point to be made is that the questions in this survey encourage the respondents to reflect upon how masculine they believe they are in relation to their peers, their experiences socialising with other men, and whether they feel comfortable revealing their emotions and feelings within this group. It also asks men to consider when they were closest to other men—in high school, sports, or their workplace—while also probing the respondents' awareness of the dynamics between men within the workplace.[31] Acknowledging the dramatic changes in the male experience in the ten years that passed from the publication of *The Hite Report on Male Sexuality,* this questionnaire not only builds upon Hite's original findings by asking American men how they see themselves, but, in light of this study of the performance of Patrick Bateman in Ellis' fictionalised Manhattan, Hite's questionnaire also places a greater emphasis upon the impact of homosocial relations in the performance of masculinity.

Hite released her reflections on the findings from the "21st Century Man Questionnaire" in the article "Today's Men." Due to the restrictive nature of an article in a magazine, the article contains a very select number of responses. As such, expanding upon the findings published in the article, I will use a wider selection of the responses from male respondents to the "21st Century Man Questionnaire" that fit the demographic of the hegemonic male represented by Patrick Bateman in *American Psycho*. The quotations that I use from the "21st Century Man Questionnaire" in this chapter can be found at the Shere Hite Archive located at the Arthur and Elizabeth Schlesinger Library on the History of Women in America, Radcliffe Institute for Advanced Study, Harvard. The research that I engaged in was focused specifically on New York respondents from the years 1987–1992.[32] Engaging with the findings of Hite's research, both from *The Hite Report on Male Sexuality* as well as from the "21st Century Man Questionnaire," provides further evidence that the scenes involving Patrick Bateman and his peers are the key scenes in the novel.

PATRICK AND HIS PEERS: HOMOSOCIAL RELATIONS AND MASCULINITY IN *AMERICAN PSYCHO*

From the opening page of *American Psycho* the importance of the male peer group in the formation and affirmation of masculine identity is abundantly clear. As the first chapter opens, with the satirically ambiguous title "April Fools," Patrick is travelling to a dinner party with Timothy Price, his friend and colleague from Pierce & Pierce. Previous analyses of *American Psycho* have overlooked the role of Price, specifically in terms of his impact on Patrick's understanding of his masculinity. The opening passages are carefully constructed to set Price as the hegemonic male figure in Patrick's peer group. Price dominates the early passages and certainly considers himself to be a hegemonic male: "I'm resourceful . . . I'm creative, I'm young, unscrupulous, highly motivated, highly skilled. In essence what I'm saying is that society can*not* afford to lose me. I'm an *asset*" (3). The emplotment of the book underscores what Ellis is doing with these Manhattan men—Ellis employs Price, from the very first page of the text, as the model of hegemonic masculinity that Patrick strives to achieve.

The off-kilter scene that plays out when Patrick and Price arrive at the dinner party sets the parameters of Patrick and Price's relationship. Joining Patrick and Price are Patrick's fiancée, Evelyn, and Patrick's "girl on the side" Courtney. Also at the party are Stash, Courtney's "artist friend" (10), and Stash's girlfriend Vanden. Looking beyond the implausibility of two people outside of this exclusive social group being invited to this party in a brownstone house on the Upper West Side of Manhattan, Stash and Vanden perform a very important function in this opening passage of the novel. Price, upon meeting Stash, mistakes him for a girl, a symbolic act that has the dual effect of undermining Stash's status while simultaneously asserting Tim's hegemonic position. At the dinner table, as Tim sits glaring at Stash "with a contempt so total" (12), Vanden is reading a copy of *Deception,* an aptly named "East Village rag" (12), in the eyes of our narrator Patrick. The glaring headline in *Deception* is "The Death of Downtown" (12), a comment on the wider social impact of the behaviour of these hegemonic male figures in Manhattan. After Vanden tosses the paper in the direction of Price in a thinly veiled attempt to alert him to the damage that the Wall Street yuppies are causing on other areas of Manhattan, Price makes his view clear: "'The Death of Downtown,' he says; then, pointing at each word in the headline, 'Who-gives-a-rat's-ass?'" (13).

The dynamics that define the positions of Patrick and Price within the internal hegemonic framework of their peer group also emerge in this early scene. It is clear that Price sees himself above Patrick, and there are subtle pointers that indicate Patrick's concern towards his subordinate position. This is nicely underlined with Patrick's awareness of the chemistry between his fiancée, Evelyn, and Price. Not only does Patrick reveal his paranoia as a result of Evelyn and Price's endless flirting throughout the dinner party, but he is also noticeably agitated when they disappear into the toilet for "perhaps twenty minutes," before Evelyn returns looking "flushed" (12). With his masculinity bruised, Patrick is humiliated further after the party in bed with Evelyn when he tries to initiate sex but finally must admit defeat: "after attempting to have sex with her for around fifteen minutes, I decide not to continue trying" (23).

Patrick's endeavour for a more dominant position is repeatedly undermined by Price's constant put-downs. One theme that emerges in the Patrick-Price-Evelyn triangle begins when Price quite flippantly calls Patrick "a dufus" (11). It is Evelyn, unsurprisingly a subordinate object in their male gaze, who speaks up for Patrick. Her comment is equally derogatory in relation to Patrick's estimation of his masculine status: "Oh leave Patrick alone . . . He's the boy next door. That's Patrick" (11). This comment draws a smirk and a nod from Price. In a later discussion Evelyn once again repeats, "Leave Patrick alone. He's the boy next door" (17), before adding, "Patrick is *not* a cynic, Timothy. He's the boy next door, aren't you honey?" (19). Patrick's reply is suggestive of his growing fury and hints at the greater symbolic significance of his performance on the streets of Manhattan later in the novel: "No I'm not, I whisper to myself. I'm a fucking evil psychopath" (19). The repeated claim of Patrick as the "boy next door" is seen, in Patrick's eyes, as a rejection of the hegemonic status that he wishes to achieve in Manhattan. His retort, to himself no less, of being an evil psychopath raises further questions of how the acts of violence committed by Patrick in the later scenes of the novel should be read. Almost all analyses of the acts of violence committed in *American Psycho* are shaped by the debate about whether they are real or imagined. A point consistently overlooked remains that the passages of graphic violence (committed on both male and female characters) encompass only 19 pages of the 384-page novel. Moreover, the first major act of violence in the novel is committed on a male and not a female figure, and this does not occur until page 126, after the social scenes in the novel are played out.[33]

This neat set-piece opening scene plays a crucial role, as it introduces the conflicts and complexities that will shape Patrick's performance in his male peer group. While Patrick and Price come together to consolidate their hegemonic status in the presence of Stash and Vanden, there are subtle hints at the tensions and conflicts that will come to shape the relationship between Price and Patrick. What appears clear, even at this early point in the novel, is that it is his status within his male peer group that underpins Patrick's view of the performance of his masculinity as success or failure in Manhattan.

One of the major findings to glean from Shere Hite's research on the social construction of masculinity is the impact of relationships between men in the formation of male identity. As well as the extensive study of men's attitudes towards women, Hite underlines the influence of the peer group in the male individual's effort to find his place in society:

> In a very real sense, relationships between men are "what matters" to most men in our culture—even more so than male-female relations. Men look to other men for approval, acceptance, validation, and respect. Men see other men as the arbiters of what is real, the guardians of wisdom, the holders and wielders of power. (*The Hite Report on Male Sexuality* 3)

Homosocial relations between men and the hierarchical internal hegemonic framework in which these men compete are crucial elements in understanding the performance of the American male. Sharon Bird recognises the significant role of homosocial gender relations in the maintenance of the pattern of hegemony in society: "delineation of relations among masculinities is important because it facilitates a better understanding of how the structural order of gender is maintained" (120). Bird references the contribution made by two of the leading figures in the study of men and masculinities—Raewyn Connell and Michael Kimmel—but fails to recognise Hite's input in the study of the social construction of masculinity. Hite underlines the fundamental rôle of the hierarchical framework in the shaping of various masculinities in society. On the one hand, she rejects the biologically essentialist argument of male domination as a normal function of male hormones, a view that has led to the naturalisation of male dominance in the social structure of society. Furthermore, Hite also rejects the notion that male domination originates in the biological nature of the reproductive family; that is to say, that it is natural for women to get pregnant and stay at home while men take on the hunter-gatherer role in the wilds of everyday society. In *Women and Love* (1987), Hite calls for further investigation into the social structures of ancient societies in order to understand how and why male-dominant hierarchies came into being. Hite's objective is to uncover at what point in history *society* normalised the aggressive and competitive behaviour of men. Hite is clear in her view of the impact of the hierarchical socialization of masculinity on men and boys: "A man should look, act and behave like other men—but be on top" (*The Shere Hite Reader* 120).[34]

If the concept of hegemonic masculinity is the framework to shape the social organization of men in American society, then it is within work organizations that hegemonic masculinity continues as the organizing principle.[35] David Collinson and Jeff Hearn, in their study of men and masculinities in work, organizations, and management, highlight the preoccupation of American men with the performance of their gendered power and status. Their contribution to the study of the shaping of the identity of the American male in this specific social arena goes further than seeing the work environment as "a white male heterosexual and largely able-bodied ruling monoculture" (Cockburn 219). The aim of Collinson and Hearn is to underline the work arena not as a place of male unity but as inherently problematic:

> These masculinities in contemporary organizations have been shown to be characterized by contradictory tensions. On the one hand, men often collaborate, cooperate and identify with one another in ways that display a shared unity and consolidated power between them. Yet on the other hand, these same masculinities can also be characterized simultaneously by conflict, competition and self-differentiation in ways that highlight and intensify the differences and divisions between men. There seem to be deep-seated tensions, ambiguities and contradictions at the heart of these dominant masculinities in the workplace. ("Naming Men as Men" 162)

Hite's research supports Collinson and Hearn's view that the conflicts and tensions that characterise the performance of the American male within homosocial groups play a major role in the shaping of their masculinity. First, a certain group of Hite's respondents underline their belief that being competitive can make them better men and, crucially, that being competitive makes them work together better (Hite 032_07_03; Hite 033_01_05). Cliff Cheng rejects the assumption that the main dynamic of the homosocial group is straightforward "male bonding." Cheng points to the negative aspects of the competitive dynamics in these relationships between men, seeing them as ultimately defined by the control and manipulation of power.[36]

Following the introduction of the relationship between Price and Patrick in the opening chapter of *American Psycho,* Ellis uses the subsequent chapters "Harry's," "Pastels," and "Tunnel" to explore in greater depth and detail the group dynamics of Patrick and his peers. Hite's research underlines the fact that the perceived homogeneity of the group is paramount to its existence. It is crucial not only that these men share common political outlooks or social interests but also that they look the same and behave similarly. The detailed descriptions of the characters' attire may first appear as

Ellis satirising the superficiality of these men in their obsession with appearance. Readings of these sections describing the brand-name attire of Patrick and his peers often focus on the atonal, affectless impression of these passages.[37] Looking at these parts of the narrative sociologically underlines the importance of their dress as a social indicator that illustrates the status of these Manhattan men and their consolidated power.[38]

As one respondent highlights in the "21st Century Man Questionnaire," the group can only work if the men are from "the same cultural make-up" (Hite 031_05_05). Furthermore, men will only join a group that is considered to be cool (Hite 031_09_08). The main attraction of being part of a group is the collective feeling of security that these men feel. Being together they act to consolidate their position in the threat from other men. What Hite's research underlines is that this group bonding occurs in activities that mask male insecurities, with these activities dominated by homophobia and gender-bashing. Most notably of all, despite being aware of this behaviour, men continue to engage in these discriminatory activities. These acts of socialising are a shared activity to reaffirm their masculine status in the face of the impending threat to their hegemonic status. Hite underlines the willingness of the male to engage in role-playing due to the need to appear strong, in control, and masculine (*Hite Report on Male Sexuality* 22–23 and Hite 031_08_04). As one respondent in *The Hite Report* remarks, "sometimes I don't show my feelings because I say to myself—I can handle this all by myself. I often feel like a robot" (60). This theme is continued in the responses to Hite's questions: "Lots of times I feel like a robot . . ." (60); "Social pressure is so enormous sometimes that I do not show emotions and behave like a robot" (60). Michael Kimmel investigates this issue in *Guyland* (2008), stating that men in groups are constantly watching the performance of other men, what Kimmel calls the "gender police" (*Guyland* 47). This pressure to conform underpins the performance of the male characters in *American Psycho*.

At dinner in Harry's, this dynamic plays out when the subject matter of their conversation turns to the recent sexual conquest of Patrick's colleague McDermott. Talking about a girl he met in Tunnel, the club that they often frequent, their conversation follows Hite's comment on the type of male bonding that takes place in these social situations. Hite points to the response of one male from her research who states: "Men together are always trying to be macho and talk about their exploits with women, and how many women they have fucked, and then they expect you to share similar stories with them" (*Hite Report on Male Sexuality* 22). This characteristic behaviour features prominently in the exchanges between McDermott and the group. McDermott mocks and ridicules the unnamed girl for not going all the way and only touching him while wearing a glove. The group's reaction to the story is to query McDermott's "inability to act more aggressively with her" (32). The sociological value of this scene, and this exchange in particular, is verified by a male respondent who Hite quotes in her research as stating: "I consider this type of behaviour a form of competition, even though it is also usually used as a form of bonding" ("Today's Men" 50).

Ellis continues to satirise the desire of these men to display how macho they can be in terms of their sexual prowess. As one respondent comments in Hite's research: "The macho thing to do is to talk about how many women you have picked up and fucked from your local bar, and whether or not she was a great fuck (meaning she did it your way), or whether she was a weirdo in bed (had her own ideas about what pleases *her*)" (*Hite Report on Male Sexuality* 23). In the face of the rising media coverage of the AIDS epidemic at this time, Van Patten's remark stands out: "It's really funny that girls think guys are concerned with that, with diseases and stuff" (33). McDermott agrees: "I'm not gonna wear a fucking condom" (33). Their distorted view of their invincibility as the hegemonic group in society is further evident with their voices at the table blending into one to claim defiantly, "Guys just can*not* get it" (33), with a final voice declaring, "Well not *white* guys" (33).

In contrast to the public display of how macho these Manhattanites are in front of the other men in the peer group by ridiculing women and treating them as sexual objects, Hite's research underlines the fact that "most men said that friendships with men were nowhere near as fulfilling as a sexual relationship with a woman they loved" (*Hite Report on Male Sexuality* 89). These conflicting ideas of what it means to be masculine are an important element of the character of Patrick Bateman. Despite engaging in the group dynamic of objectifying and belittling women, there are moments, away from his peers, in which Patrick reveals another side to his character. Out for lunch with his secretary Jean, Patrick admits, "I just want to have a meaningful relationship with someone special" (252). This is a persistent point in Hite's "21st Century Man Questionnaire." Whilst many of the participants acknowledged the importance of feeling free and being their own man, they also wanted to fall in love "with a beautiful (inside) funny, sensuous woman with 'substance'" (Hite 032_08_016). Patrick Bateman's behaviour represents this social reality that while men have a certain role to play in public, especially in front of their male friends and colleagues, they want, and need, to have a loving and caring relationship (*Hite Report on Male Sexuality* 87–91, 96–98, 102–103). At the end of the date, when Patrick leaves Jean at her door, he reports, "she embraces me and this time emanates a warmth that I'm not familiar with" (254). On his way home in a cab, still reflecting on this moment with Jean, Patrick imagines himself "running around Central Park on a cool spring afternoon with Jean, laughing, holding hands. We buy balloons, we let them go" (255). Patrick's behaviour, as well as that of his colleagues, underlines the fact that men are unable to display their emotions in front of other men in the fear that it may be perceived as weakness. The point remains, however, that men are as emotionally sensitive as women and yet, as Hite highlights in her reflection upon her findings in the "Today's Men" article, "one man explained that anger is the only truly permissible male emotion" (52).

Experiencing these internal conflicts, Patrick and his peers continue their performance as the hegemonic group in Manhattan by belittling and disparaging other male groups in terms of race, religion, or, most notably, sexuality. Comments that their peers are "homosexual" or "gay" litter the narrative, both within their exclusive group and outside of it. This is another dynamic of the male peer group that is highlighted by Kimmel in *Guyland:* "Homophobic harassment of the new guys, racial slurs, and seething sexism often lie alongside the casual banter of the band of brothers" (13). The internal conflicts that simmer beneath the surface of Patrick's façade appear at certain points in these group scenes. Patrick, in early instances in the novel, displays what might be read as counter-hegemonic views and opinions that go against the sentiments of the rest of the group. First, at Evelyn's dinner party, in contrast to Price's opening monologue that condemns the contemporary condition of New York City, Patrick launches into a mesmerizing speech that not only calls for a review of American foreign policy but also domestic issues that affect all sections of society:

> But we can't ignore our social needs either. We have to stop people from abusing the welfare system. We have to provide food and shelter for the homeless and oppose racial discrimination and promote civil rights while also promoting equal rights for women but change the abortion laws to protect the right to life yet still somehow maintain women's freedom of choice. . . . We have to encourage a return to traditional moral values and curb graphic sex and violence on TV, in movies, in popular music, everywhere. Most importantly we have to promote general social concern and less materialism in young people. (15)

One characteristic of Ellis' writing that features throughout his body of work is the intrinsic ambiguity of the tone of the prose. Ellis certainly plays upon this in this passage. Various questions emerge at this point: is Patrick serious? Is he mindlessly channelling leftist views in order to impress Evelyn's artist friends? Is he being intentionally ironic in front of Evelyn's liberal artsy friends to the benefit of himself and Price? It is difficult to say, but to reject blindly certain reflective moments is perhaps to underappreciate what Ellis is doing, very cleverly, with the character. These comments need not necessarily be insincere, inauthentic concerns but simply exist as elements of the complexity of the character. Patrick is not a faceless (de)constructed or (de)constructing subject of the multitude of discourses that define this era. As the novel progresses, Ellis is revealing a character that projects the complexities that impacted upon the Manhattan male during this period of American history.

Patrick displays further counter-hegemonic opinions in these early scenes at Harry's. When the group discuss what they view as Paul Owen's undeserved luck at handling the prestigious Fisher account, Preston calls him a "lucky *Jew* bastard" (35), to which Patrick replies, "Just cool it with the anti-Semitic remarks" (35). Later, when Price asks Patrick what bothers him about a joke Preston tells about a "nigger" (37), Patrick again replies, "It's not funny . . . it's racist" (37). It is interesting that at this stage of the novel, Patrick comes to the defence of the other male groups that will later prove to be the victims of his violent rage.

Alongside Ellis' depiction of the hegemonic group acting to consolidate their position in Manhattan society, the opening chapters also serve to illustrate the internal conflicts that shape the group. Price's position as the head of this peer group is repeatedly emphasised at Patrick's expense. When Patrick is asked a question about tasselled loafers, Van Patten moans, "Oh shit, *don't* ask Bateman" (30). In contrast to the group's attitude towards Patrick, and his subsequent short, stuttered answer, Price's address on rounded collars and tie knots stands out "with an exact, clear enunciation that can be heard over the din in Harry's" (31). The reaction of the group is unequivocal: McDermott cries: "Buy that man a drink" (31), while Van Patten, who earlier refuted Patrick's ability to answer such questions, calls Price "priceless" (31). Moreover, when Price once again produces a precise, erudite reply to another question, Preston is "stunned by Price's remarks" (34).

Following Price's snide remarks in the first chapter of the novel that establishes Patrick's subordinate position, Tim continues his ridicule of Patrick as a ploy to reassert his dominance in the affirming eyes of the other members of the group. When Tim is challenged as to why he is so sure that an up-and-coming British intern must be homosexual—"How would *you* know, Timothy?" (34)—Tim's retort is sharp and to the point: "I saw him fuck Bateman up the ass in the men's room at Morgan Stanley" (34). When Patrick makes his comment that Preston should "just cool it with the anti-Semitic remarks" (35), Price's reaction to this is to pat Patrick condescendingly on the back and call him "The voice of reason" (35) and, in an echo of Evelyn from the first chapter, "The boy next door" (35). When Patrick replies, "Yeah, a boy next door who according to you let a British corporate finance analyst intern sodomize him up the ass" (35), Price replies, "I said you were the voice of reason . . . I didn't say you *weren't* a homosexual" (35). Price also jumps on Preston, quipping half-jokingly, "Preston . . . you *are* a joke. You do know you *weren't* invited to dinner. By the way, nice jacket, nonmatching but complementary" (36). Tim's remarks in these exchanges are not simply expressions of ignorance or bigotry but are conscious attacks on the masculinity of the other members of his peer group. Kimmel makes the point that "homophobia—the fear that people might *misperceive* you as gay—is the animating fear of American guys' masculinity" (*Guyland* 50). Homophobia, in Kimmel's eyes, goes even deeper in its sense of existing as the fear that other men may view you as a failure, a fraud, in other words, not achieving the hegemonic ideal of what it means to be masculine (50).[39]

One of the displays of manhood and masculinity that Ellis plays on in *American Psycho* is the ability to reserve a table at the top restaurants in Manhattan. This appears as a major concern of the group at the beginning of the following chapter as Patrick and his peers make their way to Pastels. Ellis' satirical critique continues with the absurd yet sociologically charged discussion of where to book a table. The group democratically reach a decision but Price is "the only dissenting voice," who, after accepting defeat, eventually shrugs: "I don't give a shit" (38). When Price shuns the group by listening to Vivaldi on his Walkman, the other males use the opportunity to undermine Price's hegemonic position. As Patrick tells us, "Van Patten and McDermott made rude jokes about the size of Tim's dick and I did too" (38).

Turning away from the focus on Price, the group is notably "impressed by, maybe even envious of McDermott's prowess in securing a table" (38).[40] And yet the hierarchical framework of the group is later re-established when McDermott orders the busboy to remove their drinks. Despite McDermott's protest, "'who made *you* boss?'" (39), Price wins out. Price ultimately returns to his increasingly normalised dominant position, most notably in the eyes of Patrick. Patrick continues to turn to Tim to seek approval of his views and opinions. Once in Pastels, Patrick feels that the group is having a good time but is only able to affirm this by looking at Tim and commenting, "even Price seems relaxed though he hates the place" (38).

An interesting dynamic of the group emerges with the appearance of Montgomery, an associate outside of the close-knit group. When Montgomery, a guy worth "eight hundred million" (41) with a "definite model type" (40) on his arm, passes by, he shakes only Price's hand. Tellingly, in Patrick's flâneurial observation of this interaction, he notes that Price is "being unusually kind to someone I thought was a stranger" (40). Price tries to set up a game of squash with Montgomery but Montgomery tells him "absently" (40) to call him while he is "already moving away from the table, hurrying toward someone else" (41). Despite Price obviously admiring and trying to impress Montgomery, once Montgomery moves to another part of the room, Price demonstrates his insecurity by reacting angrily at his peers' obvious admiration for Montgomery by growling, "Go over and give the dwarf *head*—will you shut up? . . . I mean how impressed can you *get*, McDermott?" (41).

It is here in Pastels that one of the pivotal scenes in the novel takes place. One of the key images from *American Psycho* is the business card as an indicator of status. The episode that ensues at the dinner table at Pastels is loaded with sociological significance. Patrick, sick of being ridiculed by his peers, decides to pull out his business card to impress the others at the table, "to even up the score a little bit" (42): "'New card.' I try to act casual about it but I'm smiling proudly. 'What do you think?'" (42). With its bone colour and silian rail lettering, Patrick's card is much admired by his peers. The competitiveness that underpins the dynamics of the group, however, begins to surface at this point. Van Patten, who Patrick sees as "the jealous bastard" (42), takes out his card, which Price endorses by stating, "That's really nice" (42). Patrick's reaction?: "A brief spasm of jealousy courses through me when I notice the elegance of the colour and the classy type" (42). Once again Price expresses his admiration, stating, "this is really super. How'd a nitwit like you get so tasteful?" (43). Patrick's jealousy grows: "I'm looking at Van Patten's card and then at mine and cannot believe that Price actually likes Van Patten's better. Dizzy, I sip my drink then take a deep breath" (43). However, the hierarchy of the group is established once again when Price brings out his business card, which Patrick admits begrudgedly is "magnificent" (43). Patrick is fully aware of the admiration for Price's card: "Suddenly the restaurant seems far away, hushed, the noise distant, a meaningless hum, compared to this card, and we all hear Price's words: 'Raised lettering, pale nimbus white'" (43).[41] For Patrick this attempt to assert his masculinity has been a spectacular failure and Patrick can only sit and reflect, "I am unexpectedly depressed that I started this" (43).

In the subsequent chapter Patrick and his peers move on to the club Tunnel, and it is here that the group's hierarchical framework implodes with Price's apparent breakdown. In Tunnel the other guys in the group begin to turn against Price. After he ignores the attention of some girls, McDermott tells Price to "lighten up" (51), while Craig retorts, "your outlook *sucks*" (51). McDermott adds that Tim is acting "like a major asshole" (51). After Price and Patrick score some low quality cocaine, Price reaches his breaking point, telling Patrick, "I'm leaving . . . I'm getting out . . . *Disappearing*" (58). From the opening page of the novel, the tensions that have influenced Tim's attempts to negotiate his hegemonic position in Manhattan have been evident. It is Price, and not Patrick, who asks the question at the restaurant table: "If all of your friends are morons is it a felony, a misdemeanour or an act of God if you blow their fucking heads off with a thirty-eight magnum?" (34). The perception that the American male is unable to share his emotions with other male friends as it may undermine his masculinity is a finding in *The Hite Report on Male Sexuality.* As Hite comments, "only a few men mentioned being able to talk intimately with their best friend," as only "a few men described very close relationships" with other men (19). The reason for this is abundantly clear according to the narrative of the respondents: "Many men said their ability to be close is cut short by fears of 'homosexual' feelings" (20). Despite reaffirming his status in his peer group, Ellis uses the appearance of Montgomery to underscore the insecurities that Tim also experiences even as the dominant member of the group. As with many men, Tim is simply unable to share his worries with anyone else and, in his view, his only option is to disappear. In his final climactic act, Tim stands on railings above the crowd in the nightclub before escaping down the erected decorative tunnel in the club. Although this may appear at first reading a blackly comic or even absurd scene, it indicates that the only option open to these Manhattan men struggling to live out the hegemonic ideal of what it means to be a real Wall Street success is to disappear. Unable to share his problems or concerns with his peers due to the macho front that these men must maintain, the only option for Price is to vanish into a black hole of nothingness.

Tim's narrative, repeatedly overlooked in studies of *American Psycho,* is crucial in its role of contextualising Patrick's behaviour in the novel. Tim appears as more than a working colleague to Patrick—he is a role model; an exemplar, in Patrick's eyes, of the type of Manhattan male that Patrick must strive to be. There is a notable absence of parental guidance in Patrick's life. Patrick's father is mentioned only indirectly in the pivotal conversation with Bethany (227). Patrick's mother appears in the text when Patrick goes to see her in her residential home, Sandstone (351–352), but she is heavily sedated, and when Patrick visits her in the middle of April she asks him what he wants for Christmas (351). With no support from his parents, therefore, Patrick turns to his colleagues for some sense of guidance on how he should behave. Put simply, Patrick is desperate to be accepted by his peers.

Taking this into consideration, it is Patrick's reaction to the constant reassertion of his subordinate status by his peers, as well as the female characters in the text, that drives his performance in the streets of Manhattan in the core of the novel. Highly satirical and with moments of comic black humour, Ellis creates the character of Patrick Bateman as a representation of the underlying pressures experienced by these Manhattan males. Approaching a reading of the text in this manner turns away from the controversial or sensational to gauge the greater value of this novel as a sociologically charged critique of the performance of masculinity in Manhattan. It is at this point in the novel, following the breakdown and disappearance of Price, that Patrick begins to act out his frustrations of his role in society and his position in relation to other men and masculinities in Manhattan.

PATRICK THE FLÂNEUR: MASCULINITIES ON THE STREETS OF MANHATTAN

Following Ellis' depiction of the dynamics that underpin Patrick's peer group in the opening chapters, and the impact of these conflicts and tensions on Patrick's sense of his own masculinity, the disappearance of Tim Price causes a pronounced shift in the narrative. It is at this point that Patrick becomes an incarnation of the flâneur roaming the streets of Manhattan. Outside the closed environment of the restaurants and clubs, Patrick's movements in the urban labyrinth bring him face-to-face with a multiplicity of masculinities in Manhattan that are a direct challenge, in Patrick's view, to his hegemonic status. After speaking to the black Hispanic doorman in the lobby of his building, Patrick reflects:

> I am a ghost to this man, I'm thinking. I am something unreal, something not quite tangible, yet still an obstacle of sorts and he nods, gets back on the phone, resumes speaking in a dialect totally alien to me. (68)

Whereas the opening section of the novel depicted Patrick's attempt to negotiate his status within the closed social group of the Wall Street yuppies, it is at this point that Patrick becomes the flâneur reporting on the condition of his masculinity. Reflecting on his feelings of existing as "a ghost," "something unreal," or "something not quite tangible" (68), there is the suggestion of the invisibility of the hegemonic male in Manhattan; in other words, the Wall Street yuppie is no longer a reference point for other men in Manhattan. This is the beginning of Patrick's highly satirised performance that includes moments of erratic, absurd behaviour punctuated by acts of graphic violence.

Critical readings of the graphic violence in *American Psycho* have focused almost exclusively on the acts of sexual violence committed by Patrick on the female characters in the novel. While Mark Storey correctly identifies the violence in the novel as symbolic manifestations of Patrick's attempts to understand his masculinity, Storey focuses solely on attacks on the female characters. Following Storey, Berthold Schoene-Harwood also fails to look beyond the acts of violence committed on female characters. Schoene-Harwood is correct, however, to reject Carla Freccero's claim that "there is no truth to be found beneath appearances, and the accumulation of Bateman's successful, unnoticed, and ultimately deeply unsatisfying torture-murders that do not teach him—or the rest of us—anything" (52). James Annesley also argues that while "[Patrick's] murders do not represent some kind of *acte gratuite*," they remain "hollow and inexplicable acts of violence" (*Blank Fictions* 20). Reading the novel as a literary representation of the existence of multiple competing masculinities in Manhattan points to the arguably even greater significance of the acts of violence that Patrick commits on the male characters in the text. Schoene-Harwood draws on Suzanne Hatty's analysis of male violence to offer a useful reading that emphasises male violence "as a modern strategy [that] guarantees both individual and social control, while maintaining and perpetuating hierarchy and inequality" (Schoene-Harwood, "Serial Masculinity" 385). But again Schoene-Harwood fails to extend this to Patrick's attacks on masculinities in the novel. One criticism of Schoene-Harwood's reading of these passages in the novel is his ambiguity regarding how the reader should consider these acts of violence committed on the female characters, as he judges them as "hyperbolic acts of violence, both real and imagined" (381). Certainly the standard approach to reading these scenes in the novel is to cite them as evidence of Ellis' conscious blurring of reality and illusion to reflect the deteriorating psyche of the narrator, Patrick.[42] Should there not be a distinction between whether these acts are "real" or "imagined"? Should we consider these acts of violence as actual events or fantasies in Bateman's imagined attempts at asserting his hegemonic status? One of the qualities of Ellis' writing, particularly in *American Psycho,* is that what may appear at first glance to be superficial or sensational is in fact loaded with greater sociological significance. If the attacks are read symbolically, they point to the larger issues of the challenge to his goals as achieving a status of hegemonic masculinity within the internal hegemonic framework.

The first act of violence in the novel is Patrick's attack on a homeless man on Twelfth Street. From the first page of *American Psycho,* the homeless populate the streets of Manhattan. As the narrative unfolds, "beggars and homeless seem to have multiplied . . . and the ranks of the unfortunate, weak and aged lined the streets everywhere" (268). A recurring motif in the novel, which haunts these Manhattan males, are the billboards advertising *Les Misérables.* A musical based on a novel that depicts homeless poverty in nineteenth-century Paris, these billboards suggest that the suffering that has become a symptom of free market neoliberal philosophy is now a spectacle to be enjoyed by the affluent in Manhattan. Fittingly it is below a *Les Misérables* poster that Patrick encounters the "bum, a black man" (123) with the sign "I AM HUNGRY AND HOMELESS PLEASE FEED ME" (122). As Patrick begins to barrage this man with questions, the man reveals that he had a job but was laid off. Patrick is insistent: "Why don't you get a job?" (123); "Listen. Do you think it's fair to take money from people who *do* have jobs? Who *do* work?" (124); and finally, "Get a goddamn job, Al . . . You've got a negative attitude. That's what's stopping you. You've got to get your act together" (124). Patrick's final words before viciously attacking the man underline that it is the difference between these men that is the motive for the attack: "Al . . . I'm sorry. It's just that . . . I don't know. I don't have anything in common with you . . . Do you know what a fucking loser you are?" (126).

Shere Hite's research into what the men regard as the fundamental elements of American manhood offers an insight into the motives behind this attack. When Hite asks, "What does it mean to be a man?" (*Hite Report on Male Sexuality* 46), the replies are especially telling with regard to Patrick's aggression and anger towards the homeless man. To be considered a real man, the respondents make it clear that it is necessary to be "strong with a successful career"; "he should work. A man can't have much self-worth without it"; "a man is useless if he doesn't work"; and conclusively, "A man without a job is not a man, he is defeated. My conscience would bother me to unbelievable proportions if I didn't have a job" (68–69). The influence of the "breadwinning" and "self-made man" archetypes, therefore, remains as a constant in the American male's belief of what constitutes authentic manhood (Hite 032_08_09). The need to be competitive in order to appear as a real man in the gendered and gendering environment of the workplace remains as a fixed point of masculine reference (Hite 032_06_01). In the context of the projection of this ideal in the opening sections of the novel, and Patrick's struggle to assert his status within this arena, this act of violence appears as a reaction against those men who, at least in Patrick's eyes, do not adhere to the hegemonic ideal of American masculinity. Although Patrick's narration of the scene highlights the race of this man, this is not Patrick's concern. What drives the attack is Patrick's disgust that this man is not following the legitimised and legitimising path of neoliberal-era masculinity.

Patrick's next attack on another Manhattan man takes place in the chapter "Killing Dog." Patrick's attack on the "old queer" (157) is not as random as it may first appear when considered within the development of the narrative.[43] As I have demonstrated above, homophobia is a major issue in Patrick's peer group, with homosexuality existing as a shorthand for unmanliness. This is a major cause of concern for Patrick regarding the instable condition of his hegemonic masculinity. Ellis plays upon this insecurity at various points in the novel. Earlier in Harry's, Patrick, once more performing in front of his peers, broadcasts his hegemonic views that "men are only here to procreate, to carry on the species, you know?" (88). Patrick's view of homosexuality as a threat to his performance of his masculinity is further underscored when he finds himself in view of a gay pride parade on Fifth Avenue. What drives Patrick's issue with gay men is what he considers as the inexplicable conscious deviation from the hegemonic ideal: "I stood in front of Paul Smith and watched with a certain traumatized fascination, my mind reeling with the concept that a human being, a *man,* could feel pride over sodomising another man" (134). Patrick, the Manhattan male who processes his idea of his masculinity within the hierarchical internal hegemonic framework, simply cannot understand how "a *man*" (134) could feel pride in expressing his differentiation from what society has established as the hegemonic norm. The chiming refrain sung by these men, "There's a place for us / Somewhere a place for us" (134), is so unnerving to Patrick that he flees back to the safety of his apartment. Of course what Ellis is doing here is using a line from the Manhattan-based musical *West Side Story* to critique further Patrick's unwavering belief in the self-actualising power of the male peer group. *West Side Story* is set in the Upper West Side of Manhattan in the mid-1950s and plays out the rivalry between two gangs: the white, working-class Jets and the Puerto Rican Sharks. Traditionally, the gang has been the group in which males display an aggressive masculinity in order to assert their dominant status. Disputes between these groups are often settled with acts of violence that prove their masculinity. What Ellis achieves with these gay men appropriating this song as their anthem is to satirise very cleverly Patrick's belief in the legitimising power of the male peer group. Conformity underpins the performance of Patrick's masculinity, and as the narrative progresses it becomes increasingly clear that Patrick's erratic behaviour can be linked to his doubts as to whether he can achieve the hegemonic ideal of what it means to be a real man.[44]

Ellis takes this further with the development of the relationship between Patrick and his colleague Luis Carruthers. From the beginning of the novel,

Patrick and his peers ridicule Luis. Furthermore, Patrick has an affair with Luis' girlfriend Courtney. Ellis undermines this, however, with the development of Luis' feelings for Patrick, which reaches its crux when Luis Carruthers finally declares his love for Patrick (282–285). This leads Patrick to reflect upon his everyday existence in New York: "Luis' presence forces me to consider that maybe a life connected to this city, to Manhattan, to my job, is *not* a good idea" (280). Patrick's reaction to this realisation is the attack on a young boy at the zoo, the motive of which is hinted at in Patrick's sigh that prefaces the attack that he is "unable to maintain a credible public persona" (285). It is this challenge to Patrick's heterosexuality that drives his attempt to strangle Luis Carruthers in the toilet of the Yale Club. This attempt to assert his hegemonic "heterosexual" power, however, is undermined by Luis thinking that Patrick is trying to kiss him: "His right hand reaches up and tenderly touches the side of my face. I stand there, frozen, my arms still stretched out in front of me, fingers still circled around Luis' throat. 'God, Patrick,' he whispers. 'Why *here?*'" (152). This scene with Luis not only underlines the insecurities that plague Patrick in terms of his sexuality, but it also provides further evidence of the implausibility of the vicious attacks carried out by Patrick in the novel. Patrick's slow, awkward, and powerless motions in the attempted attack on Luis (152–153) are in great contrast to the precise filmic language of Patrick's swift, skilful, precise movements in the detailed passages of graphic violence on the female characters of the novel as well as the other males on the streets of Manhattan.

Attempting to come to terms with the gay pride parade and the encounter with Luis in the toilet of the Yale Club, Patrick begins to "stalk the dark, cold streets off Central Park West" (157). Patrick works himself into a frenzied, self-alienated state: he catches sight of his face reflected in a limousine, he sees his shadow cast on the pavement, and he can see his gloved hands moving and admits that "it takes an awesome amount of strength to fight down the urge to start slapping myself in the face" (157). With this rage building, he encounters an "old queer" (157) walking with his dog. Patrick's description of this man reveals a lot about the meaning of this attack within the context of his understanding of his masculinity in the novel. The contrast between these two men is underscored, with Patrick's archetypally masculine tall, dark, and handsome appearance contrasting with the "old queer's" stock homosexual characteristics of being in his "late fifties," "pudgy," with "obscenely healthy-looking pink skin" and "no wrinkles"—all of which Patrick sees as "accentuat[ing] his feminine features" (157). Throughout the novel what might be considered feminine practices play a major part in Patrick's performance of his masculinity.[45] A useful approach to understanding this problematic might be Demetrakis Z. Demetriou's concept of "dialectical pragmatism" (345). According to Demetriou, the hegemonic group, rather than existing apart from subordinated males, incorporates elements of the subordinated groups to maintain the pattern of hegemony. As the social scenes in the novel underline, it is essential that Patrick and his peers appear truly masculine in the eyes of other males. The great irony, however, which is a major focus of Ellis' satirical take of this period, is the various un-masculine obsessions of Patrick and his peers—from their knowledge of fashion, their obsessions with grooming products, and even their love of daytime TV, specifically the moral compass that is *The Patty Winters Show.* This attack on the homosexual man, therefore, stands as a symbolic act that attempts to react against the effect of these uncertainties and insecurities that underpin Patrick's sense of his masculinity in a society that is projecting conflicting ideas of what it means to be a true American male.

With Patrick's struggle to assert his masculine identity becoming ever more erratic and volatile, Patrick's attacks on other male characters continue. The arrival of the Japanese into Manhattan is a recurring theme in the novel. In Cliff Cheng's collection of essays, *Masculinities in Organisations* (1996), Tomoko Hamada suggests that Euro-American males, the hegemonic group within the world of transnational capitalism, were beginning to face the challenge to their hegemonic status for the first time from Japanese companies. Hamada makes the point that as well as Euro-American managers struggling to uphold traditional masculine values, "they are also facing logical contradictions inherent in the effeminized masculinities required by the rapidly spreading, international, corporate, hegemonic patriarchy, where transnational corporations are attempting to rediscipline managers and professionals" (Hamada 173).[46] Patrick and his peers react aggressively to this challenge. When the group are anxious that they cannot decide where to go out to eat, Hamlin suggests, "Why don't we just forget this shit and go bash some Japs?" (301). The contradictory nature of Patrick's attitude towards the ever-growing influence of other masculinities is further demonstrated in how these "others" are enriching his everyday life. The influence of the Japanese is not only accepted and acknowledged in the narrative but is celebrated by many of these Manhattan males. In the first chapter the group enjoy Japanese beer with a dinner of sushi with soy sauce, tempura, and sake (9–11). At various points Patrick boasts of the delicacy of Japanese apple-pear (27, 133). He has a Sony alarm clock (24), a Sony Walkman (107), a "huge Sony TV" (133), a Sony Watchman pocket TV (212), a Sony palm-sized handycam (236), a Sony multidisc CD player (295), a Sony CCD-V200 8mm camcorder (295), and a "Sony MDP-700 multidisc player with digital effects and universal-wireless-remote programming" (295). Patrick, after attending a U2 concert in place of Japanese clients of Luis Carruthers (137), suggests they eat at "a really top sushi bar on the Upper West Side" (139). And finally, upon meeting with his ex-girlfriend Bethany, he recites a haiku he has written for her (224). Charles Murphy's tirade on the arrival of the Japanese into Manhattan, and the preposterous suggestion that the Japanese are aiming to buy the Empire State Building and, seemingly more importantly, Nell's—"*Nell's,* can you believe it, Bateman?" (173)—moves something in Patrick. Patrick stalks the streets once more, this time on the Upper West Side, to take out his vengeance on this new group daring to further destabilise their increasingly delicate position. Patrick carries out a horrendous attack on what he believes to be a young Japanese delivery boy. The ironic futility of this demonstration of his hegemonic muscle is underlined, however, when Patrick realises that he has failed in his mission and has murdered "the wrong type of Asian" (173).

The conflicts and tensions that drive Patrick's brutal acts of violence on other Manhattan males culminate in the attack on Paul Owen. On the surface, a clear motive for the attack is the jealousy that Patrick and his peers feel towards Paul Owen for handling the coveted Fisher account. But Paul Owen also has a greater symbolic role to play. Following the acts of violence that have been committed on the "other" in this urban arena, the brutal murder of Paul Owen can be read as Patrick's reaction to the masculine hegemony of Manhattan, or, even more significantly, an attack on the image of masculinity that he is forced to embody. One of the recurring motifs of the novel is the inability of these Manhattan males to distinguish themselves from each other, and throughout the novel Paul Owen mistakes Patrick for Marcus Halberstam. As Patrick reflects:

> but for some reason it really doesn't matter and it seems a logical faux pas since Marcus works at P & P also, in fact does the same thing I do, and he also has a penchant for Valentino suits and clear prescription glasses and we share the same barber at the same place. (86)

In this scene, the likeness of Patrick and Paul Owen is emphasised repeatedly: they are similarly dressed in linen suits, cotton shirts, and silk ties (206); Paul Owen is the same age as Patrick (twenty-seven) (207); and they sound exactly the same: "My voice sounds similar to Owen's and to someone hearing it over the phone probably identical" (209). Patrick, in attacking Paul Owen, is essentially violently reacting against the role that he is expected to play. As Hite's research underlines, men are intently aware that they must play a certain role in society in order to be accepted by their peers (Hite 031_08_04). In Hite's original study on men's perception of their masculinity, the respondents demonstrated their awareness of the ideals of true American masculinity that they were expected to live up to (*Hite Report on Male Sexuality* 66–71). This external performance of ideal American masculinity, however, conflicts with their internal feelings of what it means to be true to themselves. One respondent in the "21st Century Man Questionnaire" points to this conflict: while this New York male states his admiration for his father's faith in the ideal of American manhood, that is "his dedication to his wife, family, and hard work," the respondent desires "to be free," that is to say, to be able to think and act independently and have the chance to develop his own identity (Hite 032_08_015).

Hite's research emphasises the contradictory nature of these expectations: men must be "self-assured, unafraid, in control, and autonomous or self-sufficient" (*Hite Report on Male Sexuality* 66), with "the most frequently mentioned quality [being] leadership or dominance" (67). And yet men must also "be accepted by other men as 'one of them'" (69). What emerges from Hite's research, which is reflected in *American Psycho,* is that the source of the frustration and aggression of American men is in their struggles to follow what Hite calls "the male code" (76):

> Trying to live by the male code, being totally self-sufficient, emotionally and economically, always providing shelter and food (or sex and orgasms), never receiving or needing anything, never needing a woman's love more than she needs the man's—all this hurts and stunts men. (*Shere Hite Reader* 209)

What Hite succeeds in doing in her research, notably twenty years before Michael Kimmel identified the "guy code" (*Guyland* 7),[47] is to recognise that men are conditioned to behave in a certain manner which, on various levels, goes against what they consider as being true to themselves. Moreover, this behaviour is enforced through peer influence. Hite cites one respondent's astute view:

> Men are trained at an early age to disregard any and every emotion, and be *strong*. You take someone like that and then wonder why they don't and sometimes can't express feelings. Not only that, they are supposed to be a cross between John Wayne, the Chase Manhattan Bank, and Hugh Hefner. We are only human for christsake. (*Hite Report on Male Sexuality* 76)

Reading the attack on Paul Owen within the context of Hite's research points to the symbolic power of these scenes as acts of frustration and aggression in response to the demands of adhering to the hegemonic ideal of masculinity in Manhattan. It is at this point in the novel that Patrick's narrative voice begins to fracture and become ever more unreliable. Patrick leaves an answerphone message on Harold Carnes' machine admitting all the murders that he has committed. When Patrick comes face-to-face with Carnes in a club aptly called "World's End" (371), the idea of Patrick as serial killer and mass murderer is once more rejected. Carnes, misrecognising Patrick by calling him Davis (372), laughs at the idea of Patrick the cold-blooded murderer: "Davis . . . I am not one to bad-mouth anyone, your joke *was* amusing. But come on, man, you had one fatal flaw: Bateman's such a bloody ass-kisser, such a brown-nosing goody-goody, that I couldn't fully appreciate it" (372). Carnes goes further to belittle Patrick's manhood: "Why else would Evelyn Richards dump him? You know, really. He could barely *pick up* an escort girl, let alone . . . what was it you said he did to her?" (373). Patrick, growing ever more incredulous, insists that he did murder Paul Owen. Carnes, however, repeats that that is simply not possible: "'Because . . . I had . . . dinner . . . with Paul Owen . . . twice . . . in London . . . *just ten days ago*'" (373).

It is at this point that we reach the crux of Ellis' satirical portrayal of Patrick's attempts to assert his hegemonic status. The passages of violence committed on the male characters resonate in their greater sociological significance as revelatory of the strains and anxieties placed upon these men in Manhattan. As one respondent in Hite's *Report on Male Sexuality* declares:

> Teaching men that masculinity is composed of aggressiveness, destructive competitiveness, and acquisitiveness has led men to value physical aggression and dominance; and has produced the high general level of fear, contempt, arrogance, and paranoia in men, and has contributed mightily to the high general level of interpersonal viciousness in this society. (59)

This statement on contemporary masculinity informs this reading of Patrick Bateman. Throughout the novel Patrick displays these levels of fear of other masculinities, contempt towards his peers, arrogance towards those he sees as below his status in Manhattan society, and growing paranoia towards how others see him, both inside and outside of his peer group. It is due to these issues that Patrick displays the levels of aggressiveness, both in terms of his competitiveness against other Wall Street males, and in a symbolic sense in the attacks on the males in the streets of Manhattan. The passages in the novel in which Patrick becomes the flâneur stalking the streets of the urban labyrinth should be read figuratively as Patrick's attempt to understand his identity in the urban metropolis. Ellis further sends up the idea of Patrick as an actual serial killer when Patrick goes to the office Halloween party. Patrick, of course, had decided to go "as a mass murderer, complete with sign painted on my back that read MASS MURDERER (which was decidedly lighter than the sandwich board I had constructed earlier that day that read DRILLER KILLER), and beneath those two words I had written in blood *Yep, that's me*" (317). Inevitably Patrick's public display of his secret serial killer identity is foiled, as it is Craig McDermott, and not Patrick, who wins the contest dressed as an even more deviant figure of the time—the American stock trader Ivan Boesky.[48]

Following these further rejections of his identity in his attempts to assert his hegemonic status, Patrick once again turns to his peer group for support in the restaurant aptly named "No Man's Land":

> Even after I tell the table, "Listen, guys, my life is a living hell," they utterly ignore me, the group assembled . . . continuing to argue about allocating assets, which stocks look best for the upcoming decade, hardbodies, real estate, gold, why long-term bonds are too risky now, the spread collar, portfolios, how to use power effectively, new ways

to exercise, Stolichnaya Cristall, how best to impress very important people. (333–334)

The lack of interest of Patrick's colleagues is an accurate portrayal of the attitude of the male peer group underlined by the participants in Hite's research. Hite's respondents make clear that the display of emotion is a display of weakness and not something tolerated by male social groups. Men, within the anonymous safety of Hite's questionnaires, are able to admit that they do have emotions. In their everyday lives, however, "conditioning makes men reluctant to show emotion" (Hite 033_03_03). Put simply, men are "indoctrinated to be less emotional" (Hite 032_01_04). The consequence of this social conditioning is that men must be seen to emanate what have been hardened as distinctly masculine traits: rationality, composure, and the appearance of being in control. As one respondent remarks, "I am forced to wear a mask to protect my professional status" (*Hite Report on Male Sexuality* 60).

With Patrick forced once more to internalise these issues that he has been facing throughout the novel, the narrative begins to flow into the protagonist's stream of consciousness before fracturing into a filmographic third-person narration of Patrick wreaking havoc once more on other Manhattan males. Patrick attacks a young saxophone player playing a piece from *Les Misérables* (334), a young Iranian taxi driver (335), a police officer (336), a night watchman (338), and a black janitor (338). Patrick's apparent breakdown is further represented in the fragmentation of the narrative into short, sharp chapters with Patrick in bed with Luis' soon-to-be wife Courtney (346–348); Patrick out for dinner with McDermott at Smith & Wollensky (348–349); Patrick on a date with Jeanette (349–350); Patrick's visit to see his mother in the nursing home, Sandstone (351–352); Patrick's visit to Paul Owen's apartment that is now on the market (352–354); and a trip to the gym (356). As Patrick tellingly laments when having dinner with McDermott, "how can I tell McDermott that this is a very disjointed time of my life [?]" (349).

Following these scenes in which Patrick appears to be affected by the everyday pressures of adhering to the hegemonic ideal, Patrick meets with his secretary Jean at an outdoor café, aptly named "Nowheres" (357), and it is here that Patrick's desire for a counter-hegemonic alternative to this life in Manhattan comes to the surface. At the beginning of the brunch date, their conversation is stiff and stilted. Patrick often refers to himself in the third person (358), with the narrative continuing to break off at various points into Patrick's internal thoughts. It is here that one of the most quoted passages of the novel occurs:

there is an idea of a Patrick Bateman, some kind of abstraction, but there is no real me, only an entity, something illusory, and though I can

> hide my cold gaze and you can shake my hand and feel flesh gripping yours and maybe you can even sense our lifestyles are probably comparable: *I am simply not there.* (362)

Critics of *American Psycho* are quick to jump on this section as proof of Patrick's disintegrating subjectivity. This is an understandable interpretation, especially in light of the passages of the apparent disintegration of Patrick's psyche that precede it. A more useful and constructive way of reading this passage appears when it is considered in the context of the conversation Patrick is having with Jean in this chapter. Doing so points to the interpretation that Patrick's reflection of himself as an abstraction is indicative of the fact that the inner conflicts that have affected his performance in the novel have now reached their zenith. Patrick plays a certain role in Manhattan, but behind this façade he simply does not know the Manhattan male he is meant to be.

These internalised issues contrast sharply with the actual conversation that Patrick is having with Jean during their date. It is at this moment that Jean finally admits her love for Patrick. Due to his social conditioning Patrick is simply unable to process that someone would care for him. As Patrick reveals in the dinner date that he has with his brother Sean earlier in the novel, he thinks the world would be a better place if he disappeared:

> I stare into a thin, web like crack above the urinal's handle and think to myself that if I were to disappear into that crack, say somehow miniaturize and slip into it, the odds are good that no one would notice I was gone. No . . . one . . . would . . . care. In fact some, if they noticed my absence, might feel an odd, indefinable sense of relief. This is true: the world is better off with some people gone. Our lives are *not* all interconnected. (217)

And yet this conversation with Jean offers Patrick the possibility to be happy outside of the demoralising and distressing environment of the internal hegemonic framework in which he continues to compete with other Manhattan males. Jean sees the other side of Patrick. She insists that he is "sweet," "mysterious," "considerate," and even "shy" (363). Patrick, however, cannot accept the fact that he might actually be different. As he reflects, "the lines separating appearance—what you see—and reality—what you don't—become, well, blurred" (363). Patrick finally takes Jean's hand and, walking into the street, they catch sight of a baby staring at them. As Patrick tells us: "We stare back. It's really weird and I'm experiencing a spontaneous kind of internal sensation. I feel I'm moving toward as well as away from something, and anything is possible" (365–366). After the repeated rejection of his hegemonic status by his male peers, and the social anxieties he is experiencing, there is the suggestion, however implicit, of a potential counter-hegemonic path for Patrick. Hite, in her analysis of men's views on the importance of male friendships compared to love relationships with women, underlines her findings that men state that they are happiest when in a relationship with someone who loves them (*Hite Report on Male Sexuality* 89–103). As Hite declares: "Men *need* women, especially since they cannot usually talk to other men—but many men resent that need, believing that to need affection and to like talking about feelings is a sign of weakness" (102–103). Despite Patrick wanting to be in "a meaningful relationship" (252), showering Jean with gifts on Valentine's Day (368), and asking himself the question "*Why not end up with her?*" (364), it is the fear of being dependent that underpins Patrick's struggle with accepting a relationship with Jean.

Ellis' examination of these conflicts and tensions that underpin Patrick's performance in *American Psycho* reaches full circle with the sudden return of Tim Price in the final stage of the novel. There is a figurative, as well as literal, significance of this narrative turn. Price's return is somehow strangely both real and unreal, with Patrick stating, "our conversation probably resembles something like this but is actually briefer" (369). There is also a subtle hint as to whether Price is actually there in the office with Patrick or not: "and, for the sake of form, Tim Price resurfaces, or at least I'm pretty sure he does" (369). The Price sitting in Patrick's office is not the same hegemonic Manhattan male Price that dominated the early chapters of the novel before making his dramatic exit in Tunnel. Patrick is sitting in his office reading the new bestseller, *Why It Works to Be a Jerk,* when Price strolls in. Price is vague about where he has been—"just making the rounds" (369)—and announces that he has moved on from P & P and is now working for Robinson in a subordinate position: "right-hand man, you know?" (369). As Price leaves the office, Patrick reflects on Price as the figure against which they measure their masculine identities: "I'm wondering and not wondering what happens in the world of Tim Price, which is really the world of most of us: big ideas, guy stuff, boy meets the world, boy gets it" (370).

The final chapter of the novel, with Patrick returning to Harry's one last time with his Wall Street colleagues, serves to anchor further the role of Price in the novel and, perhaps even more importantly, underline the change in the once hegemonic figure of the group. Patrick's narration moves disorientatingly from reports on their conversation: "The conversation follows its own rolling accord—no real structure or topic or internal logic or feeling; except, of course, for its own hidden, conspiratorial one" (380), to inner reflections of his own thoughts: "I am, of course, thinking about other things, asking myself my own questions: Am I a fitness junkie? Man vs. Conformity?" (380), as well as the final absurd declarations that he made "a necklace from the bones of some girls' vertebrae" (380) and his automated teller has started speaking to him (380). As the conversation develops, the dynamics of the early scenes featuring Patrick and his peers are re-established with the group's discussion of the topic of *The Patty Winters Show* that afternoon, "Does Economic Success Equal Happiness?" (381). The response of these

Manhattan males is telling: "The answer, in Harry's this afternoon, is a roar of resounding 'Definitely,' followed by much hooting, the guys all cheering together in a friendly way" (381).

There is one notable development, however, in the behaviour of one member of the group—Patrick's role model Tim Price. Price, the angry and obnoxious Manhattan male who, in the opening scenes, raged at those who did not fit in with the neoliberal ideology of the age, is indignant when the figurehead of the neoliberal era, President Ronald Reagan, appears on the TV screen. Patrick notices something "eerie" about Price, who, Patrick speculates, "was in rehab" (382). As Patrick reports, "the first and really only one to complain is Price, who, though I think he's bothered by something else, uses the opportunity to vent his frustration, looks inappropriately stunned, asks, 'How can he lie like that? How can he pull that *shit*?'" (381). Price, the one-time leader, now challenges the very neoliberal beliefs that underpinned the functioning of that group: "I just don't get how someone, *anyone,* can appear that way yet be involved in such total shit" (382). Whereas Patrick is more concerned about getting a reservation, Price is dismayed that the group does not share his awareness of the reality around them: "Price looks away from the television screen, then at Craig, and he tries to hide his displeasure by asking me, waving at the TV, 'I don't believe it. He looks so . . . *normal.* He seems so . . . out of it. So . . . *un*dangerous'" (381). Price's counter-hegemonic stance is undermined by the others in the group, particularly McDermott, who had challenged Price earlier in the scene in Tunnel. Turning to Price, McDermott rages, "He *is* totally harmless, you geek. *Was* totally harmless. Just like *you* are totally harmless. But he *did* do all that shit and *you* have failed to get us into 150, so, you know, what can I say?" (381–382). Price continues to appeal to the group, even turning to Patrick for support, but Patrick is apathetic: "I sigh, shrug, whatever" (382). Price is clearly an important character in the novel. His journey demonstrates that there is a counter-hegemonic path that these Manhattan males can take. However, as this episode underlines, the group dynamic maintains its governing power over these Manhattan males. Just as Patrick was ridiculed, particularly by Price, earlier in the novel for daring to voice counter-hegemonic views, now it is Price who is ignored and disparaged by Patrick and the group for attempting to offer an alternative opinion. Put simply, the novel ends as it begins, with the group triumphing over the individual.

CONCLUSION

The final comment in the novel is left to Patrick, our somewhat unreliable yet undeniably insightful flâneur reporting on his experience of attempting to assert his masculine status. As the voices of these Manhattan males begin to blend into one, with the refrain of "What's in it for me?" echoing over the din in Harry's, an unidentifiable voice in the group calls out, "Why?"

and Patrick, in answering, makes his final comment to the group and the reader:

> "Well, though I know I should have done *that* instead of not doing it, I'm twenty-seven for Christ sakes and this is, uh, how life presents itself in a bar or in a club in New York, maybe *anywhere,* at the end of the century and how people, you know, *me,* behave, and this is what being *Pat*rick means to me, I guess, so, well, yup, uh . . ." (383–384)

With this final speech, Ellis affirms Patrick as the flâneurial figure reporting on the impact of homosocial relations on the Manhattan male's understanding of his masculinity. An important point to make is that Patrick's questioning of his selfhood throughout the novel should not be viewed as a *negation* of his subjectivity but should be read as a reaction towards an emerging necessary *negotiation* of his hegemonic status both within his peer group and also in the challenge to this group's hegemonic position in Manhattan. What this analysis of Patrick's performance of his masculinity has aimed to demonstrate is that the social scenes in the novel are the key passages in which Ellis presents his satirically biting critique of the conflicts and tensions that impact upon the Manhattan male in his attempt to assert a dominant position within the internal hegemonic framework of the male peer group. Building upon this reading, the acts of violence committed by Patrick on male figures in the streets of Manhattan take on a greater significance in their symbolic value as representations of Patrick's conflicts with other masculinities. Ellis structures the novel very carefully to underscore this as its underlying narrative drive. From the first chapters of the novel, Patrick looks to other males, particularly Price, for guidance on the masculine role that he has to play in Manhattan. The emanating concern from the text, therefore, that underpins Patrick's anxiety is the issue of "Man vs. Conformity" (380). With Patrick's contemporaries calling him "Mr. GQ" (87), "Mr. Wall Street" (272), and even "Mr. Manhattan" (304), the centre of Patrick's anxiety is the level of discrepancy between the New York male that he feels that he is and, crucially, the New York male that he feels he should be.

NOTES

1. Key studies of *American Psycho* and Bret Easton Ellis, which remain influential in the reading of the text and the author, include Young; Annesley, *Blank Fictions*; Murphet; Mandel and Durand; Colby; Baelo-Allué, *Bret Easton Ellis's Controversial Fiction*; and Mandel.
2. An extremely useful source on the controversy created upon the release of the novel can be found online. See Brien.
3. See Freccero; Seltzer; Heyler; Baelo-Allué, "Serial Murder"; Mandel.
4. The reading of Ellis as a writer of "blank fiction" is a reference to Annesley's *Blank Fictions*.

5. This is a reference to Thomas Byers' concept of "pomophobia." As Storey writes, "[Byers'] hope is that the old ideas of an essential masculinity may fall away and a new construction of sexuality and gender will replace them" (57). Pomophobia is the (American male's) fear of things falling apart. See Byers 5–33.
6. Storey cites Vivien Burr, who, paraphrasing the theories of Harré, states: "The structure of the language we are born into determines the kinds of beliefs about personhood we acquire" (Burr 172).
7. Schoene makes his point well but fails to cite the reference to autism in the text on what becomes a cultural reference for the characters in the novel, *The Patty Winter's Show* (61–62).
8. Demetrakis Z. Demetriou, in his 2001 article "Connell's Concept of Hegemonic Masculinity: A Critique," builds upon what he identifies as a substantial simplification in Connell's initial appropriation of the concept of "hegemonic masculinity." Returning to the origin of the term "hegemony" in Gramsci's study of class hegemony, Demetriou suggests the existence of two separate forms of hegemony: "internal hegemony," that is to say, "hegemony over subordinated masculinities" (341); and "external hegemony," in other words, "hegemony over women" (341). By making these separate categories of hegemonic masculinity visible, Demetriou's proposal raises a crucial question about the production and reproduction of hegemonic masculinity.
9. Ellis states in his 2012 interview in *The Paris Review*: "*American Psycho* is a book about becoming the man you feel you have to be, the man who is cool, slick, handsome, effortlessly moving through the world, modelling suits in *Esquire,* having babes on his arm. It's about lifestyle being sold as life, a lifestyle that never seemed to include passion, creativity, curiosity, romance, pain. Everything meaningful wiped away in favour of surfaces, in favour of looking good, having money, having six-pack abs, dating the hottest porn star, going to the hottest clubs. On the surface, like Patrick Bateman, I had everything a young man could possibly want to be "happy" and yet I wasn't. . . . No one can really live up to these ideals, so there's an immense amount of dissatisfaction roiling through the collective male psyche. Patrick Bateman is the extreme embodiment of that dissatisfaction" (Goulian 180).
10. Raewyn Connell proclaims Krafft-Ebing "the founder of modern sexology" (*Masculinities* 145). Jeffrey Weeks calls him "in a very real sense the Founding Father of sexology" (*Sexuality* 155). Also see Krafft-Ebing.
11. See Havelock Ellis.
12. See Freud.
13. See Kinsey, Pomeroy, and Martin; Kinsey, Pomeroy, Martin, and Gebhard. John Gagnon makes a useful "reconsideration" of the impact of Kinsey's studies ("Reconsiderations").
14. See Masters and Johnson.
15. See Weeks, *Sexuality* 12–45.
16. See chapter 2, "The Invention of Sexuality" in Weeks, *Sexuality* 11–40.
17. Kinsey's contribution was to refute what Foucault called the "perverse implantation" of sexologists, namely Freud and his "sexual aberrations" in *Three Essays on the Theory of Sexuality.* As Kinsey states, "Biologically there is no form of outlet which I will admit as abnormal. There is no right or wrong biologically" (Pomeroy 72).
18. See Irvine 13–14.
19. See Gagnon and Simon; Simon; and Gagnon, *Interpretation of Desire.* Gagnon and Simon were influenced greatly by Mead.
20. A necessary point to make at this juncture is that this emphasis on the social construction of sexuality and masculinity is not a total rejection of biology.

Certainly the physiology of the human body provides the preconditions of sexuality, but it does not cause the patterns of everyday life. Sexuality is only given meaning within the social arena.

21. The term "sexual script" was introduced in 1973 in *Sexual Conduct* (Gagnon and Simon). As John Gagnon has suggested, "Scripts specify, like blueprints, the whos, whats, whens, wheres and whys for [a] given type of activity. . . . It is like a blueprint or roadmap or recipe, giving directions" (*Human Sexualities* 6).
22. An extremely useful recent reconsideration of the impact of Gagnon and Simon's sociological approach to studying sexuality can be found in Kimmel, *The Sexual Self*.
23. See Jackson 4.
24. Jackson also makes the point: "From a feminist perspective, this had distinct advantages: female sexuality could not be seen as a repressed version of male sexuality, and neither male sexuality nor heterosexuality could be taken as norms of human sexual being" (4).
25. It is in the third edition of *Sexuality* (2009) that Jeffrey Weeks calls for a renewed emphasis on agency: "agency in relation to erotic and intimate life—not only the agency of social movements, but the impact of the millions of individual decisions about love, sex and relations that shape the contours of contemporary life, on a global scale" (xii). For writing on the need to study sexuality as a historical construction, see Weeks, "Sexuality and History Revisited."
26. Hite is notably absent from what are considered the cornerstone studies on masculinity: Connell, *Masculinities*; Kimmel, *Manhood in America* and *The Gendered Society*.
27. The theories surrounding "sexual dysfunction" grew out of Masters and Johnson, *Human Sexual Response* and *Human Sexual Inadequacy*.
28. This overview of the impact of *The Hite Report on Female Sexuality* is indebted to Weisstein.
29. Hite discusses her methodology in the preface of *The Hite Report on Male Sexuality* (xvii–xxvi), acknowledging the reductive nature of attempting to quantify the complex behaviour of human beings, the extreme of which remains Kinsey's seven-point bipolar scale. As Hite remarks, "The act of quantifying human behaviour into a series of discrete categories reduces a complex whole to a group of oversimplified variables. And, like Humpty Dumpty, can these pieces ever be put back together again?" (xxii–xxiii). See also Engel Lang for further discussion of the concerns surrounding Hite's methodology.
30. This point is also made regarding *The Hite Report on Female Sexuality* in Singer.
31. The questions include: How 'masculine' would you say you are on a scale of 1 to 10, 10 being the most masculine?; Are you macho?; When have you been closest to other men—in high school? In military service? In sports? With your father? With your best friend?; Do you belong to, or socialise with, a group of men? Please tell us about them; Do you tell any other men, your friends and colleagues, when you fall in love? Do you discuss emotional problems in your relationship with them?; Do you prefer to work with women or with other men? Why?; Do you speak up when people are discriminated against for gender reasons? Or do you usually avoid confrontation? (Hite, "Post-modern Masculinity" 101–102).
32. This body of research involves a total of 266 questionnaires from 2,017 available in the archive. The citation format that I use is: Hite Box number_Folder number_Questionnaire number.

33. This point makes reference to the 2011 Picador edition of *American Psycho*.
34. Hite reflects on where this hierarchical ideology may have originated in *The Shere Hite Reader* 286–288.
35. This thought underpins Cheng. For comprehensive overviews of studies of masculinity in the workplace, also see Collinson and Hearn, "Naming Men" 144–169 and "Men and Masculinities" 289–310.
36. Cliff Cheng cites Seidler.
37. See Annesley, *Blank Fictions*.
38. With regard to the detailed passages on what the characters are wearing in the novel, Ellis has stated, "If you could see what the characters in *American Psycho* were wearing, they would all look like clowns" (Adams, "Brett Easton Ellis Interview").
39. Also see Hite, *Report on Male Sexuality* 20–21.
40. In a later scene Patrick meets his brother Sean. Patrick cannot believe it when Sean tells Patrick to meet him at Dorsia: "Sean calls at five from the Racquet Club and tells me to meet him at Dorsia tonight. He just talked to Brin, the owner, and reserved a table at nine. My mind is a mess" (216). Patrick is unable to book a table at Dorsia for a dinner with a girl Patricia or his secretary Jean. Patrick even makes a list of priorities, the number one being "get an eight o'clock reservation on a Friday night at Dorsia with Courtney" (170).
41. It should be noted that Price rejects the higher-quality card of Montgomery.
42. See Young 114–115.
43. Furthermore, following the incident in the Yale Club and the killing of the "old queer," in the following chapter, "Girls," Patrick reaffirms his masculinity in the highly detailed pornographic scene with two prostitutes.
44. See Hite, *Oedipus Revisited* 23–25.
45. This is more than evident in the detailed description of Patrick's daily cleansing ritual (23–29).
46. There is no direct mention of managers or directors in *American Psycho*.
47. Kimmel explores his concept of the "guy code" in further detail in *Guyland* 44–69.
48. Boesky made the news in the mid-1980s for his inside trading on Wall Street. He is famous for proclaiming, "Greed is healthy" in a speech at the University of California, Berkeley in 1986. Boesky received a prison sentence of three and a half years in 1987 and was fined $100 million after being found guilty of inside trading. It is thought that Boesky was the inspiration for the character Gordon Gekko in Oliver Stone's *Wall Street,* the highly acclaimed movie portraying the greed of the 1980s. Michael Douglas' performance as Gekko won him an Oscar for best actor.

5 "A World Citizen with a New York Pair of Balls"

The Global Hegemonic Male in Don DeLillo's *Cosmopolis*

Andrew Dix, Brian Jarvis, and Paul Jenner, in their desire to put *The Contemporary American Novel in Context* (2011), ask the question first posed by Julian Hawthorne in 1863: "what is an American book?" (113). Their answer, unsurprisingly, is that the American novel of the last twenty years has been shaped within the discourses of globalization.[1] Dix, Jarvis, and Jenner turn to Paul Giles' writing on the cartographies of American literature to argue that the focus of the contemporary American novel is the "boundaries between the local and the global, the national and the transnational" (113).[2] As such, the American novel both reflects and critically engages with, to echo Raewyn Connell, the "antinomies of globalization": the global vs. the local; homogeneity vs. heterogeneity; dispersed vs. concentrated power ("The Northern Theory of Globalization" 373). There is one writer whose work is intensely focused on the grand narratives that impact upon the American individual in the increasingly globalizing contemporary American society: Don DeLillo.

Within the parameters of this study of the literary figure of the flâneur observing, critiquing, and writing the city, DeLillo is an apposite inclusion. In many ways, DeLillo's mode follows Walter Benjamin's reading of the urban observer: in his everyday life, as well as his fiction, DeLillo inhabits the paradox of being detached and yet assimilated into American culture. To use the words of Frank Lentricchia, DeLillo's mode "is the sort of mode that marks writers who conceive their vocation as an act of cultural criticism," that is, they "invent in order to intervene," they make "an effort to represent the culture in its totality," and they are ultimately driven by the "desire to move readers to the view that the shape and fate of their culture dictates the shape and fate of the self" ("The American Writer as Bad Citizen" 240).[3] DeLillo's aim, therefore, is to not only depict the minutiae of social discourses but to critique their impact upon the individual. Building upon this, this chapter will argue that the social construction of masculinity is a central concern of DeLillo's critique of the global hegemonic male in contemporary Manhattan in *Cosmopolis*.[4]

At the time of the publication of *Cosmopolis*, the response was, at best, mixed.[5] Philipp Schweighauser and Peter Schneck (2010) make the insightful point of the contrasting nature of the European and American reactions to the novel. A quick survey of literary reviews of *Cosmopolis* supports this premise. On one side of the Atlantic, critics such as Walter Kim in the *New York Times* offer the warning: "Beware the novel of ideas, particularly when the ideas come first and all the novel stuff (like the story) comes second." Michiko Kakutani goes a step, or should that be a leap, further to declare: "*Cosmopolis,* however, turns out to be a major dud, as lugubrious and heavy-handed as a bad Wim Wenders film, as dated as an old issue of *Interview* magazine." Gail Caldwell, in the *Boston Globe,* is equally aghast: "It's irritating from its opening pages, and not just because its protagonist—a 28-year-old billionaire money guy named Eric Packer—is a spooky, cardboard narcissist. Loathsome characters can be commendable creations so long as their containing structure either justifies or elevates their existence. But *Cosmopolis* verges on parody." Bruce Bawer, in his highly critical look at "Don DeLillo's America," makes the point of "the stunning implausibility" of DeLillo's fiction:

> Representation of reality is not DeLillo's strong suit. It's hard to accept most of his characters as living, breathing human beings. But then, these novels are not meant to be true-to-life tales. They are tracts, designed to batter us, again and again, with a single idea: that life in America today is boring, benumbing, dehumanized. (22)[6]

John Updike, in his review of *Cosmopolis* for *The New Yorker,* echoes Bawer in politely underlining the "implausibility" of the narrative, with events "far-fetched and random": "Now, a reader undertaking a novel grants the writer a generous initial draft of suspended disbelief. DeLillo spends this advance payment as recklessly as his hero overinvests in loans against the yen."

Despite this reaction from critics in the United States, on the other side of the Atlantic, George Walden, comparing *Cosmopolis* with DeLillo's previous offering, *The Body Artist* (2001), writes, "In [DeLillo's] new novel the contemporary theme and lively action prevent the novel from becoming obscure." Tim Adams, in *The Observer*, lauds DeLillo's interpretation of the American contemporary: "As ever, DeLillo finds in the black comedy of these encounters excruciatingly smart parables about the logic of money and the state of the American soul." Blake Morrison, writing in *The Guardian,* acknowledges that *Cosmopolis* "has bewildered most of its reviewers" but sees the major themes that characterise DeLillo's work fuse in *Cosmopolis.* For Morrison, DeLillo's "hymn to New York" is "more prose-poem than novel." This overview of initial responses to *Cosmopolis* underlines the clear dichotomy towards DeLillo from those inside and outside of American society. The American critics' reaction to *Cosmopolis* in many ways echoes the critical response to the publication of DeLillo's *Libra* (1988). Lentricchia highlights the example of George Will, a man who called DeLillo a literary vandal for writing about real people, a bad citizen for the suggestion that John F. Kennedy's assassination was part of a conspiracy, and a bad influence because a lot of people were now reading DeLillo's fiction ("The American Writer as Bad Citizen" 241). It is apparent, therefore, that American critics attack what European scholars see as the great strength of DeLillo's work: his unwavering drive to produce sharp assessments of the condition of American society and the relationship between American society and the individual.

To engage fully with DeLillo's sociological intentions with *Cosmopolis*, it is necessary to place it within the greater social and cultural context of its time and consider the production of the novel within the backdrop of one of the major events in U.S. history: the terrorist attacks of September 11, 2001. DeLillo's immediate reaction to this event was the essay "In the Ruins of the Future" (2001). DeLillo's at times intense, at times solemn, but above all penetrating piece anchors this moment in recent American history as not only a turning point for the country and the American people but also for the storytellers of the contemporary era: "The narrative ends in the rubble and it is up to us to create the counter narrative" ("Ruins").[7] DeLillo sees New York following the terrible atrocity as an enduring collection of narratives. Of the "100,000 stories crisscrossing New York," these stories "are stories of heroism and encounters with dread" ("Ruins"). They are "stories that carry around their edges the luminous ring of coincidence, fate, or premonition." Above all, these are "stories generating others" ("Ruins").[8]

DeLillo begins "Ruins" reflecting on how, in the previous decade, "the surge of capitalist markets has dominated discourse and shaped global consciousness." Although the focus of the essay is to comment on these grand narratives, in typical DeLillian style he processes their impact through the individual stories of the people of Manhattan. Sonia Baelo-Allué, writing on the expectation and subsequent reaction to what is considered as DeLillo's 9/11 novel, *Falling Man* (2007), determines this as DeLillo's standard approach to processing the "trauma" of these historic events—his proclivity towards writing the "psychic trauma" rather than the "cultural trauma." In other words, what DeLillo looks to is the "domestic and intimate" ("9/11 and the Psychic Trauma Novel" 64). DeLillo weaves together various stories about real people: he writes of Marc and Karen, husband and wife who not only struggle to save their own children but also stop to help other members of their community; there is the man standing beside DeLillo as they look on together at what is left of the Twin Towers, who says, "Oh my God, I'm standing here" (DeLillo returns to this image in *Falling Man* [25]); DeLillo comments on the energy of the people on Canal Street; amid the mourning people there is the sound of the saxophonist playing softly; DeLillo reflects the horrific image of two women on the two planes who are best friends and who die both together and apart; and there is the powerful final image of the young woman in a headscarf kneeling in prayer. For DeLillo, the power of these stories "take us beyond the hard numbers of dead and missing and give us a glimpse of elevated being" ("Ruins").[9] DeLillo's mode, therefore, is to fulfil the responsibility that he feels as a writer to tackle these grand narratives formed in the global and demonstrate how it is in the local that the counter-narratives are written.

The idea of narratives and counter-narratives not only links "Ruins" and *Cosmopolis* but also affirms DeLillo's belief in the role of fiction in processing these major societal events. DeLillo frets on the contemporary condition of the American novel, believing that writers are "working in the margins" (Begley). He does, however, champion the potential of "the rich literature" of the contemporary canon to tackle the grand narratives of our time. DeLillo has a warning, however, for the contemporary novel:

> We have a rich literature. But sometimes it's a literature too ready to be neutralized, to be incorporated into the ambient noise. This is why we need the writer in opposition, the novelist who writes against power, who writes against the corporation or the state or the whole apparatus of assimilation. We're all one beat away from becoming elevator music. (Begley)

DeLillo echoes E. B. White, the classic chronicler of New York whom I refer to in the first chapter of this book, with his reflection on the relationship between the individual and the city. DeLillo moves through the streets of metropolis observing the reaction of the people to the attack not only on Manhattan, but their Manhattan. Just as E. B. White lauded the presence and power of New Yorkers, so DeLillo reminisces on "the spirit of Canal Street": "One month earlier I'd taken the same walk, early evening, among crowds of people, the panethnic swarm of shoppers, merchants, residents and passers-by, with a few tourists as well" ("Ruins"). In an echo of E. B. White's view of the power of the city to absorb almost every individual (*Here Is New York* 23), DeLillo also recognises that "the city will accommodate every language, ritual, belief and opinion" ("Ruins"). With "Ruins" and, I will come to argue, *Cosmopolis,* as much as DeLillo is writing about what might be considered the ephemeral or the abstract, DeLillo is also writing Manhattan.

There is an indisputable connection between "Ruins" and *Cosmopolis*. So much so that I would argue that "Ruins" can be read as a prelude to *Cosmopolis*. I feel it important to make the point at this juncture, however, that while "Ruins" is understandably a raw reaction to the events on September 11, I am not suggesting that *Cosmopolis* should be considered as a 9/11 novel. DeLillo, I think fairly, has distanced the novel from the atrocity. Although DeLillo was near the completion of the novel at the time of the attacks, he has stated: "The attacks didn't affect the novel directly, but they certainly affected me" (qtd. in Conte 179). *Cosmopolis* is more than a novel about one day in New York, or indeed its immediate aftermath. It is a concentrated critique of the end of the boom period that the United

States enjoyed in the 1990s. As DeLillo has stated, "the idea [for the novel] occurred to me just about the time the market was beginning to flatten out, which was spring 2000. I realized that the day on which the action occurs would be the last day of an era—the golden age of cyber-capital, with booming global markets" (qtd. in Heffernan 56–57). To this point I would add another important reading of the significance of the novel that was not possible to foresee upon its publication. As much as it is a reflection upon the discourses that were axiomatic of "that day in April in the year 2000" in which the novel is set, *Cosmopolis,* in light of the global economic crisis in 2008, also has a prophetic quality and now reads as an unnerving forewarning of the likely impact of the globalizing markets on the Manhattan male. It is this ability of the novel to ruminate on these processes that not only underlines the sociological value of the novel but also sets the novel apart from other forms of art. If we read DeLillo's narrative as a critical statement that depicts the irresponsible attitude and behaviour of the hegemonic males at the centre of the financial capitalist system in Manhattan that led to the global financial crisis of 2008, the worst since the Great Depression of the 1930s, then *Cosmopolis* the novel, published in 2003, is at least five years ahead of the event. Thus, DeLillo's novel not only depicts the performance of the hegemonic males of the multinational and transnational corporations over the course of one day in April 2000, but, with the protagonist Eric Packer, it also foretells the mind-set and thought processes of these hegemonic males performing within the globalized and globalizing arena of Manhattan. With its focus on the themes of technology, power, cyber-capital, time and space, and, as many critiques of the novel have overlooked, the performance of masculinity in relation to these grand narratives, *Cosmopolis* is deeply rooted in its social and historical context. *Cosmopolis* is an acute investigation into the discourses of the globalized local arena of New York City and, as I will argue, the impact of this upon the performance of the hegemonic Manhattan male.

COSMOPOLIS AND GLOBALIZATION

Looking at available collections of essays on DeLillo, globalization arises as a linking theme. The main thread running through Harold Bloom's *Critical Views on DeLillo* (2003) is DeLillo's place in the historical lineage of the heavyweights of American literature, namely Thomas Pynchon, Philip Roth, and Cormac McCarthy. DeLillo's interest in the global is seen as an indication of DeLillo as a writer of the postmodern. Dana Philips turns to *White Noise* (1985) to discuss the effect of postmodernity as the displacement of older forms by newer ones in a crowded cultural landscape: "All knowledge is local knowledge, but one must understand how shaped by the global the local has become." As various characters in the novel, attuned to the postmodern world, like to say, "We're all from New York" (121). In

"DeLillo, Postmodern, Postmodernity" (2008) Peter Knight contributes to this discussion by considering to what extent DeLillo's "aura of postmodernism" (39) is linked to the author's interests in the discourses of globalization. John Carlos Rowe, writing on *Falling Man* (2007), supports this view: "The consequences of globalization are central to Don DeLillo's fiction" (121). Furthermore, Stacy Olster's *Don DeLillo: Mao II, Underworld, and Falling Man* (2011) charts the progression of DeLillo's writing against the backdrop of the development of the author's understanding of the increasingly globalized world.

Peter Boxall, one of the most distinguished DeLillo scholars, makes the point that DeLillo's novels, particularly his latest works

> continue to reach for a comprehensive vision; they continue to offer us one of the most wide-ranging and inventive fictional analyses of the state of contemporary culture under the conditions produced by globalization, the mass market, and the development of transformative new media technologies. ("DeLillo and Media Culture" 52)

DeLillo's reach for a comprehensive vision continues, according to Boxall, in his reading of *Falling Man.* Boxall questions whether DeLillo's writing on the impact of globalization on Manhattan ultimately points to the creation of a closed system from which there is no escape, with "nowhere to retreat to, no possibility of dangling, no room in which to hide oneself away in intellectual quarantine, like Bellow's Joseph, as the war rages elsewhere" ("Slow Man, Dangling Man" 174).[10]

There have been further contributions to the analysis of globalization in DeLillo's work that have focused specifically on *Cosmopolis.* Jerry A. Varsava, writing in 2005, makes the point that "globalization has received more attention than any other single international issue over the last fifteen years or so, nearly guaranteeing that DeLillo would turn to it at some point" (93). For Varsava, *Cosmopolis* is a "cautionary tale" (104):

> DeLillo's *Cosmopolis* provides us with a revealing diagnostic of an age in which the negotiation between self and other, between self and community, was neglected wholly by many as they sought psycho-emotional gratification in the sound and fury of financial exchange and its mediating technologies, in the libertarian pursuit of cyber capitalism. (104)

Sven Cvek uses *Cosmopolis* to "look into the connection between a nation's sense of identity and the deterritorializing power of global capital" (157), a reading that Dix, Jarvis, and Jenner support with their interpretation of *Cosmopolis* as a piece that depicts Manhattan's "multicultural ethnoscape" (128).[11] Cvek sees the novel as "a critique of the effects of a market-driven, deterritorializing transnationalism on the U.S. polity" (157) that "marks the end of U.S. hegemony within the world system" (159). Cvek offers the extremely astute reading of the protagonist Eric Packer that rejects the perception of Packer as a "rogue capitalist." The rogue capitalist, in Cvek's view, is "the supposedly extreme, dark side of an otherwise well-balanced free market system" (159). According to Cvek, as well as symbolising globalization, Eric also represents what globalization is doing to America: "As the head of Packer Capital, he embodies both the forces of neoliberal globalization and the ambiguous position of the U.S. as their hegemonic propelling centre" (159). In other words, Packer is shaped by the dichotomy of the local and the global: "If Eric Packer 'is globalization' in his deterritorialised cyber-capitalist existence, he is also a New Yorker and an American ultimately defined by the memories and histories whose power over him he tries so hard to deny" (160).

In *Fictions of Globalization* (2006), James Annesley recognises that "Don DeLillo's *Cosmopolis* has globalization and the intricacies of the world market at its heart" (60).[12] The cornerstone of Annesley's argument is that although DeLillo's novels "interpret local experiences" (61), DeLillo "takes a broader view and sets out to contextualize these relationships within a reading of the global marketplace" (61). In sum, DeLillo aims to offer "a more detailed engagement with the globalization debate" (61). Annesley, however, doesn't celebrate this as a positive characteristic or strength of DeLillo's work. Structuring his argument around what many consider to be DeLillo's magnum opus, *Underworld* (1997), Annesley builds upon Peter Knight's assertion[13] that *Underworld* attempts to depict the impossibly complex relation between the individual and the system, but with unavoidably negative consequences:

> The problem with DeLillo's position, however, is that it represents globalization as an irreducible reality. There is no room for an interrogation of this vision, nor any sense that the novel can do more than offer a homological reflection of these material conditions. Globalization is, it seems, a reality that the novel is powerless either to interrogate or to resist. (68)

A possible answer to this reading of *Underworld* is to consider what DeLillo is actually doing with *Cosmopolis* and the protagonist Eric Packer. To use Annesley's words, DeLillo "literalizes [Packer's] centrality" (60) in the text, not only in terms of Packer's centrality in the global markets, but by also bringing him onto the streets of Manhattan as a flâneur. Packer is more than a cipher and certainly more than Gail Caldwell's "cardboard narcissist." Packer's narrative is a self-reflexive examination of his Manhattan roots as he travels from the heights of his East Side penthouse narrative to the working-class origins of his family name "Packer" in Hell's Kitchen. Packer's self-awareness of his masculinity begins when he becomes a flâneur observing and interpreting the discourses played out on the streets of New York City. While DeLillo's novels focus on the web of connections and contradictions, the complexities and nuances of processes and systems, the point to make is that DeLillo challenges the macro through the micro; in other words, DeLillo channels these critical analyses through the narrative of the individual. Packer, therefore, is not simply a stock character created by the multitude of discourses in an increasingly globalized and globalizing Manhattan. Packer is a complex individual and the figure through which DeLillo channels the impact of globalization on the Manhattan male's perception of his masculinity.

THE GLOBAL AND THE LOCAL: MASCULINITIES AND GLOBALIZATION[14]

In the last thirty years, masculinity scholarship, despite being diverse in subject matter and social location, has concentrated on localised case studies. Raewyn Connell terms this "the ethnographic moment" in masculinity research: "in which the specific and the local are in focus" ("Masculinities and Globalization" 4). The legacy of this approach to the study of men in the 1970s and 1980s was the initiation of the move away from sex-role theory, an approach characterised by the oversimplification and stereotyping of the construction of gender, towards the idea of the existence of plural masculinities, hierarchy and hegemony, collective masculinities, bodies as arenas, active construction, contradictions, and the dynamics that construct and reconstruct the patterns of hegemony (4–6). Connell argues for the need to take masculinity research a step further and, with the growing attention to globalization, calls for the focus of studies to move beyond the local character and consider the shaping of local masculinities in a world context.[15] As Connell states, this is by no means a rejection of localised studies; rather it is a call to study the global arena "as a venue for the social construction of masculinities and as a powerful force in local gender dynamics" (19). Put simply, "to understand local masculinities, we must think in global terms" (7).[16]

Connell defines "globalization" within the context of her study of masculinities as "the current pattern of world integration via global markets, transnational corporations, and electronic media under the political hegemony of the United States" ("Globalization, Imperialism" 72). Connell argues that the historical processes that have produced the "global society" have been, from the very beginning, gendered.[17] Colonial conquests and settlements were carried out by gender-segregated forces, while gender ideologies influenced the division of labour and racial hierarchies in the cultural defence of empire.[18] Within the contemporary context, global society creates new arenas that go beyond individual countries or regions in which gender identity politics, or, more specifically, masculinity politics, control the performance of men. Connell identifies these arenas as: transnational and multinational corporations; the international state, that is to say, the institutions of diplomacy and UN agencies; the international media; and the global market, in terms of capital, commodities, services, and labour, which are also strongly gender structured (*Masculinities* xxiii). Taking this gendered nature of globalization into consideration, men collectively benefit greatly from the "patriarchal dividend" (*Masculinities* 79) associated with the world gender order.[19]

While there is a multitude of discourse on globalization, the gendered nature of globalization is not a major influence of this research. As Esther Ngan-Ling Chow succinctly states:

> Much of the theorizing about globalization is either gender-neutral or gender blind, ignoring how globalization shapes gender relationships and people's lives materially, politically, socially and culturally at all levels and treating its differential effects on women and men as similar. Gender is basically taken for granted, as if it does not matter.[20] (Ngan-Ling Chow 444)

Carla Freeman supports this view with her argument that the gender neutrality of globalization masks the "implicit masculinization of these macrostructural models" (1008). Neoliberalism, the political and cultural promotion of free-market principles and individualism, is presented as, and considered, gender neutral. The lexicon engages with the gender-neutral language of "markets," "individuals," and "choice" (Connell, "Men, Masculinities" 1815). The world in which neoliberalism is ascendant, however, is still a gendered world, and neoliberalism has an implicit gender politics.

Connell offered what has become the enduring model of the global hegemonic male: "trans–national business masculinity" ("Masculinities and Globalization" 16). Connell sees the performance of these men as being "marked by increasing egocentrism, very conditional loyalties (even to the corporation), and a declining sense of responsibility for others (except for purposes of image-making)" (16). Joan Acker looks at how gender is embedded in the structuring and ongoing practices of globalizing capitalism. Acker identifies a contemporary "hegemonic hyper-masculinity" that is "aggressive, ruthless, competitive, and adversarial" (13). As Acker writes, "decisions made at the very top reaches of (masculine) corporate power have consequences that are experienced as inevitable economic forces or disembodied social trends. At the same time, they symbolize and enact varying hegemonic masculinities" (13).[21]

One focus of Connell's masculinization of globalization is to turn away from the standard discussions of globalization that paint the portrait of a homogenizing process driven by new technologies, global markets, and world news. What is produced, however, tends to be conflicts and tensions between gender patterns within the global and local arenas. This is what Connell calls "globalizing masculinities," to emphasise the idea of process ("Globalization, Imperialism" 74). Ultimately what Connell strives to emphasise is that "processes such as economic restructuring, long-distance migration, and the turbulence of 'development' agendas have the power to reshape local patterns of masculinity" (850). Again to understand the changing patterns in the local, we must look to the processes in the global arena.

Connell's study of globalizing and globalized masculinities underlines the difficulty of attempting to form a sound theory of the relation between the local and the global. From the first writings of sociological theory, the global has been seen in opposition to the local. Attempts have been made to resolve this dichotomy with the concepts of "glocalization"[22] and "grobalization"[23]—both of which merely reaffirm the polarity of the two terms and do not do enough to understand the nature of the dialectical relationship between the two categories. It would be tempting to assume a top-down hierarchy of power and authority, from global to regional to local, but Connell is quick to challenge this approach to underscore her reading that the limited research on global masculinities does not suggest that regional and local masculinities are overwhelmed by the global. Rather, the suggestion is that the *interrelated* nature of these levels leads to a constant redefinition and reformulation of hegemonic processes. As Connell states: "At the least, we must understand that regional and local constructions of hegemonic masculinity are shaped by the articulation of these gender systems with global processes" (Connell and Messerschmidt 849). The conflict of the shaping of masculinities between the global and local levels is one of Connell's "antinomies of globalization theory" (Connell, "Northern Theory" 373) that she identifies in Anglophone texts that attempt to theorise globalization. It is important to point out at this juncture that it is not my intention to resolve this issue within the restricted boundaries of this chapter. It is an important contextualising issue, however, in the understanding of the social construction of masculinities in an ever-increasingly globalizing society and, as I will come to argue later in the chapter, in DeLillo's depiction of Manhattan males in *Cosmopolis*. DeLillo takes Packer, a man whose masculinity is shaped within the global arena of the transnational markets, to the streets of Manhattan and places him at the centre of a text as a watcher, an observer, and a flâneur of the impact of the global on the local.

READING *COSMOPOLIS*

Cosmopolis is the story of Eric Packer, a twenty-eight-year-old multibillionaire asset manager and currency trader. Eric is the epitome of the global hegemonic male. The narrative takes place over the course of one day in April 2000 as Eric travels from one side of the island of Manhattan to the other—from the wealthy Upper East Side to the working class Hell's Kitchen of his youth. The reason for the trip is simple: Eric wants a haircut. It is difficult to resist making the connection with James Joyce's *Ulysses* (1922) or to read *Cosmopolis* as an odyssey of sorts. There is this undertone to the narrative, but the story of Eric Packer, I would argue, is firmly anchored in the social reality of contemporary Manhattan. The literal meaning of "cosmopolis" is "(capital) city of the world" ("Cosmopolis"), and New York is referred to at one point in the novel as "the world city" (88). Place is a central concern of DeLillo's works and it is the tension between the global and the local that comes to characterise Eric's journey in the novel—not simply the physical journey from east to west across one street in Manhattan, but even more significantly, the journey towards a sense of enlightenment about the construction of his masculinity.

In the opening passage of *Cosmopolis* the point is made that Packer considers himself the centre of the world: "Nothing existed around him. There was only the noise in his head, the mind in time. When he died he would not end. The world would end" (6). Packer's hegemonic status is affirmed in the novel by DeLillo's omniscient narrator: "he was rich . . . he was self-made . . . he was ruthless . . . he was strong . . . he was brilliant" (72). André Petrescu, the pastry assassin, also refers to Packer's place in the global world when hitting Packer in the face with a cream pie: "'I am three years waiting for this. Fresh baked only. I pass up president of the United States to make this strike. I crème him any time. You are major statement, I tell you this. Very hard to zero in" (142). According to Didi Fancher, the art critic with whom Packer has an intense sexual encounter, Packer is "talented. And a commanding presence as well. Dressed or undressed. Another talent, I suppose" (31). Traditional indicators of masculinity are important to Packer. He works out "stoically" (7), believing in the importance of "physical authority" (20) and maintaining "standards of force and brawn" (20).

Packer's hegemonic status is also projected through his choice of living quarters. He lives in a triplex apartment of forty-eight rooms in "the tallest residential tower in the world" (8), a tower "that soars to heaven and goes unpunished by God" (103). The novel begins here high in the Manhattan sky with Packer looking out over the city. As he stands watching the new day dawn, he envisages the city waking up to the new day. What he imagines, however, emphasises his initial feelings of detachment from Manhattan and its people. He sees images of "archaic business" (6), the old working-class roots of Manhattan beginning to stir in the city. He visualizes the "produce trucks rolling out of the markets . . . news trucks rolling out of the docks . . . bread vans . . . crossing the city" (6). The now "archaic" nature of the great technological and industrial advancement that had defined the development of Manhattan at a certain period in history is a recurring issue for Packer in the novel, an issue that is certainly linked to the overarching theme of the novel of the acceleration of time in the cyber-capital era. A fine example of this is Packer's reflections on the skyscraper. Arguably the emblem of the masculine discourses that shaped Manhattan at the beginning of the twentieth century, the skyscraper is the ultimate symbol of the drive to control and manipulate space and shape it into the image of man.[24] Packer, however, laments the "anachronistic quality of the word skyscraper" (9). Although

Packer feels that "they shared an edge or boundary, skyscraper and man" (8), which "gave him strength and depth" (9), it remains a construction that "belonged to the olden soul of awe, to the arrowed towers that were a narrative long before he was born" (9). Traditionally the skyscraper resonates in its greater symbolic significance not only of the development of the city but the masculine discourses that were driving the construction of *Manhattan*. *Cosmopolis* sets Packer as someone living in the future in which these *narratives*—a key word in the DeLillian lexicon—appear to no longer impact upon the global Manhattan male. As Packer reflects in the opening pages, "Freud is finished. Einstein's next" (6).

There is a running commentary on the outdated nature of the technologies of modernity throughout the novel: automated teller machines, or ATMs, are "anti-futuristic, so cumbrous and mechanical that even the acronym seemed dated" (54); Packer "wanted to understand why cash registers were not confined to display cases in a museum of cash registers in Philadelphia or Zurich" (71); when he sees a policeman speaking into a walkie-talkie, he wonders why the policeman was using such a "contraption" (102) and still "carrying the nitwit rhyme out of the age of industrial glut into smart spaces built on beams of light" (102); Packer also riffs on his hand device which "was an object whose original culture has just about disappeared. He knew he'd have to junk it" (9); the ear buds that Torval, his chief of security, uses are "degenerate structures . . . the word itself was lost in blowing mist" (19); "it was time to retire the word phone" (88); Packer "didn't know why stethoscopes were still in use. They were the lost tools of antiquity, quaint as blood-sucking worms" (43); Packer asks, "Why do we still have airports? Why are they called airports?" (22); and in conversation with Kinski they agree, "computers will die. They're dying in their present form. They're just about dead as distinct units. A box, a screen, a keyboard. They're melting into the texture of everyday life. . . . Even the word computer sounds backward and dumb" (104). If we read these technological inventions as manifestations of masculine drives of modernity, what Packer is indicating is that these symbols of masculinity are now obsolete. These narratives of the industrial and post-industrial era now belong to an old mechanical past. This, of course, is considered the underlying drive of capitalism. Max Page points out that in 1942 economist Joseph Schumpeter captured the essence of capitalism with his concept of "creative destruction": "Capitalism is by nature a form or method of economic change and not only never is but never can be stationary. The process of Creative Destruction is the essential fact about capitalism" (2). Kinski identifies this as symptomatic of the contemporary era, the "hallmark of capitalist thought. Enforced destruction. . . . Destroy the past, make the future" (92).

Packer leaves his Manhattan triplex on this day for a seemingly absurd reason: he wants a haircut (7). As other DeLillo scholars have noted, a "haircut" is also a term from the world of finance meaning the loss of a substantial amount of money. But the haircut that Eric wants has greater symbolic resonance in terms of the journey that Packer goes on to grasp the condition of his Manhattan masculinity, both literally and figuratively in the novel. One of the central themes of *Cosmopolis* is the idea that the processes of globalization modify the individual's sense of space and time, creating the experience of "time-space compression."[25] The impact of this upon Eric is realised in the various unnerving incidents that suggest that he is living in the future, no more so when Eric sees things take place on the computer and surveillance screens in his limo before they actually happen (22, 93–94). And yet, Packer's desire to get a haircut is also a journey into his past. He doesn't want just any haircut—the limo passes two hair salons on the trip (24)—Eric wants to go to the barbershop in Hell's Kitchen on the other side of town where both he and his father would go when they were boys. The suggestion is that Eric can only gain a sense of his masculine identity by revisiting his past on the streets of Manhattan. DeLillo's movement of Packer from the upper reaches of Manhattan, both physically and figuratively, into what will reveal itself to be the chaotic streets of Manhattan emphasises the tension between the global and the local. DeLillo does not keep Packer in the upper reaches of the corporate office or boardroom but places him in the centre of the local arena on the streets of Manhattan. And it is this journey that leads Packer to reconsider his hegemonic status. At the beginning of the novel Packer is unable to see beyond himself, but as he begins to move at a snail's pace through the streets of Manhattan he begins to notice other people and understand that the world around him has living and breathing people in it, these people have histories, and these people are affected by his moves within the technocapital markets. The plot of this alleged "novel of ideas" takes us back to the dichotomy between the global and the local that envelops the performance of Packer's masculinity in the novel. As Packer exclaims: "I'm a world citizen with a New York pair of balls" (26).

As Packer makes his first steps onto the concrete sidewalk on First Avenue he is met by a line of white limousines. Eric's limo is the centre of his operations and therefore central to his performance as the hegemonic male in global markets. Packer's performance of his global hegemonic masculinity on this day takes place inside his white limo. Packer sits in the club chair in front of an "array of visual display units" (13) that project "medleys of data on every screen" (13), information that Eric absorbs in seconds. The limousine is one of the resonating images from the novel. It is a recognised symbol of social status—of wealth, success, and power. Moreover, I would argue, the limousine is also suggestive of an imperious masculine status:

> He wanted the car because it was not only oversized but aggressively and contemptuously so, metastasizingly so, a tremendous mutant thing that stood astride every argument against it. (10)

If we approach the reading of *Cosmopolis* in terms of the gendered nature of globalization, these white limousines have an even greater sociological significance as representations of the contradictory nature of the visibility, or more accurately, the invisibility, of the global hegemonic male in Manhattan. DeLillo, through his narrator, makes the point of listing the various men who ride in these limousines:

> the investment banker, the land developer, the venture capitalist . . . the software entrepreneur, the global overlord of satellite and cable, the discount broker, the beaked media chief . . . the exiled head of state of some smashed landscape of famine and war. (10)

This list of men is not a gratuitous narrative description—these are hegemonic males who perform their masculinity in global arenas. Furthermore, these are the men who continue to dictate the lives of the everyday citizen in New York City. Shiner, Eric's chief of technology, recognises the local impact of the control and manipulation of these global power discourses when he states:

> "I know there's a thousand things you analyse every ten minutes. Patterns, ratios, indexes, whole maps of information. I love information. This is our sweetness and light. It's a fuck all wonder. And we have meaning in the world. People eat and sleep in the shadow of what we do." (14)

Cosmopolis not only depicts the impact of the network on the individual, that is to say, the complex relationship between the system and the subject; by gendering our reading of *Cosmopolis*, this (counter-)narrative illustrates the gendered nature of neoliberal globalization and the impact of this on the social construction of masculinity. Despite their incredibly and increasingly powerful hegemonic positions, these men move through the streets in complete anonymity. All "identical at a glance" (9), these "long white limousines had become the most unnoticed vehicles in the city" (11). These powerful men are invisible to the everyday person in the streets of Manhattan.

Packer enjoys this anonymity, and safety, in his white limo. As Kinski says, "evilly, [with] eyes alight" (92), when the limo is later under attack by anti-globalization protesters, "'this is controlled anger, I would say. But what would happen if they knew that the head of Packer Capital was in the car?" (91–92). In the global arena, however, Packer strives to be recognised as the most powerful and dominant figure. Packer sees no man above him, not even the man considered to be the most powerful in the world: the president of the United States. Packer's rejection of the president is certainly indicative of the highly competitive nature of hegemonic males competing within the globalized hierarchical framework. Power, and the control of power, is central to Eric's sense of his masculine status. Packer's dismissal of the power of the American president can be read figuratively in terms of the reconfiguration of the world into one globalized stateless society.[26] Eric simply hates the president for being the president:

> He hated Midwood for being omnipresent, as he himself used to be. He hated him for being the object of a credible threat to his safety. And he hated and mocked him for his gynecoid upper body with its swag of dangling mammaries under the sheer white shirt. He looked vengefully at the screen, thinking the image did the president every justice. (76–77)

The association of masculinity with power, or indeed power with masculinity, is underlined by the fact that Packer's approach to belittling Midwood is by feminizing him. Midwood's "gynecoid upper body" is of notable contrast to Packer's "overdeveloped chest" (7), the "swag of dangling mammaries" not living up to Eric's "six per cent body fat" (11). Although Eric despises the image, or indeed the idea, of a president, the reality is that the president of the United States is no direct threat to him. To Eric the president is simply "the undead" (77).

The intricacies and nuances of the construction of Eric's hegemonic masculinity within the global arena are further illustrated in the intense pleasure that Eric takes from the murders of two other global hegemonic males. The first man is Arthur Rapp, the managing director of the International Monetary Fund (33). Rapp is assassinated in North Korea, and his murder is beamed live on the Money channel. Eric watches it over and over again "in obsessive replays" (33):

> He hated Arthur Rapp. He'd hated him before he met him. It was a hatred with the purest blood-lines, orderly, based on differences of theory and interpretation. Then he met the man and hated him personally and chaotically, with sizable violence of heart. (33)

The total detestation that Eric has, or indeed, had, towards Rapp rises from the venomous prose. The pleasure that Eric takes from this spectacle borders on the maniacal: "Eric wanted them to show it again. *Show it again*" (34). There is even a degree of strange sexual gratification that Eric takes from watching the images of Rapp's death on his screen, an element of the performance of global hegemonic masculinity identified by Joan Acker. Acker builds upon Connell's conceptualisation of "trans-national business masculinity" to add her suspicions that "excitement and pleasure, perhaps bordering on the erotic are also part of this hegemonic masculinity, including the intertwined pleasures of technology and power (14).[27] Packer's performance of his sexuality is a major element of his masculinity that is tied up in these issues of technology and power. After the anti-globalization protest and the discussions with his chief of theory Vija Kinski, Eric feels "purified in nameless ways to see prices spiral into lubricious plunge" (106). And the effect on Eric? "Yes, the effect on him was sexual, cunnilingual in particular, and he let his head fall back and opened his mouth to the sky and rain" (106).

The other hegemonic male who is assassinated is Nikolai Kaganovich, "the owner of Russia's largest media conglomerate with interests that ranged from sex magazines to satellite operations" (81). Packer reveals that he and Kaganovich, at one time, were friends and had spent time together tracking wild boar in Siberia. Packer respected Kaganovich for his traditional masculine qualities: "the man was shrewd and tough, cruel in the best sense" (81). And yet, despite their friendship, Packer "was glad to see the man dead in the mud" (81):

> Eric felt good about it, seeing him there, unnumbered bullet wounds to the body and head. It was a quiet contentment, an uneasing of some specifiable pressure in the shoulders and chest. It relaxed him, the death of Nikolai Kaganovich. (82)

Kaganovich is, in many ways, the mirror image of Packer. He is physically strong, rich, dominant, and has the attention of a multitude of women. Kinski emphasises the interconnected nature of these two global forces and, even more importantly, Packer's need to defeat this hegemonic male:

> Your mind thrives on ill will toward others. So does your body, I think. Bad blood makes for long life. He was a rival in some sense, yes? He was physically strong perhaps. He had a large personality. Filthy rich, this chap. Women in his soup. Reasons enough to feel a sneaky sort of euphoria when the man dies horribly. There are always, always reasons. Don't examine the matter. . . . He died so you can live. (82)

Packer's sense of his masculine status, centred in his position as the global hegemonic male, depends upon victory over other hegemonic males. This is what the neoliberal global market demands—the survival of the fittest.

The relationship between Packer and Kaganovich has another level of symbolic significance if we read these figures as hegemonic males representing the old Cold War enemies the United States and Russia. Packer and Kaganovich have an intimate connection, a "brotherhood" as Eric calls it, wherein one could not exist without the other. Packer tells Kinski of a moment when they saw a tiger as they hunted for wild boar which was "a glimpse, a sting of pure transcendence, outside all previous experience" (81). Within the lexicon of world economics and finance a "tiger economy" is the name that was given to the countries of Southeast Asia that grew substantially in the late 1980s and early to mid-1990s due to large amounts of global investment before experiencing a financial crisis that left the majority of wealth in control of an elite few. A "tiger" is also an individual in the investment or business community that is considered aggressive. Packer reflects that this shared experience "made them feel bound to an unspoken code, a brotherhood of beauty and loss" (81). This intimate connection of hegemonic male figures takes us to the reflections of DeLillo's fictionalised J. Edgar Hoover, the director of the FBI, in *Underworld* (1997). As Hoover declares, "It's not enough to hate your enemy. You have to understand how the two of you bring each other to deep completion" (*Underworld* 51). Traditional order and meaning, therefore, particularly in the Cold War era, is constructed around the binary of "us" and "them." Klara Sax in *Underworld* also emphasises the meaning created at one time in this network:

> "Power meant something thirty, forty years ago. It was stable, it was focused, it was a tangible thing. It was greatness, danger, terror, all those things. And it held us together, the Soviets and us. Maybe it held the world together. You could measure things. You could measure hope and you could measure destruction. . . . Many things that were anchored to the balance of power and the balance of terror seem to be undone, unstuck. Things have no limits now. Money has no limits." (76)

The conversation in *Underworld* between Marvin Lundy and Brian Glassic highlights the stabilising structure of these two world powers in binary opposition, and crucially, its pivotal function in the American male's understanding of his position in society. Marvin Lundy forewarns the impact that the end of the Cold War would have, particularly on their masculine status: "And when the cold war goes out of business, you won't be able to look at some women in the street and have a what-do-you-call-it kind of fantasy the way you do today" (182). Marvin's prediction is a warning that the male "privilege" that they enjoy, what Connell calls the "patriarchal dividend" (*Masculinities* 79) that allows men to think and act as they do, "depends on the ability of the two great powers to hang a threat over the planet" (182). The role that these American men enjoy in society, therefore, is inherently connected to the fundamental binarism of these two states, the loss of which would result in the American male becoming, in the words of Lundy, "the lost man of history" (*Underworld* 182).

It is possible, therefore, to read the greater ideological implications of the death of Kaganovich. The breakdown of this binary framework would seem to suggest that the old reference points that dictated the performance of men in the mid-twentieth century have lost their narrative quality. Packer dismisses the power and influence of the Russians—"what Russians?" (103)—in this contemporary era as the multinational corporation has replaced the state and, as such, transformed the global system within which masculinity is constructed. As Connell remarks, "with the collapse of Stalinism and the end of the cold war, Big Brother (Orwell's famous parody of this form of masculinity) is a fading threat, and the more flexible, calculative, egocentric masculinity of the fast capitalist entrepreneur holds the world stage" ("Masculinities and Globalization" 17). Packer's masculinity is shaped, defined, and affirmed within the global market of cyber-capital, and it is in the limo that the discussions take place between Eric and his employees regarding the various issues that impact upon his performance within the world market.

Critiques of *Cosmopolis* read Eric Packer and his team allegorically as figures representing the various dynamics of globalization. As Jerry Varsava states, "Packer and his livery are globalization" (95). This is a fair reading of the function of these characters in the novel. Eric employs various "chiefs"[28] in his corporation. Our understanding of the role of these characters can be taken a step further, however, if we *gender* our reading to consider the implications of the gendered nature of globalization. The first expert is Shiner, Eric's chief of technology. The scene with Shiner underlines Eric's disconnection with other (male) figures in the limo. Eric simply doesn't value these people as human beings: "He did not look at Shiner anymore. He hadn't looked in three years. Once you'd looked there was nothing else to know" (11). Shiner has been with Eric since the very beginning, since the corporation was a "little bitty start up" (12) and yet Eric repeatedly questions Shiner, not trusting Shiner's repeated assertion that the system is secure and they are impenetrable. Eric even goes as far as questioning Shiner's will, within the terms of his masculinity, to do the job. Packer demands to know if Shiner still has the stamina of the single-mindedness to be a success like Packer in the cutthroat world of cyber-capitalism. Eric, displaying his anxiety regarding his hegemonic status, warns Shiner that "the phenomenon of reputation is a delicate thing. A person rises on a word and falls on a syllable" (12).

It is at this point in the novel that we are introduced to one of the major plot points in *Cosmopolis:* Eric's speculation with the Japanese yen. Within the cocoon of his white stretch limo Packer exerts his selfhood in the free market system. It is within this system that Eric finds meaning, both in terms of the behaviour of world finance, and, even more importantly, in his own masculinity. One of the major themes of the novel, as Eric states, is "the interaction between technology and capital. The inseparability" (23). It is in the first section of the novel, inside Eric's limo, that Eric views his masculinity as something inextricably linked to the confluence of technology and capital.

Packer's discussion on the yen continues with his currency analyst Michael Chin. Packer's strategy is to borrow yen at extremely low interest rates and then use this money to speculate on stocks that may yield high returns.[29] Despite Chin's warnings that Packer is "leveraging too rashly" (21) and "speculating into the void" (21), Packer is insistent that there must be a pattern, and therefore this speculation must chart. As Packer preaches, "Don't trust standard models. Think outside the limits. The yen is making a statement. Read it. Then leap" (21). Packer projects total hegemonic characteristics at this point: overconfidence, arrogance, a drive to take even greater risks, and an unwavering self-belief. Despite Chin having "advanced degrees in mathematics and economics" (21–22), Packer refutes this sound advice, as he believes he *is* the system. While Chin decides that he must look into the past in order to try and find a pattern that fits the behaviour of these currencies—"I need to back-test currencies. I don't know, like into the misty dawn" (37)—Packer, as his wife of twenty-two days, Elise Shifrin, points out, can only look to the future:

> "You know things. I think this is what you do," she said. "I think you're dedicated to knowing. I think you acquire information and turn it into something stupendous and awful. You're a dangerous person. Do you agree? A visionary." (19)

With the confluence of technology and capital accelerating his experience of time, Packer not only looks to the future or thinks in the future but also appears to live the future. As he states, "I've never liked thinking back, going back in time, reviewing the day or the week or the life" (184). As such, this incongruence creates a reality in which the market, the self-defining system, is beyond present analysis. Packer cannot accept this, however, as there has to be meaning, there has to be a way to explain why the yen keeps rising:

> The other screens showed money moving. There were numbers gliding horizontally and bar charts pumping up and down. He knew there was something no one had detected, a pattern latent in nature itself, a leap of pictorial language that went beyond the standard model of technical analysis and out-predicted even the arcane charting of his own followers in the field. There had to be a way to explain the yen. (63)

If we take *Cosmopolis,* therefore, to be Packer's journey, both physically and figuratively, through the streets of Manhattan, then the novel, rather than being a cold, abstract novel of ideas is, in fact, a novel about Packer's search for meaning in both the global and the local arenas. For Packer the information on the screens in his limo are more than numbers and figures—he believes that the data are "soulful and glowing, a dynamic aspect of the life process" (24):

> This was the eloquence of alphabets and numeric systems, now fully realised in electronic form, in the zero-oneness of the world, the digital imperative that defined every breath of the planet's living billions. Here was the heave of the biosphere. Our bodies and oceans were here, knowable and whole. (24)

Packer believes in the power of the system, as up to this point in his life it has been the system that has given him the sense of his masculinity.

Taking these readings of the male figures that interact with Packer inside of his limo into consideration, they appear to concede their subordinate status to Packer, displaying their "complicity" with the protagonist. Moreover, the narrative underlines Shiner as "small and boy-faced" (11) and Chin as "only a kid" (23). The limited contention from these subordinate males in Eric's limo is dealt with swiftly. Shiner questions Eric as to why they are in his limo and not his office. When Eric answers defensively, "How do you know we're in the car instead of the office'" (15), Shiner shrinks back and answers, "I know I'll say something that's halfway clever but mostly shallow and probably inaccurate on some level. Then you'll pity me for having been born" (15). Equally, while Chin argues strongly that "what is happening doesn't chart" (21), "we are betting big time here" (21), "we are borrowing enormous, enormous sums" (21), and finally, "Eric, come on. We are speculating into the void" (21), ultimately it is Eric who must be followed: "The two men talked and made decisions. These were Eric's decisions, which Chin entered resentfully in his hand organizer and then synced with the system" (22). Moreover, when Packer questions Chin as to why people still use airports, Chin is sheepish: "I know I can't answer these questions without losing your respect" (22). Connell makes the point that although the hegemonic category dominates the organization of masculinities within a local, or indeed global, framework, very few men actually meet this standard. Yet the majority of men gain from this hegemony and so may not wish to challenge the system, as their masculine status is formed within the system (*Masculinities* 79). When Chin reveals to Eric that he is ready to quit "the business" (23), Eric's retort emphasises his view at this point of the totality of the masculinity affirming nature of the system:

> "Put a stick of gum in your mouth and try not to chew it. For someone your age, with your gifts, there's only one thing in the world worth pursuing professionally and intellectually. What is it, Michael? The interaction between technology and capital. The inseparability." (23)

This brings us back to the debate that underpins globalization, and indeed the construction of masculinity in the globalized system: the issue between the system and singularity. Packer, at this point in the novel, inside of the metaphorical global arena of his limo, is certain that it is the system that shapes his masculine identity.

While the male figures in Eric's white limo appear to accept their complicit subordinate status within the hierarchical framework headed by Eric, the female members of Eric's staff offer a different viewpoint that both challenges the masculine nature of the global system and also forces Eric to consider the dynamics of the system that give him his masculine status. Jane Melman, Eric's chief of finance, is the third expert to enter Eric's limo. Upon sitting down, Melman immediately undermines Eric's power and status by querying the identical nature of the limos. As Eric's eyes narrow, Melman states, "All these limos, my god, that you can't tell one from another. . . . We could be kids on prom night . . . or some dumb wedding wherever. What's the charm of identical?" (39). Eric's ire is evident in his cutting reply: "That I'm a powerful person who chooses not to demarcate his territory with singular driblets of piss is what? Is something I need to apologize for?" (39). Melman continues to challenge the underlying dynamics of globalization that shape Eric's masculinity, stating that she is not "inseparable" from technology: "I like face-to-face. And I don't need to look at all those screens. . . . I know what's happening" (40).

One of the major characters in the novel is Eric's chief of theory Vija Kinski. Paul Giamio (2011), discusses at length the role of Vija Kinski (1–21). Giaimo argues that Kinski lives in "an amoral world" (5), seeing her as a "hanger-on" (5) who is "caught up in the wealth, glamour and excitement" (5) of Packer's domain. This is an incredibly reductive reading of a crucial character in the text. When Giaimo states, "Packer does not in any way benefit from her words" (5), he is criminally overlooking the implications of DeLillo placing this voice in the narrative. While Giaimo sees Kinski's "complex theoretical viewpoint" as hugely "superficial" (6), Kinski has an important role to play in the novel in terms of the significance of these gendered interpretations of globalization.

The first point to make about Kinski is to state the obvious fact that she is female. Having the chief of theory be female, I would suggest, is not a chance happening on DeLillo's part. Previous scenes with Eric and his male members of staff presented these men as being afraid to challenge Packer, to answer his confrontational questions, or assert their opinions. In other words, these passages emphasised the subordinate status of these men. Vija Kinski, on the other hand, is late for their meeting and when she does arrive she sits in Packer's chair while Packer sits looking at her, waiting patiently for her to speak. Moreover Kinski is not introduced indirectly in the novel by the narrator; she bursts into the narrative by taking control of their meeting and giving the order to Packer: "we need to think about the art of money-making" (77).

It is possible to argue that Kinski is another facet of DeLillo's voice in *Cosmopolis*—she is the channel through which DeLillo expresses his views on the performance of Packer. But this does not mean that she is a one-dimensional talking head. Kinski also challenges and undermines Packer's masculinity. Packer's previous encounters with female characters emphasised his sexual objectification of these women. Packer's wife, Elise Shifrin, at least in the early encounters, is nothing more than "great stand-up tits" (18); Didi Fancher is "a scorched blonde" (27); Eric tells Jane Melman that he can see it in her face that she is "lazy, sexy, and insatiable" (49); Kendra Hays is introduced as someone with "coral brown skin and well-defined cheekbones" who "liked to be looked at" (111). Kinski, however, frustrates Packer in resisting this form of objectification. Packer sees Kinski emerging out of the Church of Saint Mary the Virgin and he is unable to tell how old she is (78); her smile is cryptic (78) and private (94); her eyes are unrevealing (104). In the face of this challenge to Packer's "archaic" view of the role of women in his hyper-charged masculine global arena, Packer reverts to an old stereotype of the spinster living alone: "Where was her life? What did she do when she went home? Who was there besides the cat? He thought there had to be a cat" (104–105). Unable to fit Kinski into his concept of understanding the female only in terms of the physical and the sexual, he condemns her as "a voice with a body as afterthought" (105).

Kinski is employed to theorise, that is to say, not merely to analyse the behaviour of the market, or indeed Packer's performance, but to offer an interpretation that transcends the market system and to consider the "abstract linkage" of the philosophies behind globalization. Kinski presents herself as someone who knows nothing about the technological aspect of finance and capital: "I love the screens. The glow of cyber-capital. So radiant and seductive. I understand none of it" (78). Kinski is only interested in theorizing on the grand narratives that are shaping and being shaped by the forces of globalization, namely money and time. In the ever-accelerating globalized cyber-capital world, money is no longer determined by its exchange value; rather, as Kinski argues, "it's cyber-capital that creates the future" (79). This is a major reading in terms of Packer's sense of his masculinity within the global arena. David Harvey, in his reading of the move of society from modernity to postmodernity, argues that in order to fully understand the development of society towards postmodernity it is crucial to grapple with the dynamics of modernization.[30] Harvey frames his reading of the development of modernity around the idea of the shift of the processes of production from "Fordism"[31] to "flexible accumulation."[32] With the development of consumer society, exchange value replaced use value. The loss of the narrative quality of money in *Cosmopolis* is the process of modernization taken to its ultimate extreme. When Patrick takes Kinski out of the limo to look at the electronic display of market information that streaked across a tower on Broadway, Packer reflects:

> The speed is the point. Never mind the urgent and needless replenishment, the way data dissolves at one end of the series just as it takes shape at the other. This is the point, the thrust, the future. We are not witnessing the flow of information so much as pure spectacle, or information made sacred, ritually unreadable. (80)

The role of Kinski should not be overlooked. In theorising on these grand narratives that shape the contemporary era of global society, she is also critiquing the contemporary male condition by identifying it as a historical construct shaped by the grand narratives. Kinski is acutely aware of the masculine nature of the cyber-capital global markets. She is also conscious of the hyper-masculinised battleground and the consequences this has on the global society as a whole. As Kinski says to Packer disdainfully, "'there you sit, of large visions and prideful acts" (105). Kinski further critiques the hyper-charged masculinity of these hegemonic males by reflecting on Packer's need "to act." Discussing the behaviour of the yen and the sound advice that Packer has received that he should back down, Kinski initially appears to support Packer's reckless strategy. As she states, "'if you know something and don't act upon it, then you didn't know it in the first place" (85), offering the piece of Chinese wisdom that "to know and not to act is not to know" (85). Put simply, Kinski is aware that for Packer, "to pull back now would not be authentic" (85). Kinski is knowingly taunting the tenets of Packer's masculine pride. She is goading Packer with the suggestion that not acting would go against everything that Packer stands for in terms of his hegemonic status. And yet by not acting, as Packer himself knows, he will be putting the system before his individual status.

Kinski's ultimate act, after illustrating the dynamics of Packer's masculinity, is to undermine the masculine-affirming structure of the system itself. In place of the "pathology of the state" (85) that characterised the Cold War era, she postulates: "'we create our own frenzy, our own mass convulsions, driven by thinking machines that we have no final authority over. The frenzy is barely noticeable most of the time. It's simply how we live" (85). As she concludes definitively, "'it's all random phenomena. You apply mathematics and other disciplines, yes. But in the end you're dealing with a system that's out of control" (85). Finishing her persuasive speech with a "dirty" laugh that Packer feels is "scornful and coarse" (85), there is the suggestion that Kinski gets some sort of enjoyment from shattering the system that affirms Packer's masculinity. Kinski pushes Packer's buttons and forces him to consider the arbitrary, haphazard, chaotic, or perhaps even "asymmetrical" nature of the system that defines the construction of his masculinity. When Kinski insists he must have been aware of this, Packer reflects, "'he did and did not. Not to this nihilistic degree. Not to the point where all judgements are baseless'" (85). It is at this point, however, that doubts regarding the system begin to surface. This idea of "doubt" is a major development in Packer's anxiety surrounding his hegemonic status. Earlier in the novel, Didi Fancher notices an element of doubt begin to enter Packer's behaviour (31). Packer is incredulous: "'Doubt? What is doubt?' He said, 'There is no doubt. Nobody doubts anymore'" (31). And yet here with Kinski, although he still holds on to the belief that "there's an order at some deep level. . . . 'A pattern that wants to be seen" (86), Packer begins to admit to himself, "'in this case I'm beginning to doubt I'll ever find it" (86).

Kinski leaves Packer with her final comment that illustrates clearly her awareness of the gendered nature of globalization. The global arena, since the beginning of civilization, has been dominated by these masculine drives:

> "Men think about immortality. Never mind what women think. We're too small and real to matter here," she said. "Great men historically expected to live forever even as they supervised construction of their monumental tombs on the far bank of the river, the west bank, where the sun goes down." (105)

First, Kinski's downplay of the role of women should be read as her subtle irony to further satirise the American male's, and indeed Packer's, sense of masculine self-importance. Kinski's reading echoes Connell's view that gender, and from that we can say therefore masculinity, is a historical construct embedded in the processes of the modern gender order throughout the course of history.

The climatic moment in the passage between Packer and Kinski is the anti-globalization protest that takes place as they sit cocooned in the stretch limo. The protest, clearly based on the riots that took place in November 1999 in reaction to the World Trade Organization summit in Seattle, is the opportunity for Kinski to reach the crux of her analysis of the relationship between the individual and the system. While Eric enjoys the spectacle of the protest, which he watches on the screens in his limo as "it made more sense on TV" (89), Kinski makes the point:

> "This is the free market itself. These people are a fantasy generated by the market. They don't exist outside the market. There is nowhere they can go to be on the outside. There is no outside. . . . The market culture is total. It breeds these men and women. They are necessary to the system they despise. They give it energy and definition. They are market-driven. They are traded on the markets of the world. This is why they exist, to invigorate and perpetuate the system." (90)

DeLillo employs Kinski to present the case that the system is total. In other words, there is no agency within the neoliberal market system. Despite Packer's earlier belief in the all-defining power of the system in his discussions with Michael Chin (24), there is an emerging sense of tension in terms of Packer's idea of the male's degree of agency within the system. Packer's answer to Kinski's reading is the "man on fire" (97) outside of the limo. Packer, a clinically self-involved character who displays no sympathy towards any "other" up to this point in the novel, connects with the man in flames. Putting his head outside of the limo, Packer watches the man only thirty yards away and sees beyond the spectacle to grasp a sense of this man's pain and the thought processes that lead him to this decision:

> Eric wanted to imagine the man's pain, his choice, the abysmal will he'd had to summon. He tried to imagine him in bed, this morning, staring sideways at a wall, thinking his way toward the moment. Did he have to go to a store and buy a box of matches? He imagined a phone call to someone far away, a mother or lover. (98–99)

Later, in the final confrontation with Levin, Eric even imagines himself "in the body, was the body, looking out through gas and flame" (195). Eric, possibly for the first time in the novel, "sees" another person in Manhattan. Packer's inability to "see" others, particularly the faces of others, is one of the leitmotifs of *Cosmopolis*. There are many examples of this in the novel. When Packer analyses the face of Ingram, his doctor's assistant, for the first time, he realises that the man "had a moustache, for example. Eric hadn't seen it until now" (45). Packer notices that his wife Elise is not as beautiful as he had believed she would be (120). When Packer learns the name of one of his bodyguards he states, "now that he knew Danko's name, he could see him, partially" (125). Furthermore after he murders Torval, his chief of security, Packer looks at his driver Ibrahim Hamadou for the first time (157). At this moment, however, rather than seeing people as data and numbers on a screen, he puts his head outside of the limo to connect with the suffering of the people on the streets of Manhattan. It is this act that forces Eric to consider the dynamics of the system. Eric, at one point, agreed with Kinski that the protest was a "market fantasy" (99), a "transaction" (99) between the individual and the market. Eric "thought there was something theatrical about the protest, ingratiating, even, in the parachutes and skateboards, the styrofoam rat, in the tactical coup of reprogramming the stock tickers with poetry and Karl Marx" (99). He believed that the protest proved once more "the market culture's innovative brilliance" (99). However, Packer, observing this man on fire with his own eyes in his city streets, sees the individual in the market in a new light: "The market was not total. It could not claim this man or assimilate his act. Not such starkness and horror. This was a thing outside its reach" (99–100).

The man setting himself alight is an extreme demonstration that the Manhattan male still holds on to a sense of agency in the ability to make decisions and take actions that are outside of the parameters of market forces. Kinski senses Packer's reaction towards the incident but rejects it: "It's not original . . . It's an appropriation . . . All those Vietnamese monks, one after another, in all their lotus position . . . Immolating themselves endlessly . . . It's not original" (100). Packer, a man once insistent on the reality, and indeed the originality, of the pain the man must have felt in taking the decision to make his point to the system: "He did a serious thing. He took his life. Isn't this what you have to do to show them that you're serious?" (100). At this point in the narrative this is a subtle hint at the trajectory of Packer as he moves towards his final meeting with his alter ego, Benno Levin. Being a hegemonic male, the centre of the system, a faceless focus of power in the global arena is what defines Eric's existence. However, from the very first page of the novel, it is evident that Eric is not entirely comfortable with this role. It is affecting his health and well-being. Unable to sleep and with no friends to call to talk about his problems, this is the impact of his global identity on his local day-to-day existence. Looking back upon the opening pages of the novel it is now noticeable that Eric moved through the apartment "walking slowly now, and paused in every room, absorbing what was there, deeply seeing, retaining every fleck of energy in rays and waves" (8). As the narrator reveals, "he did this when he felt hesitant and depressed" (7). Before constructing his masculine identity in the global transnational markets, Packer was, and still is, a Manhattan male. The narrative is Eric's journey towards regaining a sense of his local identity within the global system. Critics have argued that DeLillo's work emphasises the totality of the system, the all-encompassing nature of the global network. If

Packer is considered the head of the system, then his journey is his counter-hegemonic reaction against this role by returning to where his family came from in Manhattan in the once working-class area of Hell's Kitchen. Certain analyses of *Cosmopolis* argue that a "death drive" (Dix 132) underpins Eric's narrative. A more useful reading can be found if we gender the novel and consider Packer's narrative as his journey towards a rediscovery of his masculine status. What DeLillo is writing is not only a counter-narrative but a counter-hegemonic narrative. It is at this point in the novel, following the discussion with Kinski, that Packer begins to move from the global arena within the white stretch limo to plant his feet firmly on the streets of Manhattan in the local arena and "begin the business of living" (107).

THE GLOBAL HEGEMONIC MALE AS FLÂNEUR ON THE STREETS OF MANHATTAN

The reconsideration of Eric's global hegemonic masculinity begins readily in part 2 of *Cosmopolis*. It is at this point that Eric destabilises his hegemonic position by borrowing even more yen and "watching his fund's numbers sink into the mist on several screens" (115). The effect on Eric is crucial here: "The yen spree was releasing Eric from the influence of his neocortex" (115). The neocortex, the outer layer of the two cerebral hemispheres and part of the cerebral cortex, is involved with higher functions such as sensory perception, motor commands, spatial reasoning, conscious thought, and language. In chapter 3 of *Cosmopolis,* Eric is consciously cutting himself off from the system that has defined him up to this point, feeling "freer than usual, attuned to the registers of his lower brain and gaining distance from the need to take inspired action, make original judgements, maintain independent principles and convictions, all the reasons why people are fucked up and birds and rats are not" (115). The self-centred nature of Packer's character is still evident, however, in his awareness of the impact that this will have. His interconnectivity to the behaviour of the whole system is emphasised as the market begins to falter with these actions: "He was so leveraged, his firm's portfolio large and sprawling, linked crucially to the affairs of so many key institutions, all reciprocally vulnerable, that the whole system was in danger" (116). Packer, rather short-sightedly, plays down his role in these "storms of disorder" (116), believing that the global financial system will recover in "a day or two" (116).

There are various interconnected acts that Eric commits in the second part of *Cosmopolis* that underline his attempt to break free from the system and the global hegemonic status. Eric and his wife of twenty-two days, Elise Shifrin, break up (122). In an act of masculine pride, Eric loses all of Elise's money to make sure that she cannot help him (123), this move a rejection of their image as "one of the great arranged marriages of old empire Europe" (26).[33] At the funeral of Brutha Fez, a Sufi rapper, Eric experiences a sense of bliss after losing his money within the throngs of people: "Eric's delight in going broke seemed blessed and authenticated here. He'd been emptied of everything but a sense of surpassing stillness, a fatedness that felt disinterested and free" (136). After the scene in the barbershop Eric decides to sit up front with his driver Ibrahim and cuts off all means of communication with the complex (170), the complex being "the intelligence unit" (58) of Packer Capital. Finally, Eric shoots his bodyguard Torval. His reasoning is clear: "Torval was his enemy, a threat to his self-regard. When you pay a man to keep you alive, he gains a psychic edge" (147).[34] As Eric reflects, all these actions have "cleared the night for deeper confrontation" (148). On a literal level this "confrontation" obviously points to Eric's final scene with Benno Levin. Taken figuratively, in terms of Eric's journey in the novel, the final confrontation is that with his own hegemonic masculine status.

Throughout the narrative Packer looks outside of his limo—in other words outside of the global arena—to the people in the streets of the metropolis. New York is his city, and Packer comes to realise the act of seeing and understanding the city is the process of understanding himself. In the first part of the novel there are subtle hints at the impact of the role of flâneur on Packer's selfhood. Sitting in the limo with Jane Melman, Packer, obviously concerned about the yen and his hegemonic status, looks wistfully out of the window at the "streaming people" (41): "These were scenes that normally roused him, the great rapacious flow, where the physical will of the city, the ego fevers, the assertions of industry, commerce and crowds shape every anecdotal moment" (41). Place has always been a major element in DeLillo's fiction, and the Manhattan of *Cosmopolis* is a powerful fluid organism. If the global arena in *Cosmopolis* is the centre of the post-industrial technocapitalist era, Manhattan is presented, at the local level, as the industrial arena of commerce, a melting pot of races, ethnicities, and religions. Eric watches the Hasidim trading on the streets and imagines the hundreds of millions of dollars passing hands, "a form of money so obsolete Eric didn't know how to think about it" (64). These men, alongside the black men wearing signboards, are presented as if traders from biblical times: "the hagglers and talebearers, the scrapmongers, the dealers in stray talk" (65). Eric's flâneurial watchings are sensitive to the energy of the people moving through these streets, and it is by observing these people that Packer looks beyond his identity in the cocoon of his white limo: "He wanted to understand, to separate one thing from another through detailed observation" (87). When breaking up with his wife, Elise, Packer admits that he is doing so as he realises that what is important is "to be aware of what's around me. To understand another person's situation, another person's feelings. To know, in short, what's important" (121). What DeLillo's critique of the global hegemonic male suggests is that by looking away from the data of the screen, Packer becomes aware of the dynamics of his hegemonic status and looks to write his individual counter-hegemonic narrative in Manhattan.

The first scene in which Packer becomes "the man of the crowd" is at the funeral of Brutha Fez. Packer is a huge fan of the African American rapper who performed "ancient Sufi music, rapping in Punjabi and Urdu and in the black-swagger English of the street" (133). Yet Brutha Fez's actual name is Raymond Gathers and, born in the Bronx, he is a fellow New Yorker. Brutha Fez is the embodiment of the multicultural Manhattan male in the global city, "a singular rapper," in Eric's eyes, "who mixed languages, tempos and themes" (134). Eric, is his flâneurial role, notes the juxtaposition of the cultures that Fez represents. While "scores of women walked alongside the limousines, in headscarves and djellabas, hands stained with henna, and barefoot, and wailing" (133), there are also Fez's bodyguards "in Western dress, dark suits and ties, polished oxfords, with combat shotguns held at port arms" (133). Eric notices the subtle changes in atmosphere in the crowd, the "melancholy . . . more regret than excitation" (134), as "even the younger people seemed subdued, over-respectful" (134). Eric reports on the number of mourners following the hearse, a selection of all sections of society including Fez's family, friends, the New York City mayor, the police commissioner, members of Congress, fellow rappers, media executives, foreign dignitaries, famous faces from TV and film, and members of world religions (134–135). Throughout the novel Eric projects his identity as a true global hegemonic male without considering his roots lying in Manhattan. As an observer of this spectacle of mass mourning, Eric comes to reflect upon his connections with others in the city:

> Then he thought about his own funeral. He felt unworthy and pathetic. Never mind the bodyguards, four versus three. What set of elements might be configured that could possibly match what was happening here? Who would come to see him laid out? (136)

Packer is clear in the idea of the people who would come to his funeral: "Men he'd crushed, to nourish their rancour. Those he'd presumed to be wallpaper, to stand over him and gloat" (136). And yet here watching the people "in communal grace" (138), he breaks down and begins to weep violently. Eric, the man who had no friends to call upon in the first page of the novel as he spent another night awake alone, is embraced by another mourner, Kozmo Thomas, a manager of many rappers who had owned a stable of horses with Eric: "Then Kozmo wrapped an arm around him and drew him in. It did not seem strange that this was happening. When people die, you weep" (139). It is notable that Eric needs to process consciously these most basic human emotions and justify them to himself, but finally Packer makes a human connection here on the streets of Manhattan.[35]

Packer's connection with the people of Manhattan is explored further in a typical DeLillian trope of the movie scene. Packer, making his way to Hell's Kitchen, sees a movie being filmed with "three hundred naked people sprawled in the street" (172). Eric is amazed by the vulnerability of these people who have both literally and metaphorically stripped themselves of all the symbolic signs that project their social status: "They were a sight to come upon, a city of stunned flesh, the bareness, the bright lights, so many bodies unprotected and hard to credit in a place of ordinary human transit" (172). Eric feels the pull to take off his clothes, leave them on the sidewalk, and connect with these people, "more naked than ever in their lives" (173). Eric once believed that the power of number and figures on a screen "defined every breath of the planet's living billions" (24), but in the symbolic departure from the limo, Eric is now realising the true essence of the human condition: "He felt that presence of the bodies, all of them, the body breath, the heat and running blood" (174). Lying here together, "people unlike each other who were now alike, amassed, heaped in a way, alive and dead together . . . the experience was a strong one, so total and open he could barely think outside it" (174). The fact that Packer "could barely think outside it" is a clever turn of phrase by DeLillo that echoes back to the theme of the relationship between the individual and the system that underpins Eric's understanding of the construction of his selfhood. Lying alongside others stripped of all their symbols of wealth, class, or ethnicity, Eric truly feels as one with the people of Manhattan. Closing his eyes he imagines the people as the camera sees them. He imagines the different bodies, the young and strong, the middle-aged and obese, the children. Eric wants to be there with them. Throughout this passage the refrain resonates: "He was one of them"; "He was one" (176).

One major element of the performance of Packer's masculinity is his sexuality, and it is at this moment that it is resolved in the novel. Despite the fact that the narrative takes place over the course of one day, Packer has time to have sexual encounters with four different women. The sexual encounters are mere transactions for Packer. In the first encounter, with the art critic Didi Fancher, they keep their clothes on, a symbolic act that underlines their disengagement: "they did not get serious about undressing until they were finished making love" (25). The sense of detachment in Packer's sexual activities also features in his encounter with one of his bodyguards, Kendra Hays. Packer defines her by her ZyloFlex body armour, asking her to keep it on while they have sex (111). The disconnection in these sexual episodes reaches its crux in the encounter with his chief of finance, Jane Melman. It is in this scene that Packer, with his sunglasses on no less, proceeds to give Melman his theory on the impact of sex on the performance of their identities: "Sex finds us out. Sex sees through us. That's why it's so shattering. It strips us of appearances" (50). Packer feels himself getting serious, reflecting intensely on his masculinity: "Is his manhood a sham? Does he love himself or hate himself? I don't think he knows. Or it changes minute to minute. Or the question is so implicit in everything he does that he can't get outside it to answer" (51). Inside the limo, in the centre of the system, in the interconnected web of power, capital, and technology, sex is something that appears to transcend the physical. As Eric theorises, "they don't even need to touch"

(51). Sex is something "beyond every model of established behaviour. He only has to say the words" (51). Like a digital transaction, sex is something abstract: "then man and woman reached completion more or less together, touching neither each other nor themselves" (52). Packer performs Connell's reading of the global hegemonic male's "growing tendency to commodify relations with women" ("Masculinities and Globalization" 16). It is this scene that fully underlines the condition of Packer's masculinity inside his white limo. There he is, the Manhattan male who is paradoxically connected to every element in the global system and yet detached from basic human contact. And yet, outside the cocoon of the limo, in the streets of Manhattan, Packer finally connects with his wife, Elise, a true connection that is of notable symbolic contrast to Eric's earlier sexual encounters.

Critics have rejected DeLillo's work, in particular *Cosmopolis,* for being nothing more than a "novel of ideas."[36] And yet, as Jerry A. Varsava rightly states, "novels of ideas invariably offer a limited number of highly concentrated scenes in which given themes and issues are more or less systematically interrogated through philosophical dialogue and social commentary" (92). The scene with Elise is one of these. Standing naked together, Eric and Elise are stripped of all that defines them. Packer reveals that he lost all of Elise's money, but she laughs it away with "her body fused to his" (178), saying "'what do poets know about money? Love the world and trace it in a line of verse" (178). It does seem, to use Updike's words in his review of *Cosmopolis,* "implausible" that Elise would simply laugh at the fact that Packer has lost her fortune. It might be possible to read this as Elise's rejection of the significance that Packer associates with financial wealth. But it is here, naked in the movie scene, that Eric is finally truly intimate with his wife Elise. They finally connect as "two lovers in isolation, free of memory and time" (177). It is here that Packer realises that he loves her but, at that very moment, she slips out of his arms and disappears.

Cosmopolis is the journey of Eric Packer into his past. Whereas Packer in the global arena defines himself by obsessively "thinking past what is new" and wanting "to be one civilization ahead of this one" (152), Eric's desire to get a haircut and return to the barbershop in Hell's Kitchen is driven by his desire to understand himself. Eric goes to the barbershop to hear stories about his father, a man who died when Eric was five years old. The scene in the barbershop is reminiscent of an old man's club, a traditional place of male camaraderie. Eric goes there to talk to Anthony Adubato, the man who first cut Eric's hair when Eric's father brought him here as a kid. The inclusive nature of this social club is underlined when Eric invites his driver, Ibrahim Hamadou, to join them. While in the first section of the novel Eric reveals that he "did not look at the driver" (32), he invites him to share food, drink, and stories about their lives. Anthony and Ibrahim reminisce about their time driving cabs around Manhattan in their attempts to live up to the breadwinner role to support their wives and children, a million miles away from Eric's experience as a Manhattan male. In contrast to Eric's position of the hegemonic male sitting at the back of his limo controlling the global markets of finance, these men drove their cabs all day and all night, even eating at the wheel and only stopping to use the bathroom, in order to provide a service to the people of Manhattan.

While Eric, in the first part of the novel, projects the image of the hypermasculine hegemonic male within the global market who believes in the centrality of traditional masculine traits such as ruthlessness, competitiveness, and taking risks, Anthony subverts this image by stating that Eric actually got his intelligence from his mother: "Your mother was the brains of the outfit. That's where you get your mentality. Your mother had the wisdom" (162). As Kinski also points out to Packer, "Your genius and your animus have always been fully linked" (82), a comment that appears as a play on the double meaning of *animus* as a feeling of hostility towards others (which Eric clearly displays against the other hegemonic males in the global markets), as well as the *animus,* in Jungian psychology, being the unconscious feminine psychological qualities that a male possesses. It is here within the security of these men talking about the men they once were, with their voices "becoming a single vowel sound" (165), that Eric finally drops off to sleep. Upon awaking, and continuing their bonding conversation, Eric, feeling comfortable in their presence, "confided in them" (166) about the threat to his safety. Despite being cocooned in the limo, with numerous high-tech security measures in place, it is in this place of Packer's past that Eric truly feels safe. This feeling of safety comes not only from detaching himself from the world but from connecting with these two other Manhattan men from distinctive classes, cultures, and religious backgrounds in the archetypal male social club of the barbershop: "It felt right to expose the matter in this particular place, where elapsed time hangs in the air, suffusing solid objects and men's faces. This is where he felt safe" (166). The only thing left for Eric is his haircut. As they slip into typical barbershop conversation, Eric, imitating himself as a boy when his father had to hold him down for Anthony to cut his hair, suddenly jumps up out of the seat with his asymmetrical haircut, exclaiming, "I need to leave. I don't know how come. That's how come" (169). It is at this point that Eric Packer's journey into understanding the dynamics of his global hegemonic masculinity reaches its climax.

FINAL CONFRONTATION WITH BENNO LEVIN

It is in the final scene with Richard Sheets, or as he prefers to be known, Benno Levin, that Eric comes face-to-face with his hegemonic status in Manhattan. Richard Sheets was a one-time employee at Packer Capital.[37] In contrast to Eric Packer trying to return to his Manhattan identity, Richard Sheets creates an alias in an attempt to escape from the hierarchical framework in Manhattan. DeLillo has revealed that he chose the name as "[Sheets] would use a name that would sound like a European anarchist or revolutionary from the early 20th century" (Krasny). Levin makes his first appearance in the novel with his self-penned diary, entitled "The Confessions of Benno Levin" (55). A secondary narrative acting as a counterpoint to the main narrative is a recurring feature in DeLillo's more recent works, namely *Underworld* and *Falling Man*. DeLillo plays with the temporality of these narratives: while Packer's story is characterised by his insistence on not only speculating or predicting the future but actually seeing the future, Benno Levin's diary entries are reflective pieces on his past. But there is something more to these parallel storylines. While Packer's narrative is that of the hegemonic male separated from the gritty reality of Manhattan, Levin's story is that of the everyday male, the subordinate within the great hierarchical framework, not only in Packer Capital but also in the great metropolis of Manhattan. Ultimately, these two separate strands dovetail in the final confrontation between the two contrasting male figures in the derelict building that Benno Levin calls home.

Reading the final passage in *Cosmopolis* as the final confrontation between two opposing masculinities underlines its similarities with the work of another New York writer: Paul Auster. *Cosmopolis* is dedicated to Paul Auster, and the thread of the novel featuring Benno Levin is conspicuously Austeresque. There are many similarities in the sensibility of these two New York writers that stand out in terms of their depictions of contemporary masculinity. The act of writing as a form of self-actualisation is a recurring theme in Auster's work. The prototypical Austerian protagonist is the detached Manhattan male writing alone in a room with only his words as his way of reflecting upon his existence. Likewise in *Cosmopolis* we find Benno Levin, alone in a derelict room, writing what he calls his "mind speeches" (57). Just as in Auster's fictional worlds, for Levin the act of writing is a form of self-study. Levin reveals that he wrote letters to Packer knowing that Packer would never read them. This does not matter to Levin, as "the fact that he would never see the letters was not an issue. I would see them. The issue was writing them and seeing them myself" (59). As Levin later admits:

> I think about myself too much. I study myself. It sickens me. But this is all there is to me. I'm nothing else. My so-called ego is a little twisted thing that's probably not so different from yours but at the same time I can say confidently that it's active and bursting with importance and has major defeats and triumphs all the time. (60–61)

The Packer/Benno Levin doubling echoes the construction of male figures in Auster's fiction. As I will come to discuss in the subsequent paragraphs, Levin's very masculine existence is affirmed in his relation to the hegemonic male Packer. The final battle between these two Manhattan males echoes the climactic confrontation that occurs at the end of Auster's most widely regarded work, *The New York Trilogy* (1987). The final confrontation between the unnamed narrator and Fanshawe in *The Locked Room*, the third instalment of the trilogy, is Auster's dramatization of the conflict between the opposing hegemonic and counter-hegemonic masculinities. Auster employs these characters in his fictionalisation of the conflicts and tensions that underpin the experience of the contemporary American father. Likewise the final scene in *Cosmopolis* is DeLillo's final confrontation between two conflicting models of Manhattan masculinity: the global hegemonic male and the everyday Manhattanite.

Levin's first-person narrated "Confessions" underlines the contrast in masculine status between these two men. Levin sees Packer as a Manhattan male who "did not really separate life and work" (56). Levin, evoking the role of a Manhattan flâneur, reveals that he watched Packer obsessively both on screen and in the street. Packer is affirmed not only as the hegemonic male but also as the male figure against which Levin judges the status of his own masculinity: "It was important to know where he was, even for a moment. It put my world in order" (151). Levin sees himself as Eric's "human sensor, reading his thoughts, knowing the man in his mind" (153). Levin suggests the historical nature of Packer's hegemonic behaviour in likening it to old tribal chiefs: "In the old tribes the chief who destroyed more of his property than the other chiefs was the most powerful" (193–194). Levin is suggesting the historical precedent of this performance of hegemonic masculinity, a performance that has defined the social construction of masculinity throughout history.

In contrast to Packer's hegemonic masculine status, Levin is the everyman. A former assistant professor of computer applications, he left his job to chase the American dream: "to make my million" (56). He had a normal job and was married briefly but "struggled to love and provide" (55). Levin experienced the great difficulty of living up to the archetypal masculine role of the breadwinner: "How many of you know the true and bitter force of that simple word provide?" (55). As Levin reveals, "I used to look at her child, who was barely out of infancy, and think I'd fallen down a hole" (150). Levin provided Packer Capital with "generic labour" (60) and was demoted to work with the baht. In that subordinate role he felt "derived": "I felt inserted there, a person in a situation not of his choosing, even though I'd made the choice to be there" (153–154). Levin wallows in his subordinate status. He feels he has nothing to live for (194). He ultimately feels lost in the technocapitalist system: "I'm helpless in their system that makes no sense to me. You wanted me to be a helpless robot soldier but all I could be was helpless" (195). As he tells Packer in their final scene, "I began to hate my work, and you, and all the numbers on my screen, and every minute of my life" (191). While Packer's sense of the time and space is shaped by the confluence of technology and capital, Levin thinks of his "personal time-span set against the vast numerations, the time of the earth, the stars, the incoherent light-years, the age of the universe, etc." (59–60). In contrast to Packer who sees twentieth-century technology as "archaic" (6), for Levin, "cash machines have a charisma that still speaks to me" (60). He feels that his "sex organ" (192), the symbol of his masculinity and manhood, is receding into his body (192). Finally, when Packer questions Levin about the name of an attachment on his gun, Levin replies, "All right. I don't have the manhood to know these names. Men know these names. You have the experience of manhood. I can't think that far ahead. It's all I can do to be a person" (196).

The flâneurial theme that underpins *Cosmopolis* also features in the final confrontation between these two male figures. When Packer enters the room, he is unable to "see" Levin. When Levin asks, "do you recognise me?" Packer responds, "I can't see you clearly" (187). In contrast to Packer, who believed that nothing existed outside of his hegemonic self, Levin believes that identity, or masculinity, is created in how other people "see" the person: "I was always aware of what they said in words or looks. It is what people think they see in another person that makes his reality" (57). Despite appearing at times indistinguishable, their divergent places within the masculine hierarchy are reaffirmed. When Levin reveals his real name is Richard Sheets, Packer's remark that it meant nothing to him gives him "a trace of the old stale pleasure, dropping an offhand remark that makes a person feel worthless" (192). At this stage of his journey, however, Packer is aware of the impact of such hegemonic behaviour when he states, "so small and forgettable a thing that spins such disturbance" (192).

Despite these distinct differences, at various points during their conversation these two figures appear to merge and become indistinguishable from each other. When "the man" fires a shot into the ceiling, the narrator has to state, "Not Eric; the other, the subject" (187). They also share a similar physical affliction: their prostates are asymmetrical. When Levin reveals that having an asymmetrical prostate "means nothing. . . . It's harmless. A harmless variation" (199), this brings them together for a brief moment, transcending their socially shaped roles in society. But Levin uses the symbolic power of this asymmetry to undermine Packer's hegemonic behaviour, that is, his obsession with being all powerful and all knowing:

> "The importance of the lopsided, the thing that's skewed a little. You were looking for balance, beautiful balance, equal parts, equal sides. I know this. I know you. But you should have been tracking the yen in its tics and quirks. The little quirk. The misshape." (200)

Levin, the subordinate male figure, reveals to Packer that it is his search for perfection that has led to his failing. Levin barrages Packer for his hegemonic behaviour: "The huge ambition. The contempt. I can list the things. I can name the appetites, the people. Mistreat some, ignore some, persecute others. The self-totality. The lack of remorse. These are your gifts" (191). In Levin's mind, it is Packer's global hegemonic position that justifies the killing:

> "Even if a fungus told me to kill you, even then your death is justified because of where you stand on the earth . . . you're a figure whose thoughts and acts affect everybody, people, everywhere. I have history, as you call it, on my side. You have to die for how you think and act. . . . For how much you had and how much you lost, equally. No less for losing it than making it." (202)

It is Packer's hegemonic behaviour, rather than his wealth, that drives Levin's desire to eliminate Packer. It is Packer's self-construction as a global hegemonic male that motivates Levin to assassinate him. As Levin retorts absurdly, this act is justified "for the limousine that displaces the air that people need to breathe in Bangladesh. This alone" (202). Packer, following his journey through Manhattan, tries to tell Levin on two occasions (202?203) that his mind-set has changed, that the move from the global arena of the limo to the local streets has had an effect on his view of his Manhattan roots. Even if we look at the moment in which Eric shoots himself in the hand, Eric does so after feeling "enormous remorseful awareness" (196). Sitting there, thinking of "others down the years, hazy and nameless" (196), Eric appears to feel a sense of regret or contrition for his performance as the global hegemonic male in Manhattan: "It moved through him, called guilt, and strange how soft the trigger felt against his finger" (196). There is a sense of counter-hegemonic awareness at this time and a degree of inevitability surrounding the final moments of Packer's existence in the streets of Manhattan.

As with Fanshawe and the unnamed narrator in Auster's *The Locked Room,* there is undoubtedly an intimate connection between these men. As Levin reveals, "I wanted you to heal me, to save me . . . I wanted you to save me" (204). It is at this moment of a "terrible intimacy, a nearness of feeling and experience that Eric could not reciprocate" (204) that Eric looks at his watch and sees the body of a man, his body, in long shot on the screen. Looking at the watch again he sees the inside of an ambulance and the body tagged Male Z. It is at this moment that Packer reflects upon the tenets of the technocapitalist desire to transcend his body mass:

> It was the natural next step. It would never happen. It is happening now, an evolutionary advance that needed only the practical mapping of the nervous system onto digital memory. It would be the master thrust of cyber-capital, to extend the human experience toward infinity as a medium for corporate growth and investment, for the accumulation of profits and vigorous reinvestment. (207)

However, the fundamental feature of the human condition—pain—interferes with this philosophy. Following his experience among the naked bodies in the movie scene, Packer realises at this moment that pain is "crucial to his distinctiveness, too vital to be bypassed and not susceptible, he didn't think, to computer emulation" (207). At this final moment Packer reflects, "the things that made him who he was could hardly be identified much less converted to data" (207). It is at this moment, the moment of his apparent death no less, that Packer finally recognises that what defines him is not his self-made global hegemonic identity, but his roots as a Manhattan male.

Cosmopolis is clearly a novel that sets out to critique the discourses of globalization and their impact upon the island of Manhattan. Manhattan aspires to be the globalized city through the control and manipulation of the world's financial markets. And yet, despite the novel being named *Cosmopolis,* i.e., "world city," it is important that we do not let this cloud the fundamental significance of the Manhattan dimension and the importance of this local arena in Eric Packer's understanding of his masculinity. The very narrative of the novel takes Eric from the upper reaches of this global city in his penthouse suite to the gritty streets of Hell's Kitchen. This narrative development is a journey that resonates on three interconnected levels: first, the main premise of the novel is Eric's journey from the upper-class East Side of Manhattan to the working-class area of Hell's Kitchen on the West Side of the island; second, it is a journey into Eric's past as he returns to his roots to remember where both he and his father came from; and third, it is also a journey into Eric's sense of his masculine selfhood. These three elements dovetail and drive the narrative towards Eric's realisation that despite his creation of the global hegemonic male persona, he is in essence still a Manhattan male.

Taking a look at the naming of the protagonist, Packer, adds weight to this reading. DeLillo's choice of the name Packer hints at the working-class element of this Manhattanite in its suggestion of "packer" in terms of meatpacker or dockworker. Eric's father was clearly proud of the Packer family's working-class background, and Eric's return to Hell's Kitchen is his attempt to feel a sense of that pride as a working-class Manhattan family. As Eric reflects, "this had never been his home or street" (159); but this is where the Packer name comes from and Eric feels compelled to return to this place to "let the street breathe on him" (159). Eric's flâneurial journey into this area of Manhattan has a simple yet significant objective. Packer's journey in the novel is his attempt to reconnect with the Manhattan dimension in his identity. Eric offers acute flâneurial observations that serve to contrast where he now lives in the East Side and where he came from here in Hell's Kitchen: "The garbage cans here were battered metal not the gentrified rubber products on the streets to the east" (158). He sees "the truck lot lying empty" (158), "two cars parked on the sidewalk, shrouded in torn blue tarp" (158), and, hinting at Hell's Kitchen's history as a place where immigrants would come to try and follow their "American Dream," he sees "steel shutters marked with graffiti in Spanish and Arabic" (159). Eric stands in front of the "grim building" (159) where his father once lived but imagines the life and energy of the people that lived here in his pocket of Manhattan together:

"It was a grim street but people used to live here in loud close company, in railroad flats, and happy as anywhere, he thought, and still did, and still were" (159). With the death of his father when he was a boy, it was Eric who was left to carry the Packer name. Despite still living in Manhattan, Eric's performance in the transnational financial markets has resulted in the name Packer becoming synonymous with Eric's global hegemonic identity, "Packer Capital." As Packer stands on the gritty street watching all around him, "he was feeling what his father would feel, standing in this place" (159). Eric's desire to get "a haircut," therefore, is Eric's return to where the Packer name originated in Manhattan to shed the hegemonic identity that had come to define him.

CONCLUSION

Cosmopolis is Eric Packer's journey towards counter-hegemonic enlightenment. Inside the white stretch limo, Packer's masculinity is characterised by his literal and figurative detachment from other individuals in Manhattan. It is in the act of stepping outside of the limo and adopting the role of flâneur that Packer not only begins to "see" other people in Manhattan, but also to see himself. It is in becoming a flâneur that Packer observes the impact of his performance as a hegemonic male in Manhattan. As a global financier Packer's masculinity is shaped through his drive towards not only speculating on the future but also actively seeing the future. Packer's pathway towards a sense of self-awareness is to return to his past. At first reading, Packer's wish to get a haircut on the other side of town appears absurd; and yet, by approaching the novel as an illustration of the contemporary hegemonic male, the desire to get a haircut appears as Packer's desire to look beyond his place at the centre of a system and understand where he came from and who he actually is.

There is no question that DeLillo has created Packer in order to explore the impact of the grand narratives linked to globalization on the contemporary hegemonic Manhattan male. This need not mean, however, that Packer is a cipher or a one-dimensional device; rather, as this critical reading of *Cosmopolis* has demonstrated, Packer is a complex character who must work through the conflicts and tensions that define the experience of the contemporary global hegemonic Manhattan male. Gendering Packer's performance—his performance within the world markets, his relationships with other hegemonic and subordinate males, his relationships with his female colleagues, his off-kilter relationship with his wife, and perhaps most critically of all, his connection to Benno Levin—underscores the gendered nature of globalization and the impact of this upon the performance of his masculinity in the globalized and globalizing island of Manhattan. The inevitability that appears to underpin Packer's move towards his final confrontation should not be dismissively read as Packer's "death drive"; conversely, engaging in a gendered reading of *Cosmopolis* underlines Packer's narrative as his desire to know himself, in other words, to look beyond the world that he defines inside of the stretch white limo, and in these Manhattan streets, as he makes his way to the final confrontation with Richard Sheets/Benno Levin, Eric comes face-to-face both literally and figuratively with his global hegemonic masculinity.

NOTES

1. For an extremely useful introduction to the issue of globalization and the American novel see Dix, Jarvis, and Jenner 108–114. Also see Gray 2011.
2. See Giles, *Virtual America* and *Global Remapping*.
3. This article is republished in Lentricchia, *Introducing Don DeLillo* 1–6.
4. Masculinity is not a major concern in the study of DeLillo's fiction and is mostly tied in with other approaches to reading his novels. One article that does look specifically at the representations of masculinity in DeLillo's writing is Ruth Heyler's "DeLillo and Masculinity." Although useful, Heyler's study is more of an overview rather than an in-depth analysis of masculinity in DeLillo's novels.
5. An overview of the media's reaction to *Cosmopolis* can be found at "The Cosmopolis Media Watch" from Curt Gardner's website *Don DeLillo's America*. Gardner offers an overview of the "DeLillo Detractors": Dale Peck, B. R. Myers, George Will, Jonathan Yardley, and Bruce Bawer.
6. Bawer continues by reading DeLillo's answer to this condition of contemporary society as the suggestion of a return to "primitivism": "To find oneself one must, like the Missouri caveman, return to primitivism; and in the world according to DeLillo, returning to primitivism means, in essence, entering into a community, conspiracy, or subculture governed largely by primitive violence" (22).
7. Also see Abel for a literary appraisal of DeLillo's essay.
8. The importance of the act of storytelling as a form of processing the impact of the September 11 attacks also features in *Falling Man:* "They worked into themselves, finding narratives that rolled and tumbled, and how natural it seemed to do this, tell stories about themselves" (30)
9. Donovan (144–181) makes a worthy contribution to this discussion on the power of the counter-narrative in DeLillo's fiction.
10. Boxall also discusses how time has lost its narrative quality in *The Body Artist* (2001) and *Cosmopolis* (2003) in Boxall, *Don DeLillo* 215–232.
11. What Dix, Jarvis, and Jenner fail to acknowledge, despite their systematic analysis of the novel, and indeed their concise outline of the major debates surrounding the development of globalization, is the issue of masculinity and globalization. While they discuss the performance of Packer in terms of the major tropes of globalization, they fail to gender Packer and to question what his performance demonstrates regarding the impact of globalization on the social construction of masculinity.
12. See chapter 4, "The Fictions of Globalization," in Annesley, *Fictions* for further discussion on *Cosmopolis* and *Underworld*.
13. See Knight, "Everything Is Connected" and "DeLillo, Postmodern."
14. A selected group of texts on globalization that Connell references in her work include Featherstone; Appadurai, *Modernity at Large* and *Globalization*; Hirst and Thompson; Bauman, *Globalization*; Giddens; Brennan; Eriksen.

15. See Connell, *The Men and the Boys.*
16. In contesting this trend, Connell and Messerschmidt offer a useful framework for conceptualising the existence of local, regional, and global masculinities in Connell and Messerschmidt:

    1. Local: Constructed in the arenas of face-to-face interaction of families, organizations, and immediate communities, as typically found in ethnographic and life-history research.
    2. Regional: Constructed at the level of the culture or the nation-state, as typically found in discursive, political, and demographic research.
    3. Global: Constructed in transnational arenas such as world politics and transnational business and media, as studied in the emerging research on masculinities and globalization (849).

17. See Connell, "Masculinities, Change" and "Masculinity Research and Global Society."
18. See chapter 8 of Connell, *Masculinities* 185–203. This is also developed in Connell, "Masculinities and Globalization."
19. Even before the publication of "Masculinities and Globalization," Connell's first manifesto on the study of masculinities within a global context, she intimated the need to consider the gendered nature of the large-scale institutions in the world in "The State, Gender, and Sexual Politics."
20. Key writings on masculinities and globalization include Collinson and Hearn; Connell, *The Men and the Boys*; Pease and Pringle; Connell, *Gender*, "Masculinities, Change," and "Men, Gender, and the State"; Ngan-Ling Chow; Connell and Wood; Connell, "Globalism, Imperialism," "Men, Masculinities," "Northern Theory," "Lives of the Businessmen," "Masculinity Research and Global Society," "Gender, Health and Theory," and "Masculinity Research and Global Change."
21. Acker refers to Connell, "Masculinities and Globalization" to support this point.
22. See Robertson.
23. See Ritzer.
24. See Berman. E. B. White also reflects in *Here Is New York* that the skyscraper is the outstanding innovation of the city of modernity: "Manhattan has been compelled to expand skyward because of the absence of any other direction in which to grow. This more than any other thing is responsible for its majesty" (30).
25. Harvey, *Condition of Postmodernity* defines "time-space compression" as "processes that so revolutionise the objective qualities of space and time that we are forced to alter, sometimes in quite radical ways, how we represent the world to ourselves. I use the word 'compression' because a strong case can be made that the history of capitalism has been characterised by speed-up in the pace of life, while so overcoming spatial barriers that the world sometimes seems to collapse inwards upon us" (240).
26. As John W. Meyer states, "The world society is a stateless polity" (236).
27. Acker also points to Hacker and to Hearn, "Emotive Subjects" as studies in the pleasure in domination within the context of the business world.
28. There are juxtaposing inferences from the word "chief." While it harks back to the old Indian tribes, it is also a term associated with contemporary American politics of the time of the writing of the novel, particularly the president of the United States of this era, George W. Bush, styling himself as the "commander-in-chief."
29. Packer offers an overview of his strategy to Kinski (84).

30. See Harvey, *Condition of Postmodernity* 99–112.
31. Harvey (*Condition of Postmodernity*) writes that in its very essence, Fordism believed that "mass production meant mass consumption, a new system of the reproduction of labour power, a new politics of labour control and management, a new aesthetics and psychology, in short, a new kind of rationalised, modernist, and populist democratic society" (125–126).
32. Harvey (*Condition of Postmodernity*) defines "flexible accumulation" as being "marked by a direct confrontation with the rigidities of Fordism. It rests on flexibility with respect to labour processes, labour markets, products and patterns of consumption. It is characterised by the emergence of entirely new sectors of production, new ways of providing financial services, new markets, and, above all, greatly intensified rates of commercial, technological, and organizational innovation" (147). See *Condition of Postmodernity* 141–197 for an in-depth analysis of the concept.
33. Eric states: "Let it all come down. Let them see each other pure and lorn. This was the individual's revenge on the mythical couple. . . . Let them see each other clean, in killing light" (123–124).
34. "This acte gratuite recalls a host of characters from existentialist and protoexistentialist fiction: Dostoevsky's Raskolnikov, Gide's Lafcadio, and Camus' Meursault form an intertextual lineage that both confirms Packer's outsider status and tonally reorients DeLillo's novel so that its satiric hyperbole shades into existential absurdity" (Chandler 243).
35. I think it's important to make the point that I am not suggesting that Packer has suddenly become a sympathetic character. I would argue that Packer's narrative in the novel can be read as a journey of enlightenment. In the move from the global arena of his limo to the local arena in the streets of Manhattan, Packer becomes aware of the human condition.
36. See, in particular, the reaction to *Cosmopolis* from the U.S. literary critics that I cite earlier in this chapter.
37. Although the character's actual name is Richard Sheets, I use Benno Levin to refer to the character, as this is the identity he adopts and it also features in the title of his diary entries in the novel.

Bibliography

PRIMARY AUTHORS

Auster, Paul. *The Invention of Solitude*. 1982. London: Faber & Faber, 2005. Print.
———. *The New York Trilogy*. London: Faber & Faber, 1987. Print.
———. *Moon Palace*. 1989. London: Faber & Faber, 2004. Print.
———. *The Music of Chance*. 1990. London: Faber & Faber, 2006. Print.
———. *Leviathan*. 1992. London: Faber & Faber, 2011. Print.
———. *Mr. Vertigo*. 1994. London: Faber & Faber, 2006. Print.
———. *The Red Notebook*.1995. London: Faber & Faber, 1996. Print.
———. *Timbuktu*. 1999. London: Faber & Faber, 2008. Print.
———. *The Book of Illusions*. London: Faber & Faber, 2002. Print.
———. *Oracle Night*. 2003. London: Faber & Faber, 2005. Print.
———. *The Brooklyn Follies*. 2005. London: Faber & Faber, 2011. Print.
———. *Man in the Dark*. 2008. London: Faber & Faber, 2009. Print.
———. *Invisible*. London: Faber & Faber, 2009. Print.
———. *Sunset Park*. London: Faber & Faber, 2010. Print.
———. *Winter Journal*. London: Faber & Faber, 2012. Print.
DeLillo, Don. *White Noise*. New York: Viking, 1985. Print.
———. *Underworld*. 1997. London: Picador, 1998. Print.
———. "In The Ruins of The Future." *Harpers Magazine*. Dec. 2001. Web. 18th June 2012.
———. *Cosmopolis*. 2003. London: Picador, 2004. Print.
Ellis, Bret Easton. *American Psycho*. 1991. London: Picador, 2011. Print.
———. *Falling Man*. London: Picador, 2007. Print.
———. *Lunar Park*. London: Picador, 2005. Print.

ARCHIVAL MATERIALS

Auster, Paul, and Bill Corbett. "Interview with Paul Auster." c. 1997. TS. Auster Archive at the Henry W. and Albert A. Berg Collection of English and American Literature, Stephen A. Schwarzman Building, New York Public Library. Accessed 13 Mar. 2012. Print.
Hite, Shere. "21st Century Man Questionnaire." Shere Hite Archive located at the Arthur and Elizabeth Schlesinger Library on the History of Women in America, Radcliffe Institute for Advanced Study, Harvard. Accessed 27–28 Apr. 2012. Print.

SECONDARY CRITICAL WORKS

Abel, Marco. "'In the Ruins of the Future': Literature, Images, and the Rhetoric of Seeing 9/11." *PMLA* 118.5 (2003): 1236–1250. Print.

Acker, Joan. "Gender, Capitalism and Globalization." *Critical Sociology* 30.1 (2004): 17–41. Print.

Ackroyd, Peter. *Dickens*. New York: Harper Collins, 1990. 443–444. Print.

Adams, Ariel. "Bret Easton Ellis Interview." *Askmen.com*. Web. 1 Apr. 2012.

Adams, Tim. "A Big Apple a day . . ." Rev. of *Cosmopolis*. *The Observer*. 4 May 2003. Web. 16 June 2012.

Alford, Steven E. "Mirrors of Madness: Paul Auster's *The New York Trilogy*." *Critique: Studies in Contemporary Fiction* 37.1 (Fall 1995): 17–33. Print.

Annesley, James. *Blank Fictions: Consumerism, Culture and the Contemporary American Novel*. London: Pluto Press. 1998. Print.

———. *Fictions of Globalization*. London: Continuum, 2006. Print.

Appadurai, Arjun. *Modernity at Large*. Minnesota: University of Minnesota Press, 1996. Print.

———. *Globalization*. Durham: Duke University Press, 2001. Print.

Applewhite, Ashton. "Reading Guides: Paul Auster." *Penguin.com*. Web. 24 Feb. 2012.

Armengol, Josep M. "Where Are the Fathers in American Literature?" *Journal of Men's Studies* 16.2 (Spring 2008): 211–226. Print.

Auster, Paul, and Michel Contat. "The Manuscript in the Book: A Conversation." *Yale French Studies* 89 (1996): 160–187. Print.

Baelo-Allué, Sonia. "Serial Murder, Serial Consumerism: Bret Easton Ellis' *American Psycho*." *Miscelánea: A Journal of English and American Studies* 26 (2002): 71–90. Print.

———. *Bret Easton Ellis's Controversial Fiction: Writing Between High and Low Culture*. London: Continuum, 2011. Print.

———. "9/11 and the Psychic Trauma Novel." *Atlantis* 34.1 (2012): 63–79. Print.

Balzac, Honoré de. *La Comédie humaine*. Ed. P. G. Castex. Vol. 11. Paris: Gallimard-Pléiade, 1980. 12 Vols. Print.

———. *Physiology of Marriage*. 1829. Charleston: Bibliobazaar, 2009. Print.

Barone, Dennis. "Auster's Memory." *Review of Contemporary Fiction* 14.1 (Spring 1994): 32–34. Print.

———. Ed. *Beyond the Red Notebook: Essays on Paul Auster*. Philadelphia: University of Pennsylvania Press, 1995. Print.

Baudelaire, Charles. "The Painter of Modern Life." 1863. *The Painter of Modern Life and Other Essays*. Ed. and Trans. Jonathan Mayne. London: Phaidon, 1964. Print.

Baudrillard, Jean. *America*. Trans. Chris Turner. London: Verso, 1988. Print.

Bauman, Zygmunt. "Desert Spectacular." *The Flâneur*. Ed. Keith Tester. New York: Routledge, 1994. 138–157. Print.

———. *Globalization: The Human Consequences*. Cambridge: Polity, 1998. Print.

Bawer, Bruce. "Don DeLillo's America." *Don DeLillo: Bloom's Modern Critical Views*. Ed. Harold Bloom. Philadelphia: Chelsea House, 2003. 21–28. Print.

Baxter, Charles. "The Bureau of Missing Persons: Notes on Paul Auster's Fiction." *Review of Contemporary Fiction* 14.1 (Spring 1994): 40–43. Rpt. in *Bloom's Modern Critical Views: Paul Auster*. Ed. Harold Bloom. Philadelphia: Chelsea House, 2004. 3–7. Print.

Begley, Adam. "The Art of Fiction No. 135: Interview with Don DeLillo." *Paris Review* 128 (1993). Web. 16 June 2012.

Benjamin, Walter. "On Some Motifs in Baudelaire." *Illuminations: Essays and Reflections*. Ed. Hannah Arendt. Trans. Harry Zohn. New York: Schocken, 1968. 155–200. Print.

———. *The Arcades Project*. 1982. Trans. Rob Tiedermann. Cambridge: Harvard University Press, 1999. Print.

———. *Charles Baudelaire: A Lyric Poet in the Era of High Capitalism*. London: Verso, 1983. Print.

———. *Selected Writings: 1927–1934*. Eds. Edmund Jephcott, Howard Eiland, and Michael W. Jennings. Vol. 2. Cambridge: Harvard University Press, 2003. Print.

———. *Selected Writings: 1938–1940*. Eds. Edmund Jephcott, Howard Eiland, and Michael W. Jennings. Vol. 4. Cambridge: Harvard University Press, 2003. Print.

Berger, Meyer. *Meyer Berger's New York*. New York: Fordham University Press, 2004. Print.

Berman, Marshall. *All That Is Solid Melts into Air: The Experience of Modernity*. New York: Simon and Schuster, 1982. Print.

Bigar, Sylvie. "A Zingone in Every Aisle." *New York Times*. 7 Nov. 2013. Web. 13 Nov. 2013.

Bigsby, Christopher. "In Conversation with Paul Auster." *Writers in Conversation*. Vol. 2. Norwich: The Arthur Miller Centre, 2001. Print.

Bird, Sharon. "Homosociality and the Maintenance of Hegemonic Masculinity." *Gender and Society* 10.2 (April 1996): 120–132. Print.

Blazer, Alex E. "*American Psycho, Hamlet* and Existential Psychosis." *Bret Easton Ellis: American Psycho, Glamorama, Lunar Park*. Ed. Naomi Mandel. London: Continuum, 2011. 36–49. Print.

Blauner, Robert. *Alienation and Freedom*. Chicago: Chicago University Press, 1964. Print.

Bloom, Harold, ed. *Don DeLillo: Bloom's Modern Critical Views*. Philadelphia: Chelsea House, 2003. Print.

———. Ed. *Paul Auster: Bloom's Modern Critical Views*. Philadelphia: Chelsea House, 2004. Print.

Boxall, Peter. *Don DeLillo: The Possibility of Fiction*. New York: Routledge, 2006. Print.

———. "DeLillo and Media Culture." *The Cambridge Companion to Don DeLillo*. Ed. John Duvall. Cambridge: Cambridge University Press, 2008. 43–52. Print.

———. "Slow Man, Dangling Man, Falling Man: DeLillo and the Ethics of Fiction." *Terrorism, Media, and the Ethics of Fiction: Transatlantic Perspectives on Don DeLillo*. Eds. Philipp Schweighauser and Peter Schneck. London: Continuum, 2010. 173–183. Print.

Bradbury, Malcolm. *The Modern American Novel*. Oxford: Oxford University Press, 1992. Print.

Brand, Dana. *The Spectator and the City in Nineteenth-Century American Literature*. Cambridge: Cambridge University Press, 1991. Print.

Brennan, Teresa. *Globalization and Its Terrors: Daily Life in the West*. London: Routledge, 2003. Print.

Brien, Donna Lee. "The Real Filth in *American Psycho:* A Critical Reassessment." *MC Journal: A Journal of Media and Culture* 9.5. Nov. 2006. Web. 1 Apr. 2012.

Brooker, Peter. *New York Fictions: Modernity, Postmodernism, the New Modern*. London: Longman, 1996. Print.

Brown, Mark. *Paul Auster*. Manchester: Manchester University Press, 2007. Print.

———. "A 'Portrait of a Soul in Ruins': Paul Auster's *The Book of Illusions*." *The Invention of Illusions: International Perspectives on Paul Auster*. Eds. Stefania Ciocia and Jesus A. Gonzalez. Newcastle: Cambridge Scholars Publishing, 2011. 219–238. Print.

Bruckner, Pascal. "Paul Auster, or the Heir Intestate." *Beyond the Red Notebook: Essays on Paul Auster*. Ed. Dennis Barone. Philadelphia: University of Pennsylvania Press, 1995. 27–33. Print.

Buck-Morss, Susan. "The Flâneur, the Sandwichman and the Whore: The Politics of Loitering." *New German Critique* 13.39 (1986): 99–140. Print.

Bueno, Eva Paulino, Terry Caesar, and William Hummel, eds. *Naming the Father: Legacies, Genealogies, and Explorations of Fatherhood in Modern and Contemporary Literature*. New York: Lexington Books, 2000. 276–287.

Burr, Vivien. *An Introduction to Social Constructionism*. London: Routledge, 1995. Print.

Burrows, Edwin G., and Mike Wallace. *Gotham: A History of New York City to 1898*. New York: Oxford University Press, 1999. Print.

Burton, Richard D. E. *The Flâneur and His City: Patterns of Daily Life in Paris 1815–1851*. Manchester: Manchester University Press, 2010. Print.

Byers, Thomas. "Terminating the Postmodern: Masculinity and Pomophobia." *MFS: Modern Fiction Studies* 41.1 (1995): 5–33. Print.

Caldwell, Gail. "Bonfire of Inanities." Rev. of *Cosmopolis*. *Boston Globe*. 6 Apr. 2003. Web. 16 June 2012.

Carrigan, Tim, Raewyn Connell, and John Lee."Toward a New Sociology of Masculinity." *Theory and Society* 14.5 (1985): 551–604. Print.

Chandler, Aaron. "'An Unsettling, Alternative Self': Benno Levin, Emmanuel Levinas, and Don DeLillo's *Cosmopolis*." *Critique* 50.3 (2009): 241–260. Print.

Cheng, Cliff, ed. *Masculinities in Organizations*. Thousand Oaks: Sage, 1996. Print.

Ciocia, Stefania, and Jesus A. Gonzalez, eds. *The Invention of Illusions: International Perspectives on Paul Auster*. Newcastle: Cambridge Scholars Publishing, 2011. Print.

Cockburn, Cynthia. *In the Way of Women: Men's Resistance to Sex Equality in Organizations*. London: Macmillan, 1991. Print.

Colby, Georgina. *Bret Easton Ellis: Underwriting the Contemporary*. New York: Palgrave Macmillan, 2011. Print.

Cole, Teju. *Open City*. New York: Random House, 2011. Print.

Collinson, David L., and Jeff Hearn, eds. *Men as Managers, Managers as Men: Critical Perspectives on Men, Masculinities and Managements*. London: Sage, 1996. Print.

———. "Naming Men as Men: Implications for Work, Organization and Management." *The Masculinities Reader*. Eds. Stephen M. Whitehead and Frank J. Barrett. Cambridge: Polity, 2000. 144–169. Print.

———. "Men and Masculinities in Work, Organizations, and Management." *Handbook of Studies on Men and Masculinities*. Eds. Michael Kimmel and Jeff Hearn. London: Sage, 2005. 289–310. Print.

Connell, Raewyn. *Ruling Class, Ruling Culture: Studies of Conflict, Power and Hegemony in Australian Life*. Cambridge: Cambridge University Press, 1977. Print.

———. "The Concept of 'Role' and What to Do with It." *Australian and New Zealand Journal of Sociology* 15 (1979): 7–17. Print.

———. *Which Way Is Up? Essays on Sex, Class and Culture*. Sydney: Allen & Unwin, 1983. Print.

———. *Gender and Power: Society, the Person, and Sexual Politics*. Stanford: Stanford University Press, 1987. Print.

———. "The State, Gender and Sexual Politics: Theory and Appraisal." *Theory and Society* 19 (1990): 507–544. Print.

———. *Masculinities*. 1995. 2nd ed. Cambridge: Polity, 2005. Print.

———. "Masculinities and Globalization." *Men and Masculinities* 1.1 (1998): 3–23. Print.

———. *The Men and the Boys*. Cambridge: Polity, 2000. Print.

———. *Gender*. Cambridge: Polity, 2002. Print.

———. "Masculinities, Change and Conflict in Global Society: Thinking about the Future of Men's Studies." *Journal of Men's Studies* 11.3 (2003): 249–266. Print.

———. "Men, Gender and the State." *Among Men: Moulding Masculinities*. Eds. Soren Ervoand Thomas Johansson. Aldershot: Ashgate, 2003. 15–28. Print.
———. "Globalization, Imperialism, and Masculinities." *Handbook of Studies on Men & Masculinities*. Eds. Michael Kimmel, Jeff Hearn, and Raewyn Connell. Thousand Oaks: Sage, 2005. 71–89. Print.
———. "Men, Masculinities, and Gender Equality in the Global Arena." *Signs: Journal of Women in Culture and Society* 30.3 (2005): 1801–1825. Print.
———. "The Northern Theory of Globalization." *Sociological Theory* 25.4 (2007): 368–385. Print.
———. "Lives of the Businessmen: Reflections on Life-History Method and Contemporary Hegemonic Masculinity." *ÖZS* 35.2 (2010): 54–71. Print.
———. "Masculinity Research and Global Society." *Analyzing Gender, Intersectionality, and Multiple Inequalities: Global, Transnational and Local Contexts*. Eds. Esther Ngan-Ling Chow, Marcia Texler Segal, and Lin Tan. Bingley: Emerald Group Publishing, 2011. 51–72. Print.
———. "Gender, Health and Theory: Conceptualizing the Issue, in Local and World Perspective." *Social Science & Medicine* 74.11 (2011): 1675–1683. Print.
———. "Masculinity Research and Global Change." *Masculinities and Social Change* 1.1 (2012): 4–18. Print.
Connell, Raewyn, and James W. Messerschmidt. "Hegemonic Masculinity: Rethinking the Concept." *Gender and Society* 19.6 (Dec 2005): 829–859. Print.
Connell, Raewyn, and Julian Wood. "Globalization and Business Masculinities." *Men and Masculinities* 7.4 (2005): 347–364. Print.
Conte, Joseph M. "Conclusion: Writing amid the Ruins: 9/11 and *Cosmopolis*." *The Cambridge Companion to Don DeLillo*. Ed. John N. Duvall. Cambridge: Cambridge University Press, 2008. 179–192. Print.
Coreno, Annie. "*American Psycho* at 20: Catching up with Bret Easton Ellis." *Publisher's Weekly*. 13 June 2011. Web. 12 Aug. 2011.
"Cosmopolis." *Oxford English Dictionary*. Web. 22 June 2012.
Critique: Studies in Contemporary American Fiction 39.3 (Spring 1998). Print.
Critique: Studies in Contemporary American Fiction 49.2 (Winter 2008). Print.
Cvek, Sven. "The Market Moves Us in Mysterious Ways: DeLillo's Critique of Transnationalism in *Cosmopolis*." *The Americanist* 25 (2010): 157–170. Print.
De Cortanze, Gérard. "Le monde est dans ma tête, mon corps est dans le monde." Trans. Carl-Carsten Springer. *Magazine Littéraire* 338 (Dec. 1995): 18–25. Print.
Demetriou, Demetrakis Z. "Connell's Concept of Hegemonic Masculinity: A Critique." *Theory and Society* 30.3 (June 2001): 337–361. Print.
Demos, John. "The Changing Faces of Fatherhood: A New Exploration in Family History." *Father and Child: Developmental and Clinical Perspectives*. Eds. Stanley Cath, Alan Gurwitt, and John M. Ross. Boston: Little, Brown, 1982. 425–450. Print.
Dickens, Charles. *American Notes*. 1842. London: Oxford University Press, 1957. Print.
Dix, Andrew, Brian Jarvis, and Paul Jenner. *The Contemporary American Novel in Context*. London: Continuum, 2011. Print.
Donovan, Christopher. *Postmodern Counternarratives: Irony and Audience in the Novels of Paul Auster, Don DeLillo, Charles Johnson, and Tim O'Brien*. New York: Routledge, 2004. Print.
Dow Adams, Timothy. "Photography and Ventriloquy in Paul Auster's *The Invention of Solitude*." *True Relations: Essays in Autobiography and the Postmodern*. Eds. G. Thomas Couser and Joseph Fichtelberg. Westport: Greenwood, 1998. 11–32. Print.
Dow, William. "Paul Auster's *The Invention of Solitude*: Glimmers in a Reach to Authenticity." *Critique: Studies in Contemporary Fiction* 39.3 (Spring 1998): 272–282. Print.

Drenttel, William, ed. *Paul Auster: A Comprehensive Bibliographic Checklist of Published Works, 1968–1994*. New York: Delos Press, 1994. Print.

Dupont, Jocelyn. "'The Nechanics of Reality': Paul Auster Speaks about His Work and Inspiration." *La Clé des Langues.com*. 15 Jan. 2009. Web. 4 Sept. 2011.

Ellis, Havelock. *The Psychology of Sex*. 1933. London: William Heinemann, 1946. Print.

Engel Lang, Gladys. "Methodological Observations on the Hite Report Trilogy." *The Shere Hite Reader*. Ed. Shere Hite. New York: Seven Stories, 2006. 485–498. Print.

Eriksen, Thomas Hylland. *Globalization: The Key Concepts*. New York: Berg, 2007. Print.

Featherstone, Mike. *Undoing Culture: Globalization, Postmodernism and Identity*. London: Sage, 1995. Print.

Ferris, Joshua. *Then We Came to the End*. New York: Viking, 2007. Print.

———. "The Dinner Party." *The New Yorker*. 11 Aug. 2008. Web. 14 May 2010.

———. *The Unnamed*. London: Penguin, 2010. Print.

Ferry, Peter. "Reading Manhattan, Reading American Masculinity: Reintroducing the Flâneur with E.B. White's *Here Is New York* and Joshua Ferris' *The Unnamed*." *Culture, Society & Masculinities* 3.1 (2011a): 49–61. Print.

———. "Review of Josep M. Armengol's *Richard Ford and the Fiction of Masculinities*." *Atlantis: Journal of the Spanish Association of Anglo-American Studies* 33.1 (June 2011b): 191–196. Print.

Fiedler, Leslie A. *Love and Death in the American Novel*. 1960. Champaign: Dalkey Archive Press, 2008. Print.

Ford, Mark. "Inventions of Solitude: Thoreau and Auster." *Journal of American Studies* 33 (1999): 201–219. Print.

Foster, Hal. "Rem Koolhass: From Manhattan to the City of Exacerbated Difference." *Geographies of Modernism: Literatures, Cultures, Spaces*. Eds. Peter Brooker and Andrew Thacker. New York: Routledge, 2005. Print.

Foucault, Michel. *The History of Sexuality Vol. 1: An Introduction*. 1976. Trans. Robert Hurley. London: Penguin, 1981. Print.

Fox, Kenneth. *Metropolitan America*. London: Macmillan, 1990. Print.

Freccero, Carla. "Historical Violence, Censorship, and the Serial Killer: The Case of *American Psycho*." *Diacritics: A Review of Contemporary Criticism* 27.2 (1997): 44–58. Print.

Fredman, Stephen. "'How to Get Out of the Room That Is the Book?' Paul Auster and the Consequences of Confinement." *Bloom's Modern Critical Views: Paul Auster*. Ed. Harold Bloom. Philadelphia: Chelsea House, 2004. Print.

Freeman, Carla. "Is Local: Global as Feminine: Masculine? Rethinking the Gender of Globalization." *Signs* 26.4 (2001): 1007–1038. Print.

Freeman, John. "*Granta* Paul Auster Interview." *Youtube.com*. 20 May 2009. Web. 4 Oct. 2011.

Freud, Sigmund. *Three Essays on the Theory of Sexuality*. 1905. *The Standard Edition of the Complete Psychological Works of Sigmund Freud*. Vol. 7. Trans. James Strachey. London: Hogarth, 1953. 130–243. Print.

Frisby, David. "The Flâneur in Social Theory." *The Flâneur*. Ed. Keith Tester. London: Routledge, 1994. 81–111. Print.

———. *Cityscapes of Modernity: Critical Explorations*. Cambridge: Polity in association with Blackwell, 2001. Print.

Gagnon, John. *Human Sexualities*. Glenview: Scott, Foresman and Co., 1977. Print.

———. "Reconsiderations: The Kinsey Reports." 1978. Repub. in *Interpretation of Desire: Essays in the Study of Sexuality*. Ed. John Gagnon. Chicago: University of Chicago Press, 2004. 88–94. Print.

———. *An Interpretation of Desire: Essays in the Study of Sexuality.* Chicago: University of Chicago Press, 2004. Print.
Gagnon, John, and William Simon. *Sexual Conduct: The Social Sources of Human Sexuality.* London: Hutchinson, 1973. Print.
Gardner, Curt. "The Cosmopolis Media Watch." *Don DeLillo's America.* 3 Feb. 1996. Web. 16 June 2012.
———. "DeLillo Detractors." *Don DeLillo's America.* 28 June 2002. Web. 16 June 2012.
Giamio, Paul. *Appreciating Don DeLillo: The Moral Force of a Writer's Work.* Westport: Praeger, 2011. Print.
Giddens, Anthony. *Runaway World: How Globalization Is Reshaping Our Lives.* 2nd ed. London: Profile Books, 2002. Print.
Giles, Paul. *Virtual Americas: Transnational Fictions and the Transatlantic Imaginary.* Durham: Duke University Press, 2002. Print.
———. *The Global Remapping of American Literature.* Princeton: Princeton University Press, 2011. Print.
Gilloch, Graeme. "'The Return of the Flâneur': The Afterlife of an Allegory." *New Formations* 38 (Summer 1999): 101–109. Print.
Gilloch, Graeme, and Jane Kilby. "Trauma and Memory in the City: From Auster to Austerlitz." *Urban Memory: History and Oblivion in the Modern City.* Ed. Mark Crinson. London: Routledge, 2005. 1–22. Print.
Goulian, Jon-Jon. "Bret Easton Ellis: The Art of Fiction No. 216." *Paris Review* 200 (Spring 2012): 168–196. Print.
Gray, Richard. *After the Fall: American Literature since 9/11.* London: John Wiley, 2011. Print.
Griswold, Robert L. *Fatherhood in America.* 1992. New York: Basic Books, 1993. Print.
Hacker, Sally. *Pleasure, Power, and Technology.* Boston: Unwin Hyman, 1989. Print.
Hamada, Tomoko. "Unwrapping Euro-American Masculinity in a Japanese Multinational Corporation." *Masculinities in Organizations.* Ed. Cliff Cheng. Thousand Oaks: Sage, 1996. 160–176. Print.
Harvey, David. *The Condition of Postmodernity: An Enquiry into the Origins of Cultural Change.* Oxford: Blackwell, 1989. Print.
———. *Paris: Capital of Modernity.* London: Routledge, 2005. Print.
Hearn, Jeff. "Emotive Subjects: Organizational Men, Organizational Masculinities and the (De) constructions of 'Emotions'." *Emotions in Organizations.* Ed. Stephen Fineman. London: Sage, 1993. 142–166. Print.
———. "From Hegemonic Masculinity to the Hegemony of Men." *Feminist Theory* 5.1 (2004): 49–72. Print.
Heffernan, Nick. "'Money Is Talking to Itself': Finance Capitalism in the Fiction of Don DeLillo from *Players* to *Cosmopolis.*" *Critical Engagements* 1.2 (2008): 53–78. Print.
Heise, Thomas. "*American Psycho:* Neoliberal Fantasies and the Death of Downtown." *Arizona Quarterly* 67.1 (2011): 135–160. Print.
Helmreich, William B. *The New York Nobody Knows: Walking 6,000 Miles in the City.* Princeton: Princeton University Press, 2013. Print.
Heyler, Ruth. "Parodied to Death: The Postmodern Gothic of *American Psycho.*" *MFS: Modern Fiction Studies* 46.3 (2000): 725–746. Print.
———. "DeLillo and Masculinity." *The Cambridge Companion to Don DeLillo.* Ed. John Duvall. Cambridge: Cambridge University Press, 2008. 125–136. Print.
Hirst, Paul, and Grahame Thompson. *Globalization in Question: The International Economy and the Possibilities of Governance.* Cambridge: Polity, 1996. Print.
Hite, Shere. *The Hite Report on Male Sexuality.* 1981. New York: Random House, 1982. Print.

———. *Women and Love: A Cultural Revolution in Progress.* New York: Knopf, 1987. Print.

———. "Post-modern Masculinity." *Penthouse* Feb. 1992: 101–102. Print.

———. "Today's Men." *Penthouse* Jan. 1993: 47–52. Print.

———. Ed. *The Shere Hite Reader.* New York: Seven Stories, 2006a. Print.

———. "Where Does Our Men-On-Top Society Come From?" *The Shere Hite Reader.* Ed. Shere Hite. New York: Seven Stories, 2006b. 286–288. Print.

———. *Oedipus Revisited: Sexual Behaviour in the Human Male Today.* London: Acardia, 2007. Print.

———. "Gender Conformity: How Boys Learn They Have to 'Be Like Other Guys'." *Oedipus Revisited: Sexual Behaviour in the Human Male Today.* London: Arcadia, 2007. 23–25. Print.

Hollington, Michael. "Dickens the Flâneur." *Dickensian* 77.2 (1981): 71–87. Print.

Howson, Richard. *Challenging Hegemonic Masculinity.* London: Routledge, 2006. Print.

Irvine, Janice. *Disorders of Desire: Sexuality and Gender in Modern American Sexology.* 1990. Rev. ed. Philadelphia: Temple University Press, 2005. 13–14. Print.

Irwin, Mark. "Memory's Escape: Inventing *The Music of Chance*—A Conversation with Paul Auster." *Denver Quarterly* 28.3 (1994): 111–122.

Jackson, Stevi. "The Sexual Self in Late Modernity." *The Sexual Self: The Construction of Sexual Scripts.* Ed. Michael Kimmel. Nashville: Vanderbilt University Press, 2007. 3–5. Print.

Jenks, Chris. *Visual Culture.* New York: Routledge, 1995. Print.

Kakutani, Michiko. "Books of the Times: Headed Toward a Crash, of Sorts, in a Stretch Limo." Rev. of *Cosmopolis. New York Times.* 24 Mar. 2003. Web. 16 June 2012.

Kim, Walter. "Long Day's Journey into Haircut." Rev. of *Cosmopolis. New York Times.*13 Apr. 2003. Web. 16 June 2012.

———. "Invisible Masculinity." *Society* 30.6 (1993): 28–35. Print.

———. "Masculinity as Homophobia: Fear, Shame and Silence in the Construction of Gender Identity." *Theorizing Masculinities.* Eds. Harry Brod and Michael Kaufman. Newbury Park: Sage, 1994: 119–141. Print.

———. *Manhood in America.* 1996. 2nd ed. New York: Methuen, 2006. Print.

———. *The Gendered Society.* Oxford: Oxford University Press, 2000. Print.

———. Ed. *The Sexual Self: The Construction of Sexual Scripts.* Nashville: Vanderbilt University Press, 2007. Print.

———. *Guyland.* New York: Harper Collins, 2008. Print.

———. *Angry White Men: American Masculinity at the End of an Era.* New York: Nation Books, 2013. Print.

Kinsey, Alfred C., Wardell B. Pomeroy, and Clyde E. Martin. *Sexual Behaviour in the Human Male.* Philadelphia: W. B. Saunders, 1948. Print.

Kinsey, Alfred C., Wardell B. Pomeroy, Clyde E. Martin, and Paul H. Gebhard. *Sexual Behaviour in the Human Female.* Philadelphia: W. B. Saunders, 1953. Print.

Kirkegaard, Peter. "Cities, Signs and Meaning in Walter Benjamin and Paul Auster; or, Never Sure of Any of It." *Orbis Litterarum* 48.2–3 (1993): 161–179. Print.

Knight, Peter. "Everything Is Connected: *Underworld's* Secret History of Paranoia." *MFS: Modern Fiction Studies* 45.3 (1999): 811–836. Print.

———. "DeLillo, Postmodern, Postmodernity." *The Cambridge Companion to Don DeLillo.* Ed. John Duvall. Cambridge: Cambridge University Press, 2008. 27–40. Print.

Krafft-Ebing, Richard von. *Psychopathia Sexualis.* 1894. Trans. Arthur Vivian Burbury. London: Panther, 1965. Print.

Krasny, Michael. "KQED interview with Don DeLillo." *Youtube.com.* 24 Feb. 2009. Web. 9 July 2012.

Lentricchia, Frank. "The American Writer as Bad Citizen—Introducing Don DeLillo." *South Atlantic Quarterly* 89.2 (1990): 239–244. Print.

———. Ed. *Introducing Don DeLillo*. Durham: Duke University Press, 1991. Print.

Lethem, Jonathan. "Jonathan Lethem Talks with Paul Auster." *Believermag.com*. Feb. 2005. Web. 11 July 2011.

Mandel, Naomi, ed. *Bret Easton Ellis: American Psycho, Glamorama, Lunar Park*. London: Continuum, 2011. Print.

Mandel, Naomi, and Alain-Philippe Durand, eds. *Novels of the Contemporary Extreme*. London: Continuum, 2006. Print.

Marling, William. "Paul Auster and the American Romantics." *Literature Interpretation Theory* 7.4 (March 1997): 301–310. Print.

Martin, Brendan. *Paul Auster's Postmodernity*. New York: Routledge, 2008. Print.

Martin, Clancy. "Love Crimes." *New York Times*.15 Nov. 2009. Web. 10 Aug. 2011.

Masters, William H., and Virginia E. Johnson. *Human Sexual Response*. Boston: Little, Brown & Co., 1966. Print.

———. *Human Sexual Inadequacy*. Philadelphia: Lippincott Williams and Wilkins, 1970. Print.

McCaffery, Larry, and Sinda Gregory. "An Interview with Paul Auster." *Contemporary Literature* 33.1 (Spring 1992): 1–23. Print.

Mead, George Herbert. *Mind, Self, and Society: From the Standpoint of a Social Behaviourist*. Chicago: University of Chicago Press, 1934. Print.

Mercier, Louis Sébastien. *Panorama of Paris: Selections from "Le Tableau de Paris."* Ed. Jeremy D. Popkin. Trans. Helen Simpson. University Park: Pennsylvania State University Press, 1999. Print.

Merivale, Patricia. "The Austerized Version." *Contemporary American Literature* 38.1 (Spring 1997): 185–197. Print.

Merlob, Maya. "Textuality, Self, and World: The Postmodern Narrative in Paul Auster's *In The Country of Last Things*." *Critique* 49.1 (2007): 25–45. Print.

Messerschmidt, James. "Engendering Gendered Knowledge: Assessing the Academic Appropriation of Hegemonic Masculinity." *Men and Masculinities* 15.1 (2012): 56–76. Print.

Meyer, John W. "Globalization: Sources and Effects on National States and Societies." *International Sociology* 15.2 (2000): 233–248. Print.

Moller, Michael. "Exploiting Patterns: A Critique of Hegemonic Masculinity." *Journal of Gender Studies* 16.3 (2007): 263–276. Print.

Morawski, Stefan. "The Hopeless Game of Flânerie." *The Fla^neur*. Ed. Keith Tester. London: Routledge, 1994. 181–197. Print.

Morrison, Blake. "Future Tense." Rev. of *Cosmopolis*. *The Guardian*. 17 May 2003. Web. 16 June 2012.

Müller, Monika. "From Hard-Boiled Detective to Kasper Hauser? Masculinity and Writing in Paul Auster's *The New York Trilogy*." *Subverting Masculinity: Hegemonic and Alternative Versions of Masculinity in Contemporary Culture*. Eds. Russell West and Frank Lay. Amsterdam: Rodopi, 2000. 144–162. Print.

Murphet, Julian. *American Psycho: A Reader's Guide*. London: Continuum, 2002. Print.

Nealon, Jeffrey T. "Work of the Detective, Work of the Writer: Paul Auster's *City of Glass*." *Modern Fiction Studies* 42.1 (1996): 91–110. Print.

Neary, Lynn. "Paul Auster Tackles Homelessness and Broken Hearts." *Npr.org*. 10 Nov. 2010. Web. 9 Aug. 2011.

Ngan-Ling Chow, Esther. "Gender Matters: Studying Globalization and Social Change in the 21st Century." *International Sociology* 18.3 (2003): 443–460. Print.

O'Neill, Joseph. *Netherland: A Novel*. New York: Pantheon, 2008. Print.

Olster, Stacy. *Don DeLillo: Mao II, Underworld, Falling Man*. London: Continuum, 2011. Print.

Page, Max. *The Creative Destruction of Manhattan, 1900–1940: Historical Studies of Urban America*. Chicago: University of Chicago Press, 1999. Print.

Parkhurst Ferguson, Priscilla. "The *Flâneur* On and Off the Streets of Paris." *The Flâneur*. Ed. Keith Tester. London: Routledge, 1994. Print.

———. *Paris as Revolution: Writing the Nineteenth Century City*. Berkeley and Los Angeles: University of California Press, 2007. Print.

Parsons, Deborah. *Streetwalking the Metropolis*. Oxford: Oxford University Press, 2000. Print.

Peacock, James. *Understanding Paul Auster*. Columbia: University of South Carolina Press, 2010. Print.

———. "The Father in the Ice: Paul Auster, Character, and Literary Ancestry." *Critique* 52 (2011): 362–375. Print.

Pease, Bob, and Keith Pringle, eds. *A Man's World? Changing Men's Practices in a Globalized World*. London: Zed, 2001. Print.

Petersen, Alan. *Unmasking the Masculine: 'Men' and 'Identity' in a Sceptical Age*. London: Sage, 1998. Print.

Philips, Dana. "Don DeLillo's Postmodern Pastoral." *Don DeLillo: Bloom's Modern Critical Views*. Ed. Harold Bloom. Philadelphia: Chelsea House, 2003. 117–128. Print.

Pleck, Joseph. "American Fathering in Historical Perspective." *Changing Men: New Directions in Research on Men and Masculinity*. Ed. Michael Kimmel. Newbury Park: Sage, 1987. 83–97. Print.

Poe, Edgar Allan. "The Man of the Crowd." *Edgar Allan Poe Annotated and Illustrated Entire Stories and Poems*. Ed. Andrew Barger. Memphis: Bottletree Books, 2008. 294–299. Print.

Pollock, Griselda. *Vision and Difference: Feminism, Femininity and the Histories of Art*. New York: Routledge, 1998. Print.

Pomeroy, Wardell B. *Dr Kinsey and the Institute for Sex Research*. New York: Harper & Row, 1972. Print.

Porter, Roger J. *Bureau of Missing Persons: Writing the Secret Lives of Fathers*. Ithaca: Cornell University Press, 2011. Print.

Ramalho de Sousa Santos, Maria Irene. "Plagiarism in Praise: Paul Auster and Melville." *Revista Portuguesa de Literatura Comparada* 1 (December 1991): 105–114. Print.

Review of Contemporary Fiction 14.1 (Spring 1994): 7–96. Print.

Ritzer, George. "Rethinking Globalization: Glocalization/Grobalization and Something/Nothing." *Sociological Theory* 21.3 (2003): 193–209. Print.

Robertson, Roland. "Glocalization: Time-Space and Homogeneity and Heterogeneity." *Global Modernities*. Eds. Mike Featherstone, Scott Lash, and Roland Robertson. London: Sage, 1995. 25–44. Print.

Rotundo, E. Anthony. "American Fatherhood: A Historical Perspective." *American Behavioral Scientist* 29 (Sept/Oct 1985): 7–25. Print.

Rowe, John Carlos. "Global Horizons in *Falling Man*." *Don DeLillo: Mao II, Underworld, Falling Man*. Ed. Stacey Olster. London: Continuum, 2011. 121–134. Print.

———. "Serial Masculinity: Psychopathology and Oedipal Violence in Bret Easton Ellis' *American Psycho*." *MFS: Modern Fiction Studies* 54.2 (2005): 378–397. Print.

Schweighauser, Philipp, and Peter Schneck, eds. *Terrorism, Media, and the Ethics of Fiction: Transatlantic Perspectives on Don DeLillo*. London: Continuum, 2010. Print.

Seidl, Christian. "'Regeneration through Creativity': The Frontier in Paul Auster's *Moon Palace*." *PhiN* 31 (2005): 60–78. Print.

Seidler, Victor. *Recreating Sexual Politics: Men, Feminism and Politics*. London: Routledge, 1991. Print.

Seltzer, Mark. *Serial Killers: Death and Life in America's Wound Culture*. London: Routledge, 1998. Print.

Sharpe, William. "A Pig upon the Town: Charles Dickens in New York." *Nineteenth Century Prose* 23.2 (1996): 12–24. Print.

———. *New York Nocturne: The City after Dark in Literature, Painting, and Photography, 1850–1950*. Princeton: Princeton University Press, 2008. Print.

Simmel, Georg. "The Metropolis and Mental Life." *The Sociology of Georg Simmel*. Trans. Kurt Wolff. New York: Free Press, 1950. 409–442. Print.

Simon, William. *Postmodern Sexualities*. New York: Routledge, 1996. Print.

Simonetti, Paolo. "Loss, Ruins, War: Paul Auster's Response to 9/11 and the 'War on Terror'." *The Invention of Illusions: International Perspectives on Paul Auster*. Eds. Stefania Ciocia and Jesus A. Gonzalez. Newcastle: Cambridge Scholars Publishing, 2011. 13–38. Print.

Singer, Linda. "Controversies over the Nature of Love." *The Shere Hite Reader*. Ed. Shere Hite. New York: Seven Stories, 2006. 477–484. Print.

Smith, Grahame. "Dickens and the City of Light." *The Victorian Web*. 2000. Web. 7 Jan. 2011.

Springer, Carsten. *A Paul Auster Sourcebook*. New York: Peter Lang, 2001. Print.

Storey, Mark. "'And as Things Fell Apart': The Crisis of Postmodern Masculinity in Bret Easton Ellis' *American Psycho* and Dennis Cooper's *Frisk*." *Critique: Studies in Contemporary Fiction* 47.1 (2005): 57–72. Print.

Swope, Richard. "Approaching the Threshold(s) in Postmodern Detective Fiction: Hawthorne's 'Wakefield' and Other Missing Persons." *Critique: Studies in Contemporary Fiction* 39.3 (Spring 1998): 207–227. Print.

Tester, Keith, ed. *The Flâneur*. London: Routledge, 1994. Print.

"The Dinner Party." *Seinfeld*. Writ. Larry David. Dir. Tom Cherones. Sony Pictures, 2005. DVD.

Tindall, Gillian. "The Countryside of Balzac and Sand." *New York Times*. 2 June 1991. Web. 9 Aug. 2010.

Updike, John. "One Way Street." Rev. of *Cosmopolis*. *The New Yorker*. 31 Mar. 2003. Web. 16 June 2012.

van Nijnatten, Carolus. "The Invention of Fatherhood: The Therapeutic Effects of Writing a Father's Biography." *The Family Journal* 15 (2007): 244–250. Print.

Varsava, Jerry A. "The 'Saturated Self': Don DeLillo on the Problem of Rogue Capitalism." *Contemporary Literature* 46.1 (2005): 78–107. Print.

Varvogli, Aliki. *The World That Is the Book: Paul Auster's Fiction*. Liverpool: Liverpool University Press, 2001. Print.

———. "Exploding Fictions." *Bloom's Modern Critical Views: Paul Auster*. Ed. Harold Bloom. Philadelphia: Chelsea House, 2004. 191–207. Print.

———. "'The Worst Possibilities of the Imagination Are the Country You Live In.'" *The Invention of Illusions: International Perspectives on Paul Auster*. Eds. Stefania Ciocia and Jesus A. Gonzalez. Newcastle: Cambridge Scholars Publishing, 2011. 39–54. Print.

Wahlström, Helena. *New Fathers? Contemporary American Stories of Masculinity, Domesticity, and Kinship*. Newcastle: Cambridge Scholars, 2011. Print.

Walden, George. "Life and Death in a Stretch Limo." Rev. of *Cosmopolis*. *The Telegraph*. 11 May 2003. Web. 16 June 2012.

Wedgwood, Nikki. "Connell's Theory of Masculinity—Its Origins and Influences on the Study of Gender." *Journal of Gender Studies* 18.4 (2009): 329–339. Print.

Weeks, Jeffrey. "Sexuality and History Revisited." *Sexualities in History.* Eds. Kim M. Phillips and Barry Readys. New York: Routledge, 2002. 27–41. Print.

———. *Sexuality.* 3rd ed. New York: Routledge, 2009. Print.

Weisenburger, Steven. "Inside *Moon Palace.*" *Review of Contemporary Fiction* 14.1 (Spring 1994): 70–79. Rpt. in *Bloom's Modern Critical Views: Paul Auster.* Ed. Harold Bloom. Philadelphia: Chelsea House, 2004. 171–183. Print.

Weisstein, Naomi. "An Introduction to *The Hite Reports:* Theory and Importance." *The Shere Hite Reader.* Ed. Shere Hite. New York: Seven Stories, 2006. 457–465. Print.

Werner, James. *American Flâneur: Cosmic Physiognomies of Edgar Allan Poe.* New York: Routledge, 2004. Print.

Wesseling, Elisabeth. "*In the Country of Last Things:* Paul Auster's Parable of the Apocalypse." *Neophilologus* 75.4 (Oct 1991): 496–504. Print.

White, E. B. *Here Is New York.* 1949. New York: The Little Bookroom, 1999. Print.

White, Edmund. *The Flâneur: A Stroll through the Paradoxes of Paris.* London: Bloomsbury, 2001. Print.

Whitehead, Colson. *The Colossus of New York.* New York: Anchor Books, 2003. Print.

Whitehead, Stephen. "Hegemonic Masculinity Revisited." *Gender, Work, and Organization* 6.1 (1999): 58–62. Print.

Wilson, Elizabeth. *The Sphinx in the City: Urban Life, the Control of Disorder, and Women.* Berkeley and Los Angeles: University of California Press, 1991. Print.

———. "The Invisible Flâneur." *New Left Review* I/191 (1992): 90–110. Print.

Wolff, Janet. "The Invisible Flâneuse: Women and the Literature of Modernity." *Theory, Culture and Society* 2.3 (1985): 37–46. Print.

Wood, James. "Shallow Graves: The Novels of Paul Auster." *The New Yorker.com.* 30 Nov. 2009. Web. 8 Nov. 2011.

Woods, Tim. "'Looking for Signs in the Air': Urban Space and the Postmodern in *In the Country of Last Things.*" *Beyond the Red Notebook: Essays on Paul Auster.* Ed. Dennis Barone. Philadelphia: University of Pennsylvania Press, 1995. 107–128. Print.

Young, Elizabeth. "The Beast in the Jungle, the Figure in the Carpet." *Shopping in Space: Essays on American Blank Generation Fiction.* Eds. Elizabeth Young and Graham Caveney. New York: Atlantic Monthly Press, 1992. 85–129. Print.

Index